MURPHY'S MISSION

MURPHY'S MISSION

COLIN MURPHY – FOOTBALL ADVENTURES FROM SINCIL BANK TO SAIGON

SALLY MEARS

Mersea
Press

Cover design by Freya Mears.

Mersea
PRESS

For Cory and Freya.
And for Neil, who would have been so proud of you both.

You, me, we, all of us have been forced to breakfast on travesty, lunch on objection and insult, dine on inflicted pressures. High Tea we daren't sit still long enough to take, and by supper we were still expected to have been victorious.

— MURPH'S MESSAGE. LINCOLN CITY VS LEYTON ORIENT. 6 MAY 1989.

CONTENTS

FOREWORD BY DAVID PLEAT

Colin Murphy's journey has been a catalogue of wonderful experiences. Colin loved football and was bright enough to understand his strengths and acknowledge his weaknesses. Not a 'star' name, he worked hard, studied coaching and was a most intelligent, highly motivated and humble man.

Colin progressed from a working-class background to have a career that thousands would envy. He encountered all the trials and tribulations of the beautiful game. As his wife Judith remarked, when asked what it was like to be married to a football nut; she didn't know, as he was rarely home!

Murph, as he is affectionately known, is a one-off. After his successful stewardship of his first love, Lincoln City, he became the ultimate football wanderer. Full of inventive ideas, self-belief and a love of coaching, his limited success as a player spurred him on to achieve as a coach.

His life has been a kaleidoscope of amazing adventures, gathering a network of warm friends along the way. With his command of English and sometimes eccentricity, he never established roots between 'his' Lincoln and his last club, Hull City.

A brave traveller, Colin journeyed to the likes of Vietnam, Myanmar and Saudi Arabia, successfully flying the flag for British coaching. His single-mindedness and humility in success were admirable traits, as was his dedication.

There are few, if any, like Murph in football. I was privileged to work with him and have appreciated and admired his colourful career.

Enjoy the book.

David Pleat, March 2022

FOREWORD BY JOHN INVERDALE

Colin Murphy. A man apart. Apart from the norm. From the regimented, routine response to the standard journalistic footballing question. A man who when asked how he would assess John Fashanu's performance the previous weekend, replied,

'It was a mixture. He was good and he was bad, but he looked good all match. He was mercurial but sartorial, so I'll say his performance was sarcurial.'

A man who when asked in November how he'd assess the season so far, replied,

'If we're still top of the table on January 1, we'll have thought Christmas has come early!'

A man who kept you waiting for every – every – interview, and yet somehow you didn't mind because you knew there'd be a golden nugget just round the corner. Anyone who can describe a player as 'running around like a deranged ferret' is worth waiting for.

Colin remains one of my favourite people in sport ever, and it is a genuine joy to have known him for so many years.

John Inverdale
London, 2022

AUTHOR'S NOTE

I have met with Colin Murphy many times over the past few years. In Lincoln pubs and London restaurants, at Sincil Bank and the Emirates Stadium, we have chatted and laughed about Colin's tempestuous career.

Following his stroke in 2007, much detail has been lost from Colin's memories of his 35 years in football management. The Murphy family scrapbooks were an invaluable starting point for researching Colin's biography, and conversations with his family and former colleagues revealed the real-life dilemmas of the professional game. Unless otherwise specified, quotations included in the text are taken from these interviews.

To supplement these sources, and to tell Colin's story as faithfully as possible, I have read newspaper articles, matchday programmes, football magazines and fanzines from the 1960s through to the early 2000s. Quotes from Colin's matchday programme notes are included in their original form. Football websites, blogs and podcasts have also formed part of my research into this period of football history.

There may be some surprises in store. I hope you enjoy the read.

INTRODUCTION

'What's the word, Ben?' Colin's memory stumbled. 'It's because of my stroke. I can't always get the right word.'

My first meeting with Colin Murphy and his son Ben was late in the summer of 2015. Ben told me his dad always wore a Lincoln City tracksuit, but he arrived at my house, wearing a lilac polo shirt and navy pinstriped suit. 'Expect the unexpected,' I later discovered, is one of Colin's favourite expressions.

Ben, who had been my son's football coach, showed great kindness to my family when my husband had died of cancer four years before. We had spoken at length of the unbreakable bond between fathers and sons, of my children's East End-born West Ham-supporting dad, and of Ben's relationship with Colin, whom he clearly revered.

In the strange, chaotic symmetry of life, in the months before Colin and I first met, I received my own diagnosis of cancer. Chemotherapy and surgery beckoned. It's in the darker recesses of life that your greatest friendships flourish. And faced with many months of treatment, a dear, inspirational friend suggested there was more fun to be had than a hospital project. She offered a much-needed injection of positivity. This was my chance to write.

I'm a linguist by background, a researcher at heart, and an

Arsenal season ticket holder. What better way to combine my interests than writing a sports biography? And what better person to write about than Colin Murphy? A lower-league legend, the bard of English football with an eccentric personality to match.

And so, wearing a burgundy wig, I sat at my kitchen table and explained to Colin that 'the lady' as he called me, would like to write his life story. The conversation didn't quite go according to plan. Colin told me he had turned down a previous offer to write his biography because of one word. I searched his face, hoping for a hint, nervous about providing the wrong prompt. What was the word?

He hesitated.

'Trustworthiness.'

I thought I was going to interview Colin but realised the two hours would actually be spent with him interviewing me. It was time to lay out my stall of integrity.

'I'm a football fan. A wordsmith. I'd love to tell your story. I promise not to make you out to be a saint!'

We chatted and when Colin's memory failed him, Ben filled in the blanks.

When the time came for them to leave, I asked Colin, 'What's your biggest weakness?'

'Algebra!' he laughed.

He clapped and clasped my hand. A stroke may have stolen his career, but it hadn't taken his charisma. I seemed to have passed the trustworthiness test. And I sensed we were going to have fun.

That meeting marked the start of a six-year journey, with many unscheduled stops along the way. An odyssey which took me from interviews in Lincoln pubs, to the newspaper archives of the British Library, via the Hang Day Stadium in Hanoi. There is something curiously addictive about writing someone else's life story. The anticipation of a hidden find.

What better place to start my research than at the National Football Museum in Manchester? A shiny, interactive, touchscreen celebration of the beautiful game. If you pass through the Hall of Fame and walk up to level one, you can research the history of your favourite club, a choice of players, records, history, or facts.

I wondered how the museum had embodied Lincoln City's past. The Lord of the Imps, Bill Anderson? Record-winning hero and future England manager, Graham Taylor? No, their most salient artefact, in dazzling monochrome, was *The Banker*. Issue 4. 1989. 'The boys are back. Murphy's mission' with an advertisement for, 'Murphman ... a new superhero ... only £9.99!'

A glorious, tongue-in-cheek, fanzine celebration of Colin's 1987/88 promotion-winning season. And a biographer's delight.

I made my way down to the museum shop, where the partisan Mancunian bookshelves bulged with City and United and made a cursory nod to the north-south divide. A single Arsenal tome and a mis-filed Wenger, nestled self-consciously among the As. On a wall of signed collectibles, Eric Cantona rubbed shoulders with Alan Shearer. The entire history of English football, in ten square metres of retail space.

And then I caught sight of it, in a small pile, on a pink podium: a glossy, slim pamphlet. A neon sticker partly obscured the title, *Stand up if you love the Boss. A collection of poems written in support of the Lincoln City Football Club.*

I thumbed through 48 pages of homage to a Lincoln past, the work of lifelong Imps fan Geoffrey Piper. And there I found them, 'Clean Sheets', 'Want Promotion?', and 'Murphy's Mission'. Three poems dedicated to Murph, the bard of Lincoln City. Of all the bookshops in all the cities, in all the world, what were the chances of that?

I texted my inspirational friend.

'The stars are aligned,' she replied.

Colin's story was meant to be told.

Sally Mears
London, 2022

1

THE CROYDON BOYS

THE NON-LEAGUE DAYS

'What's your problem, pal?'

Alf Ackerman shouted across the mud-caked pitch at Stonebridge Road. His full-back Colin Murphy and goalkeeper Brian Hughes were yelling in each other's faces. The chisel-jawed South African manager strolled across the turf to see what was going on. One of Murphy's Southern League colleagues remembers the incident well. In the bitter winter of 1970, outside the unheated changing rooms of Gravesend & Northfleet, his fellow teammates stood on the half-way line and froze. The 26-year-old Murphy, known to everyone as Murph, had recently returned from a Football Association (FA) coaching course at Lilleshall. He was arranging defensive set pieces, and couldn't agree with his goalkeeper, where he should stand on the goal line for a free kick.

As the argument escalated, Ackerman strode over to intervene. Murph explained his tactical thinking and Ackerman agreed. Hughes, his chest thrust out in indignation, argued that if Murph stood where he told him, the opposition couldn't score. Ackerman, a former Millwall striker with over 200 professional goals to his name, had enough of the sideshow. He placed the muddy ball at his feet, rolled up his trouser legs and told Hughes to organise his defence for a free kick.

The old pro took his run up, powered the ball into the back of the net, and sauntered back to the bench. Yelling over his shoulder, as he went, 'I told you f***ing Murphy was right!'

'Coaching at its most effective,' Murph's teammate concluded. His name? Roy Hodgson. Gravesend & Northfleet full-back. And future England manager.

~

MURPH'S FLEDGLING FOOTBALL CAREER STARTED almost a decade before he won the stormy argument over a free kick. In the summer of 1960, ready to leave mainstream education behind, he received the golden ticket for any football-mad local lad: an invitation from youth team coach Jess Willard to trial with Fourth Division Crystal Palace. Murph still keeps the sepia-tinted letter in a box of treasured mementoes. Foolproof written instructions for the young hopeful to take green bus no. 403 from Croydon to the Good Companions Hotel opposite Kingswood Lane. Murph survived the trial at The Civil Service Sports Ground and signed schoolboy forms. A dream come true for the 16-year-old Croydon boy from the Waddon Estate. Until a devastating leg break, a footballing injury 18 months into his contract destroyed his hopes of progressing from youth to first team football.

Released by the club before his 18th birthday, Murph learnt a lesson which would serve him well in the years ahead. He couldn't allow a temporary setback to derail his long-term ambition. He had a three-month trial with Fourth Division Exeter City, but when no contract was forthcoming, he settled for Isthmian League Wimbledon instead. It marked the start of a decade-long journey through the backwaters of non-league football. A journey which would feature the inglorious sights of south-east England: Croydon Amateurs, Folkestone, Bexley United, Tunbridge Wells Rangers, Hastings United, and Gravesend. Each club contributed to Murph's dog-eared notebook, rammed full of useful contacts in the game.

Murph celebrates his non-league background. His football story interwoven with a string of characters who have enjoyed more success in their management careers than their playing days. Among his keepsakes lies a typed and stapled matchday programme (price 3d) from the first game of the 1966/67 season. Murphy (Colin V.) from Tunbridge Wells Rangers pitted against Gravesend & Northfleet's Barry Fry. Two men whose paths would cross repeatedly in the years ahead, as combative Conference challengers in the late 1980s and later, co-conspirators at First Division Southend.

An early taste of footballing success with Croydon Amateurs. Colin Murphy, front row, third from left. (Photograph from the Murphy family collection)

A photograph of the Tunbridge Wells Rangers first team squad shows a fresh-faced Colin V. Murphy, standing arms folded in the second row, beaming at the camera. Four spots away from him stands a rather more imposing looking Colin E. Murphy (no relation). The image and the accompanying initials were a useful find. Match reports I'd read of an agile centre-forward, Colin Murphy, puzzled me when Murph had described himself as a 'not very good full-back'. What were the chances of having two players of the same name in one team? And that ten years later, one of them (Colin E.) would award the other one (Colin V.) his FA Coaching Licence? They both went on to teach on the London schools' programme, much to the confusion of a generation of pupils who didn't know which version of Colin Murphy they would get.

The two men built a lifelong connection. Players formed strong bonds in the Southern League. Murph appeared alongside teammates who were climbing up or dropping down the football ladder. Every Southern Leaguer delighted in pitting himself against an ex-England or First Division player, seeing out his career in the hinterland of non-league. Murph was no exception. As left-back for Tunbridge Wells Rangers, he looked forward to facing Bobby Smith, the prolific ex-England centre-forward, playing for Hastings United. Smith had won the Football League and FA Cup Double with Tottenham Hotspur only six years before.

The former apprentice blacksmith, come football legend, arrived at Culverden Stadium in a fanfare of expectation. For the first time that season, the home gate for the match against Hastings United passed 1,000. The local paper, the *Kent and Sussex Courier*, delighted in reporting how 'the chunky Smith' had pitched up to the changing room only 15 minutes before kick-off. His teammates greeted his arrival with loud cheers. Smith had done little preparation since his suspension for missing training two months before. And in the closing minutes of an otherwise uneventful game, Murph upended his famous opponent on the park. Half a century later, Murph still laughs at the memory, 'I didn't get to do that very often!'

Smith took the challenge in good humour. It didn't change the result. Tunbridge lost 1-0. The last game Rangers played before the club folded under financial pressure and Murph was forced to move clubs once again. Useful preparation for the nomadic life of a manager in the Football League.

While Murph was playing for Bexley United, struggling sixth-tier Gravesend & Northfleet came in for him. The Fleet had bumped along the bottom of Southern League First Division for the previous five years. The board of directors had resigned en masse, and the new chairman and local newsagent Vic Troke needed to steady a sinking ship. He turned to ex-Dartford boss and fellow shopkeeper Alf Ackerman to take over as manager.

Ackerman, lured from his native Pretoria to play football for Clyde, ended his professional career with Millwall. Anti-aircraft guns were still fresh in the mind when the bruising forward arrived in Scotland after World War Two. Nicknamed 'Ack Ack' Ackerman for his artillery power in front of goal, he brought the same aggressive energy to the role of manager. Murph admired this straight-talking, sometimes fearsome figure, who wasted no time in rebuilding the Gravesend & Northfleet team. Alongside Murph, he signed Brian Hughes, a former junior at Arsenal. A year later, he brought Colin Toal from Tonbridge, and signed Roy Hodgson from Crystal Palace, a wing-half who had never played a first-team game.

Ackerman couldn't have predicted that three of his non-league signings, Murph, Hodgson, and Toal, would develop into a First Division manager, the winner of seven European league titles, and the technical director of Indian football, respectively. And none of them would forget their outspoken manager from the Fleet. In the *Gravesend & Northfleet Football Club Official Golden Jubilee Year Book* from 1996, Hodgson credits training nights with Ackerman for helping to forge his future ideas. And Murph acknowledges that Ackerman had a major influence on his own career, alongside east Midlands legends Jimmy Sirrel and Brian Clough.

Murph and his teammates trained at Stonebridge Road twice a week. On Thursday nights in the Supporters' Club, they received a small brown pay packet containing roughly £20 a week. A decent part-time wage when beer cost 20p a pint and you could buy a brand-new mini for £600. Murph didn't take the extra wages for granted. His parents had been grafters all their working lives. In his second season at the Fleet, Murph's dad, George Victor Murphy, received a letter from the mayor's parlour. An invitation to a reception to mark 30 years' faithful service to the London Borough of Croydon and a commemorative clock.

A labourer turned painter and decorator, George had lived in the same semi-detached council house with his shop assistant wife for all his married life. Murph's childhood home in Crowley Crescent stood less than two miles from the house where George was born. He had no wish to move further afield, but he couldn't have been more supportive of his only child's sporting ambitions. George accompanied his six-year-old son, the first footballer in the family, to weekly football practice and took him on his first trip to Selhurst Park. Although the detailed memory of the trip has been ravaged by time, 70 years later, Colin remembers his father with obvious affection.

'My dad was my biggest influence. He really was.'

From the age of ten, Murphy Junior donned his boxing gloves to represent Croydon Primary Schools in tournaments across the south of England. Weighing in at 4st 10lbs, he picked up his first winner's certificate for Croydon Schools Amateur Boxing Association – eight years before boxing fell out of favour and dropped off the schools' curriculum. At John Newnham, the local secondary modern in South Croydon, sport featured more prominently in Murph's school days than academic subjects. A district footballer and one of the younger members of the Croydon Secondary Schools' Cricket XI, in one outing, his slow-bowling prowess took five for 15. And in the last summer of his secondary education, The Star Cricket Competition recognised his talents for an 'outstanding performance' scoring 54 not out. Murph never lost his love for cricket. He played it at club level throughout his adult life, but it couldn't match the buzz he got from football. It wasn't just a sport for Murph, it was a way of life.

When I first met Colin, I asked him if there were a friend from his school days I might speak to.

He laughed.

'I never really had one. I've only ever done football all my life!'

Gravesend & Northfleet gave Murph his first taste of footballing success. Ackerman's tough management style brought steady progress at the Kent-based club. When I spoke to Roy Hodgson in 2021, he remembered an early FA Trophy game he played in shortly after his debut. The competition was launched in the 1969/70 season to give non-league teams a chance to play in a Wembley cup final. In the second-round qualifying tie, Gravesend & Northfleet faced lowly Newmarket Town, an Eastern Counties League side. Hodgson and Murph arrived at Cricket Field Road. It was little more than a roped-off field.

'It wasn't the stadium we were used to,' Hodgson laughed, 'and at Gravesend we weren't exactly playing at San Siro!'

Ackerman based his team talks on one very simple principle: who was marking which opponent. The gaffer didn't believe in coaching, but he made it his business to know everything about the opposition. In the Newmarket team, he recognised a fast and tricky right-winger who had played with him as a youngster at Millwall. Ackerman gave Murph his pre-match instructions.

'You've got to upset him early on. Make certain you give him a birthday present!'

The game kicked off and the Newmarket midfield whizzed the ball out to their star player on the right wing. Murph came deep inside to play close to the centre-backs. When the ball went out to his man, Murph hurtled towards him. Just as he was about to arrive on the ball, the winger played it past him. Murph couldn't stop his momentum. He smashed into the player and catapulted him over the touchline.

Hodgson didn't remember the result of the match, but over 50 years later, he still remembered the riot that ensued.

'There couldn't have been that many people at the game, but all of them ran on to the field.'

The match was held up while the referee tried to restore order.

'It was one of my early experiences of non-league football,' Hodgson said. 'I was thinking, is this how it's going to be? Is there not going to be a bit more football involved? I think I fancied myself as being far too talented to be involved in that!'

At the end of the season, Fleet reached a long-awaited cup final. It wasn't the FA Trophy, and it wasn't played at Wembley. But after a 12-year wait for silverware, 2,486 supporters watched Murph and Hodgson raise the Kent Floodlight Cup at Stone-bridge Road.

Fast forward 12 months. With one match left to play, Ackerman's efficient and experienced team only needed one point to take them out of the Southern League First Division for the first time in eight years. In the last game of the club's silver jubilee season, with Hodgson playing at number ten and Murph on the subs' bench, Fleet grabbed the third of four promotion slots. Both men quit while they were ahead. Murph transferred to Hastings United, while Hodgson moved to Southern League newcomers Maidstone United, later nicknamed by Barry Fry as 'the Manchester United of the non-league'. As player and assistant manager to his close friend Bob Houghton, Hodgson persuaded Colin Toal to join them from Wimbledon. The three amigos, reunited from their school days, were all products of the John Ruskin Grammar School in Croydon.

The fourth alumni, Lennie Lawrence, future promotion-winning manager at Charlton Athletic, moved into a house share with Murph.

Lennie remembers how his old pal was well known in the Croydon area, bombing around town in a bottle-green soft top MG. The Croydon boys were a tight-knit squad. Murph was working on the schools' programme with his namesake Colin Murphy, coaching football, cricket, and rugby at the Coldharbour

Leisure Centre in Greenwich. Lennie recalls the house share arrangement with Murph.

'He was never there. Nor was I come to that!'

Both men worked by day, trained by night, and sometime in between, pursued their FA coaching qualifications. Murph was the more outgoing, Lennie the more measured, but the relationship worked well. And before the decade was out, they would seize the opportunity to combine their talents in the Football League.

Gravesend & Northfleet Football Club celebrate promotion from the Southern League First Division in the 1970/71 season. Colin Murphy stands bare chested, back row left, next to Roy Hodgson, fourth from left, and a bespectacled Alf Ackerman, in front. (Photograph from the Murphy family collection)

Murph lived and worked with like-minded characters, a group of people linked by a common belief. Howard Wilkinson, chairman of the League Managers' Association (LMA), recalls how in the 1960s and 1970s, coaching was a growing phenomenon.

'Colin and I were disciples of coaching,' Wilkinson told me. 'The coaching bond was very strong because there weren't many of us.'

The glue which bound the group together was the FA coaching scheme, set up by Walter Winterbottom. After World War Two, the former schoolteacher was appointed as the national director of coaching, a position which later merged into the role of first England team manager. When Winterbottom left the FA in 1963, Allen Wade took over as head of the department of education. He expanded the coaching scheme with Charles Hughes as his assistant, directing the FA courses and examining and assessing candidates.

Four years after Wade took charge, he published the seminal text, *The FA Guide to Training and Coaching*. He wrote that the main purpose of the book was not to provide categorical answers or suggest cut-and-dried methods,

'Its purpose is to present ideas and principles which will require coaches to think.'

He believed that unthinking coaches and players led to stagnation in the game. Wade offered a dire warning, 'Stagnation produces complacency, and this must never again be permitted to occur in this country.'

Murph and his fellow candidates on the preliminary coaching course pored over chapters from the *FA Guide* on principles of team play, modern tactical development and reading the game. They sat a theory examination and a practical assessment. And from the preliminary course they progressed to the full badge course, now known as the UEFA A Licence. Wilkinson is not keen on the expression 'full badge' — a term which is still used colloquially today.

'Badges don't convey what coach education is. It's a totally different connotation. That was the problem we had at the time.

We were swimming against the tide but recognising that the tide would turn.'

Murph, alongside his Croydon colleagues, was an early advocate of coaching. It was difficult at first for the merit of coaching qualifications to gain acceptance; the fault of a long-held belief that footballers were born with an innate skill, and coaching would stifle their individuality. Some negativity also came from candidates who failed their preliminary award.

'They might start to change in what they did,' Wilkinson said, 'but they didn't change in what they thought, whereas coaches understood how people learn.'

The FA coaching scheme gradually taught the football community that to become a coach was to become educated in the science of learning. The FA ran a managers' and coaches' week every summer, from Sunday night to Friday morning.

'That week was not about getting a formal qualification,' Wilkinson explains. 'It was about coming together, discussing ideas, looking at new ways of doing things. A subliminal way of getting those who were non-converts or partial converts into the pen.'

David Pleat, former manager at Tottenham Hotspur, recalls how he first met Murph on one of these annual courses,

'The reason I got on so well with him was because he was a thoughtful man. He would be interested in things other than the round ball. Once you meet someone on a coaching course, it becomes ingrained in your mind. That often happens in football. First impressions are important. I liked Murphy; he was a bit off the wall. Slightly eccentric, although I didn't really find that out until his later days.'

Wilkinson has a similar memory,

'The big thing about Colin Murphy, he was so authentic. He was not afraid to be himself. That was one of his great strengths. "This is me. Yes, I'm different, but I have your interests at heart".'

There were different groups of converts around the country. The northern hotbed of coaching was in Sheffield, where future influential coach educators, including Howard Wilkinson, Dick Bate, and John Adams, joined the Sheffield Coaches Association. The southern group included Roy Hodgson, Bob Houghton, Dario Gradi, and Mike Kelly, the future England goalkeeping coach. As a member of the Surrey Football Coaches Association, Murph was involved in the London coaching scene, alongside his fellow converts.

'That's a very big part of the person who became Colin Murphy,' Wilkinson explains. 'We were part of a group, to use a loose saying, who could be called believers. We saw that as the way forward. That's what football needed to be.'

Murph kept in regular contact with his FA coaching and non-league contemporaries. When Hodgson left Gravesend & Northfleet, he was halfway through completing a two-year Certificate in Education at Avery Hill Teacher Training College. Murph signed up for the same physical education course in Greenwich, a year behind his Croydon pal. Murph can't quite remember how he talked his way onto a course in Further Education.

'I've only got one O level, and that was in sociology!' he laughed.

An early sign of his gift of the gab. The physical education course kept Murph in London and allowed him to pursue his second love of cricket. On the courts of the Dulwich Cricket Club, he pursued his third love: a 19-year-old Avery Hill student from Torquay, Judith Ridehalgh, eight and a half years his junior.

'Was it love at first sight?' I asked Judith the first time we met.

'No,' she laughed, 'he taught me to play squash!'

After Hodgson left for Maidstone, Bobby Drake, player-manager for Southern League Hastings United, came in for Murph. Drake admitted to the local press he didn't sign the Fleet's full-back for his defensive skills, but because his future captain was a 'terrific chap to have in the dressing room and a great morale booster'. A disastrous start to Hastings' season threatened the future of professional football in the town. Playing against Tonbridge on Boxing Day, with Murph once again consigned to the bench, the two men talked at length about match play and tactics. Impressed by his full-back's thoughtful vision, the manager invited his new recruit to run an evening training session. Murph impressed his fellow teammates, and Drake saw something he liked. With Murph coaching from the subs' bench, the team became tighter and better organised. The rookie coach benefited too. The Hastings job secured his FA Coaching Certificate: a mock burgundy leather passport, the first step towards a long-term career in the professional game.

From sub to team coach, nine points from a possible 12; the *Hastings and St. Leonards Observer* ran with the story. Murph savoured the attention-grabbing headline, 'Murphy appointed United coach in surprise move'.

Judith preserved the clipping in the first of an extensive library of Murph-related scrapbooks. The local paper optimistically pointed out that many of the country's more successful clubs benefitted from similar manager-coach partnerships.

'Nobody is comparing United with the Arsenals and Manchester Citys of this world, but supporters will follow the Drake-Murphy link-up with great interest.'

Drake's gamble had paid off. If Murph bided his time, there would be much bigger surprise appointments in store. He didn't need to complete his Avery Hill Certificate in Education. He just needed to pick up the phone.

2

THE GHOST OF BRIAN CLOUGH
NOTTINGHAM FOREST AND DERBY COUNTY

T he shrill sound of the house phone pierced the early morning air. Holding his usual mug of builder's tea in his hand, Murph picked up the receiver.

'Colin, it's Des Anderson here. Dave and I are moving to Nottingham Forest. There's a coaching job going, do you fancy it?'

Murph didn't hesitate, 'When do I start?'

Murph struck up a friendship with Anderson at Gravesend & Northfleet, when the former Millwall wing-half was playing for Hastings United. Anderson was impressed by reports coming out of the FA's headquarters about Murph's coaching ability and recommended his Southern League pal to Dave Mackay. The Heart of Midlothian and Tottenham legend had taken on the player-manager role at Second Division Swindon Town, and invited his old friend, Anderson, to join him as assistant. The two men, both born and bred in Edinburgh, enjoyed a close personal and professional bond. Anderson referred to his boss as 'the Laird'. After a year together at Swindon, the duo moved north up the Second Division rankings to Nottingham Forest. The club had been relegated after 15 years in the top flight, and they relished the challenge of returning the Reds to their former glory.

The Laird invited Murph to join them as Forest's youth team coach.

Dave Mackay, second from left, and Colin Murphy, seventh from right, line up for a charity match with Nottingham Forest, in the 1972/73 season. The football kit shows the leaping stags of the Forest badge before its re-design in 1974. (Photograph from the Murphy family collection)

It was October 1972, and Murph was 28 years old, when he accepted the job offer which would change his life. After what felt like a lifetime playing non-league football and teaching on the schools' programme, this was his big break; his first coaching job in the Football League. Within seven months, the trio bedded in at the City Ground and took Forest to a respectable 14th-placed finish. At the end of the football season, Judith graduated from Avery Hill and moved to Nottingham to be with Murph. The 20-year-old bride and her 29-year-old groom got married in West Bridgford, just down the road from Trent Bridge. They held the reception in a hotel owned by Alan Hill, the Reds' former goalkeeper. Murph chose the date for the nuptials: 12 August 1973. A

Sunday. He didn't want to interrupt Forest's pre-season training. He went back to work the next day.

Two months later, Murph faced an even bigger life-changing event. A move which would catapult him 15 miles west of Nottingham to its less glamorous sister town of Derby. A new chapter in a complex story which had begun seven years before. In the rain-drenched winter of 1966, Derby County appointed Sam Longson, a local Derbyshire farmer's son, as chairman. In his search for a new manager, the Rolls-Royce-owning entrepreneur received a nudge in the right direction from the sardonic Len Shackleton, former Sunderland forward, turned sports journalist with the *Daily Express*. Shackleton suggested that Longson should look at a young management team in charge of Fourth Division Hartlepools United (before the club changed its name to Hartlepool and later, Hartlepool United). It would be a gamble for Derby to sign two relative unknowns, two divisions below them in the Football League, but the duo had a compelling record. The chairman took Shackleton's advice and signed two names which would be forever etched in the heart of every Derby fan: Brian Clough and Peter Taylor. A formidable force who would kick start the most successful decade in the Rams' history. And haunt their successors at the Baseball Ground for years to come.

The honeymoon period for Longson and Clough was brief but idyllic. Clough and Taylor restructured the Derby squad, and in the summer of 1968, struck football gold. They made a canny £4,000 signing to bring Double-winning Dave Mackay from Tottenham Hotspur, dropping their new captain out of midfield, to lead the team from behind. In Clough's first season in charge, Derby finished fifth from bottom, but 12 months later he exceeded Longson's wildest dreams. Derby were no longer seasoned mid-tablers. They were seven points clear at the top of the table, and Second Division champions. Clough's attacking style of football and scathing opinions on the football hierarchy made him a media sensation. The Derby fans adored him and watched him turn a miracle in the east Midlands over the next three years. Not content with grabbing one piece of silverware, Clough lifted the First Division trophy at only the third attempt. But his flirtation with the press soured his relationship with his long-suffering chair.

Longson wanted his manager to change, to become part of the Establishment, which the younger man despised. Irritated by gagging clauses, aimed at taming his outspoken comments, Clough refused to sign his contract renewal, and issued the board with an ultimatum. Either Derby's president should replace Longson, or Clough would resign. The threat ripped the board apart. With huge reluctance, the directors accepted their management duo's resignations. Clough couldn't believe they wouldn't ask him back. And a legion of fans couldn't believe it either. Horrified at losing the manager they worshipped, The Derby Protest Movement was born. An army of 800 signed-up members, determined to keep their living legend at the Baseball Ground.

Despite the rumblings from Clough's disciples, the Derby board began their search for a replacement manager. Turned down by Bobby Robson at Ipswich Town, they approached the club's former captain, Dave Mackay. The Derby Protest Movement acknowledged Mackay as the team's defensive saviour, but they converged on Nottingham to warn the former Footballer of the Year against re-joining the Rams. They wouldn't allow him to get in the way of Clough coming back. Angry fans gathered in the car park at the City Ground, but they couldn't intimidate the former Scottish international. Despite his diminutive stature, Mackay commanded an impressive physical presence.

'The hardest man I ever played against, and certainly the bravest,' George Best, European Player of the Year, would later recall. A tribute which subsequently appeared in many of Mackay's obituaries.

Undeterred by the protestations of the pro-Clough lobby, in October 1973 Mackay signed a four-year contract with the Rams. He accepted the invitation to bring his assistant and youth team coach from Nottingham Forest with him. Mackay couldn't quite believe his luck. He didn't know if it was a fabulous opportunity for an inexperienced manager or a poisoned chalice. But it was a dream come true for Murph, the young coach from Croydon; launched from the Southern League to the First Division in just one season.

The trio didn't enjoy an easy start at the Baseball Ground. Twelve first team players signed a letter to the board, demanding that they reinstate Clough and Taylor. The players threatened to refuse to train, but Mackay was unswayed by their protest. If they carried out threats of a rebellion, he would report them to the FA and field Murph's reserve team instead. The players buckled, regrouped under their new boss, and concentrated on making headway in the league. Within a year, Mackay had moulded a squad whose attacking power could compete at any level. Former England forward Francis Lee joined from Manchester City, a brilliant addition to the side. At the season's close, Derby took an implausible 15 points out of a possible 18 and raised the championship trophy for the second time in four years. The hand of Brian Clough was momentarily lifted from Mackay's shoulder.

Murph was riding the same wave of success with the Derby reserves. The team competed in the Central League, a competition which fielded clubs from the Midlands, North Wales and the north of England. The reserve league was a stepping stone for many young players from youth to first team football. In his first full season in charge, Murph led the Rams to the runners-up slot, one point behind Liverpool, with 90 goals apiece. A year later, Liverpool racked up their sixth win in seven seasons, and Murph finished third. But while Liverpool had fielded only 27 players during the season, Derby had used 38, including 12 teenagers playing their Central League debuts. Murph never fielded the same team in consecutive matches. This lack of continuity might have sacrificed a win for the sake of the youngsters' development, but the reserve team coach didn't mind losing his best players if it gave them a chance in the first team.

The three amigos with the First Division championship trophy at Derby County, in 1975. From left to right, Des Anderson, Colin Murphy, and Dave Mackay. (Photograph from the Murphy family collection)

The FA liked Murph's thinking. Although by no means a household name, they called him up as an instructor on a 'full badge' coaching course at Bisham Abbey. The recognition meant a great deal to Murph. He wasn't a well-known name in football, but he had earned the FA's respect through hard graft and technical ability. His success with the reserves showed what could be achieved with tight organisation and the right team spirt. A young Joe Lovejoy, then sports reporter at the *Derby Evening Telegraph*, wrote an in-depth piece about Derby's youth team coach. From the shadows of the reserves, Murph was getting noticed.

In the same season, Mackay took Derby to their first FA Cup semi-final in 28 years. It ended in disaster; a 2-0 defeat against Tommy Docherty's young Manchester United side. And by November 1976, despite all of Mackay's past successes, Derby sat in 19th place, one spot above the relegation zone. Barely 18 months after securing the First Division title, and a mere six weeks after thrashing Tottenham 8-2, Mackay paid the price for winning only three out of 18 league matches through the end of the previous season and the start of the new one. The turmoil which he inherited after Clough and Taylor's departure was long forgotten. When Mackay read in *The Sun* newspaper that an east Midlands manager was about to lose his job, he knew who they meant. He was incensed that the directors hadn't spoken to him first, confronted the board and asked for a vote of confidence. They turned it down.

Three years, one month and two days after they were appointed, Mackay and Anderson were on their way out of the Baseball Ground. The announcement came as no surprise; speculation had circulated for some time that Mackay would pay the price for a lack of discipline in the squad. The management role at Derby was still one of the top jobs in English football, and the rumour mill surged into overdrive. Alan Durban, the former Derby midfield star, looked to be a frontrunner. Likewise, a young Graham Taylor, who had romped to the Fourth Division title with Lincoln City the season before. Former West Ham captain Bobby Moore and Middlesbrough manager Jack Charlton were mentioned in despatches. But for the Rams' faithful, only one person could fill Mackay's shoes: Brian Clough.

Vice-chairman George Hardy dampened speculation of Clough's return. The chance was 'very remote' he said. And then he shocked the whole of the football community with his choice of Mackay's replacement. Instead of a big-name draw to fill the big man's shoes, he opted for a 32-year-old virtual unknown. On 25 November 1976, Colin Victor Murphy was no longer Derby County reserve team coach. He had just become the youngest man in charge in the First Division.

The broadsheets didn't get the chance to run with the story. Gary Newbon, a sports reporter from *ATV Today*, was handpicked by Murph to announce the breaking news. It was unusual for members of the media to bother to speak to a reserve team coach, but Newbon, of a similar age to Murph, had given him his phone number when they first met. As soon as Murph heard of his promotion to acting manager, he rang the young sports reporter and told him he would make his way to the studios. Newbon should get ready for an exclusive. Murph enjoyed the cloak-and-dagger operation, and his contact took a leap of faith in persuading his TV bosses to reschedule the day's filming. Newbon had treated a young unknown with respect, and Murph gave him his reward, an exclusive breaking story. The media circus had begun.

The 1,000-1 career opportunity of managing a First Division club, forced Murph to battle with his own conscience. He owed everything to Mackay and Anderson, the two men who gave him his first break in the professional game. Murph felt the utmost respect for both men but had to choose between personal relationships and personal opportunity. This was the chance he had always dreamed of, to put all his creative energies into managing at the highest level. Murph accepted the acting manager's job, but it took him six weeks before he could bring himself to sit in Mackay's chair.

Over a decade later, in a post-Christmas fixture at Lincoln City, Murph played host to Doncaster Rovers, managed by Dave Mackay. In Murph's matchday programme notes, he paid tribute to the man who had given him his first taste of the Football League.

'My thanks for this opportunity are eternal,' Murph wrote, 'and somehow, sometime and somewhere, there will be an opportunity for me to discuss these sentiments, but being a believer in fate, then the time and place will either arrive or thrust itself upon within convenience.'

If the prose was a little difficult to understand, the younger manager's gratitude was genuine and long lasting. In an interview with Tony Hardisty from the *Sunday Express* in 1997, he said Mackay was, 'As nice a man, as football ever produced.'

When I first met Colin, he told me of his admiration for the determined Scottish manager.

'Dave was a really decent chap. He knew his football inside out. He got on very, very well with the players. He had camaraderie, and he had respect.'

Mackay didn't blame Murph for his decision to take the Derby job; he gave the younger man his blessing. But when the all-time great published his autobiography almost three decades later, he made no mention of who replaced him at Derby; either a genuine omission or a deliberate snub.

At the Derby Book Festival in 2017, Stuart Webb, the sleek, former club secretary (later chief executive, director and chairman) of Derby County, had his own story to tell. Promoting his autobiographical account of *Clough, Maxwell and me: Explosive, the Inside Track*, Webb suggested that Murph had engineered his own promotion. A few directors travelled to away matches on the reserve team bus, and Murph as reserve team coach had talked his way into one or two of them to say he could do the job. The directors thought if Mackay left, they had a young guy, successful in the Central League, who could take over.

'A great mistake. A terrible mistake,' in Webb's opinion.

Murph remembers things a little differently.

The Derby board promised him a fair trial and an open mind about his long-term appointment.

The club needed a manager who could organise the talent they already had. The reserve team looked in great shape and the directors put their faith in Murph's coaching and organisational abilities. But the fans weren't happy. In the pre-internet age, they used the Sportsbox letters page of the *Derby Evening Telegraph* to register their complaints. They had watched Murph's reserve team play. One fan described them as 'well drilled – just like robots'. He didn't want a team of automatons turning out for his beloved Rams. Murph ignored the criticism and justified his selection. He didn't have a playing pedigree, but he opposed the long-held belief that there was an automatic correlation between playing ability and management ability; only talented players made good managers.

When I spoke with Howard Wilkinson in 2021, he agreed with Murph's opinion.

'If you're in the game long enough, once you stop playing and become a coach, if you didn't realise it before, you'll realise it soon after. Being a good player might give you a two or three per cent better chance of being a successful manager. It might. Because they are two completely different occupations; one's about "me" the other's about "we".'

Murph thought his appointment might have broken the system a bit, given other coaches the chance to achieve their ambitions in a management role. Something of a pattern was emerging. Within a six-month period, top clubs Everton and Spurs parted company with big-name managers, Billy Bingham and Terry Neill respectively, and replaced them with virtual unknowns, coaches from within their own clubs. Steve Burtenshaw was caretaker for only four games at Everton, but Keith Burkinshaw made the job his own at Spurs. Two successive FA Cups and one UEFA Cup within eight years. Proof that the progression from coach to manager could be seamless.

Back at the Baseball Ground, Murph was unfazed by his new responsibilities. The only reason he was a reserve team coach was because he wanted to become a first team manager.

'The quicker I get on with the job, the better,' he told Derby journalist Ian Vickers. 'I want to get to the top, if not I'll get out.'

The rookie manager moved into the transfer market at breakneck speed. Within two weeks, he sold Scottish international Bruce Rioch to Everton for £200,000. Murph believed you had to be able to make decisions, not ponder over whether they were right or wrong. Acting chairman Hardy announced that he had asked acting manager Murph to name the player he most wanted to buy. It sounded like a vote of confidence but in hindsight, was more likely a deft passing of the buck in case the signing went awry.

Murph's appointment came at a time of internecine wrangling among the Derby board. Seven months earlier, after

Derby's disastrous FA Cup semi-final defeat, Longson stepped down from the chair. He agreed with club secretary Stuart Webb that he would carry on for a further season if George Hardy would take on the role of vice-chair; a decision the outgoing chairman would come to regret. Hardy, a scrap millionaire, soon usurped him and became chairman in everything but name. Longson wanted Mackay to stay, Hardy didn't. Hardy wanted Murph to take over, Longson didn't. Hardy had almost total control of the board, so Mackay left and Murph stayed. But what Hardy really wanted was for Derby's messiah, Brian Clough to return to the Baseball Ground. Murph was an interim appointment, keeping the manager's seat warm. Only Murph didn't know that yet.

Longson had nothing against Derby's caretaker manager. He described him as 'a bright young man with a fine record' but he doubted Mackay's replacement would have the experience to handle a difficult situation. Derby needed a stronger man in charge. The chairman underestimated the resolve of Derby's quiet man. Thrust into the spotlight, Murph had no fear of making big decisions. When a Saturday morning fixture against West Ham was cancelled, Murph, Hardy and Webb headed straight down to London in Hardy's white Rolls-Royce. A conspicuous emblem of his success, it sported a personalised number plate — GH 2000.

The trio wanted to sign Charlton's leading striker, Derek Hales. If Murph believed the newspapers, he wasn't the only interested party in cutting a deal for the Second Division forward. West Ham, Spurs, Anderlecht and perhaps more significantly, Brian Clough at Nottingham Forest were all rumoured to be circling the bearded front man. A penalty box predator who was terrifying defences in the Second Division, the top scorer in the Football League, with 28 goals, the previous season. And back in his Southern League days at Dartford, he put a goal past Murph at Gravesend, although the gaffer chose not to remember that! In a midnight signing in Suite 1202 of the five-star Carlton Tower Hotel, Hales agreed terms with Derby. Or as Murph told the

Daily Mirror, 'We went down there and nicked him, just like Dick Turpin!'

Murph wasn't worried about being involved in transfer dealings of almost £500,000 in his first three weeks in charge. He believed that ability counted for far more than experience. He had the confidence to back his own judgement. It looked like a copper-bottomed deal. The most expensive player to leave the Second Division would be the ideal man to link with former Arsenal forward Charlie George and Welsh international Leighton James up front. Murph expected the trio to do a long-term job for Derby. Somewhat rashly, Hales told the press, 'If I don't score more than 20 a season, I'm not earning my money.'

The striker didn't earn his money. Hales scored only four goals in 23 appearances: a disastrous first signing for the caretaker manager. But the change of personnel brought some short-term respite to Derby's woes. Murph's men took six points (in the days of two points for a win) from his first five league games. They went three games without conceding a goal. The club had moved out of the bottom four and the board was making noises about offering Murph a more permanent appointment. They wanted to smooth the transition, to guide him through the early months in charge, with a general manager at his side, an adviser for the rest of the season. Longson and Webb had an elder statesman in mind, one with an immaculate pedigree, who might be tempted by a seat on the board. They were courting the holder of three First Division titles, two FA Cups and one UEFA Cup: Liverpool legend Bill Shankly.

Shankly, who retired from football two years before, had no desire to return to full-time management, but he had a successful track record in an advisory role. While still managing at Anfield, he helped Ron Yeats, his former colossus of a Liverpool captain, to take over as player-manager at Tranmere Rovers. Shankly had not lost his passion for the sport. He started at Derby in an unofficial capacity over the Christmas period, attended the clash with Leicester City and joined the team in the dressing room, before and after the game. The players, in particular fellow Scot Archie Gemmill, welcomed the veteran's involvement. If, as Webb later suggested, Murph felt threatened by Shankly's arrival, he didn't let on.

In January 1977, after a three-and-a-half-hour board meeting, Murph threw off the title of acting manager and accepted a full-time post. A 20-1 outsider, he had come through the field with a £15,000-a-year salary, a 12-month trial, but no long-term contract. He knew that some people would think he was a puppet manager, but he said it would be up to him to select the team, decide the tactics, and deal in the transfer market.

'They've brought Bill Shankly here in an advisory capacity and if I don't listen to a man like that, I'd be a bloody fool,' he told Peter Batt from the *Evening News*, 'but I still know that it's down to me. If I make it, I'm going to have to make it on my own. And I know who'll be leaving if the decisions and results aren't right.'

With Shankly as general manager and Murph in charge of team affairs, it should have been the perfect arrangement, but it didn't work out. No matter what Shankly had achieved, no matter how much he could have helped him, Murph just didn't want the Liverpool legend at the Baseball Ground. They travelled around together for a month, shared hotel rooms and discussed their views on the game, but Murph couldn't delegate, and he paid the price. The relationship drifted apart. Four years later, after Shankly's sudden death, Murph acknowledged his mistake in his weekly column for the *Lincolnshire Echo*. He admitted that as a young manager, he thought he knew it all. And as a slightly older manager, he probably still did. By failing to capitalise on what Shankly had to offer, Murph missed the opportunity to do what Graham Taylor did at Watford. By bringing in former Double-winning Arsenal supremo Bertie Mee as his assistant, Taylor leapfrogged from the Fourth Division to the First in just five years. Perhaps if Murph had welcomed Shankly as general manager, his Derby County story might have ended differently.

Colin Murphy shakes hands with cigar-wielding chairman Sam Longson, at the Baseball Ground. 6 January 1977, the date of Colin's permanent appointment as manager of First Division Derby County. (Photograph from the Murphy family collection)

After accepting the full-time job, Murph felt confident that 12 months with Derby would be enough to make his name as a manager. He couldn't wait to put a lifetime of footballing thoughts and theories into practice, and he would run things his own way. The press delighted in the rags-to-riches story. A flurry of national headlines suggested that this Cinderella was going to have a ball. But the priority for the season would be First Division survival.

For six weeks, Murph and Richie Norman, the youth team coach, had juggled three teams. The boss needed an assistant manager, 'a talented guy, not a yes man' as Murph put it, so he could execute his plans to restructure the coaching setup. It was time to call up Dario Gradi, former Chelsea reserve team coach under Dave Sexton. Gradi, who was born in Milan, and grew up in Croydon, was one of only a handful of FA staff coaches. With more First Division experience than Murph, both men were excited by what they could achieve with the Derby team. Murph, outwardly at least, appeared undaunted at managing a group of England internationals and household names. Roy McFarland, Archie Gemmill, Charlie George and Colin Todd, were all respected players throughout Europe. Murph didn't care that he had spent his own football career in the non-league game.

'Why should they frighten me?' he said to Peter Batt. 'They might be world-class players, but in my days in the Southern League, I ran into skivers, conmen, mercenaries, villains and a lot of nice guys too. So, you could say I know the ways of the world.'

Murph was a tracksuit manager of the new generation. He didn't sit down unless he had to, never walked when he could run, blinked repeatedly as he spoke. At his first away game at Black-pool, the players still called him 'Murph' rather than football's more deferential 'boss'. Murph said he didn't care what the players called him so long as they continued to play for him, and he had their respect. If management was about motivating and managing all types of people, he had the best grounding. Batt, a seasoned sportswriter with a lacerating tongue, wasn't often impressed. But when he met Murph after Derby's cancelled third-round FA Cup replay, the Fleet Street hellraiser showed an unprecedented respect for his fellow Londoner. The journalist reported that Murph displayed a 'finely balanced blend of matey-ness and aggression which to our jaundiced eye gave him an even chance of survival'.

Murph's harsher critics said the Derby players wouldn't play for him because he had no reputation in the game. The gaffer disagreed. He wasn't a big-name manager, but he knew how to scuffle. And he had a theory on successful management; good managers made more good decisions than bad ones. It was as simple as that. He had 12 months to prove to his detractors that he could make some good decisions. At least that was what the board had told him. But the directors were working from an alien calendar. Only 47 days after Murph accepted the full-time job, Stuart Webb returned from a publicity trip to Sweden, and announced arguably the biggest volte-face in English football history. The board had voted. Forget the resignations and the recriminations. After three years and four months away from the Baseball Ground, they had invited the self-styled 'Ol' Big 'Ead' and his running mate back. Clough and Taylor were coming home.

Hardy, the power behind the Derby board, doled out platitudes. Murph was one of the nicest men he had ever met, a man of integrity and moral fibre, but he wanted the best for Derby County, and the best was his former management team. If Murph thought they had set him up as a fall guy, he kept it to himself. He cleared his desk, left the Baseball Ground and took Gradi home with him. They opened a couple of bottles of wine, sat down in Murph's sitting room, and waited for the inevitable.

The following morning, they drove to the Raynesway training ground, assessed the mood of the players and told them all to go home. Boardroom politics had overridden FA Cup preparation. Murph and Gradi spent the day in Murph's office, waiting for the outcome of the talks; mere bystanders as the press and television cameras descended on the Baseball Ground. Longson as chairman was equally powerless. He was stunned by the news that the board had approached Clough. In his autobiography, *Sam's Story*, published by his family 24 years after his death, Longson wrote that he asked the board to allow Murph to stay on. He argued that Murph had picked up the pieces after Mackay's departure. The team was taking shape and they should give him more time. The claims seem disingenuous now, a piece of political manoeuvring. It's unlikely that Longson positively wanted Murph, the newly promoted reserve team coach. It's much likelier that he simply didn't want Clough, the thorn in his side. No wonder the press viewed Murph as a pawn in a high-stakes game played out by the Derby board.

Longson needn't have worried. The board had dangled the First Division carrot in front of Brian Clough's nose. Twenty-four hours later, he rejected it and walked away. He wouldn't be returning to the Derby he loved. His reasons were unclear. Perhaps out of loyalty to Nottingham Forest who came in for him, after his 44 ill-fated days in charge at Leeds United. More likely, the move was a bloody-minded two fingers up to the Derby board who had accepted his resignation in the first place. Clough said it would be impossible to build a better team than the one he had left at Derby, but he returned to the City Ground with one aim: to take Nottingham Forest back to the First Division. Three months later, he did exactly that. Within 12 months of promotion, the unfancied east Midlands team won the 1977/78 First Division title. And roll forward another 12 months, they were champions of Europe.

In what might seem to us now as an almost comical show of arrogance, Clough's rejection of their offer stunned the Derby board. Reeling from his prophecy that Forest could be a bigger club than Derby, they held an emergency board meeting, skulked back to their management duo and offered them formal contracts to the end of the calendar year. Murph's fellow league managers told him he should refuse the offer and walk away, but he believed he was finally in the driving seat. With a formal agreement on the table, his and Gradi's short-term futures would be secure. Murph knew he was jeopardising his family's security by staying without a long-term contract, but he couldn't bring himself to leave the job he had always wanted. He returned to the training ground the next morning, faced the press and batted away the chairman's comment that you couldn't put an apprentice in charge of tradesmen. The younger man recognised he lacked experience, but this was different from a lack of talent.

'If a youth player has the ability to get into the first team, he is still called an apprentice,' he told the *Express Sport*.

Murph ignored the slight from the cigar-smoking chairman, 44 years his senior, and knew that it had required more strength of character to stay than to leave. He believed the experience had made him stronger, both as a man and as a manager. Gradi was sanguine about the effect on the players. The excitement wouldn't have done them any harm. If anything, it would have geed them up a bit. It had done more than gee up the board. Longson's resistance to Clough's return marked the death knell of his 11 years as chair. The board proposed and seconded Hardy to take over. Longson received the consolation prize of honorary president, to add to his New Year's Honours OBE.

Murph asked for the opportunity to get on with the job, without constant speculation about his future. There were more pressing problems to face; an FA Cup fifth-round tie against Blackburn, and a midfield department stricken with injury. The manager kept his team talk before the Blackburn game, short and sweet, 'Forget me. Forget Cloughie and forget the club. Go out there and play for yourselves.'

Brevity did the trick. The team played their most relaxed football for months, and with a 3-1 win romped through to the last eight of the FA Cup.

'Let's just say it was my most consoling 90 minutes of the week,' Murph said to Jeff Farmer, the *Daily Mail's* football man in the north. The beleaguered manager had come through the week's drama with his dignity intact, perhaps now he could start to make plans.

Looking for a goalscorer to replace Bruce Rioch, Murph didn't have time to dwell on the result. For three weeks he badgered Tommy Docherty at Manchester United to release the 22-year-old visionary midfielder, Gerry Daly. At £175,000, the deal was done. Murph was gradually putting together a team, but little did he know that what Docherty gave with one hand, he could take away with another. As the season continued, Murph picked up praise from his First Division opponents. After a 2-2 home draw against Norwich City, manager John Bond admired Derby's way of playing their way out of trouble. Almost every other side at the bottom of the table would try to hoof their way from the back as the only line of attack. Despite all the problems Murph had endured in the previous four months, he was still intent on playing football; passing the ball around, building up moves, keeping possession.

Murph exerted more control over some things than others; he could determine the style of play, but not the quality of the pitch. If they hoofed the ball up in the air at the Baseball Ground, it landed with a thud. For 17 years, groundsman Bob Smith suffered the torments of a surface which stood four feet below street level and refused to drain. The mud was covered in sand and the pitch markings were indistinguishable. With five games to go of the 1976/77 season, 3-0 up against Manchester City, Daly came forward to take a penalty. Except he couldn't, because the penalty spot had disappeared in a quagmire of mud. Smith appeared at the side of the pitch, dressed in a grey flannel jacket, flared trousers and black tie, carrying a metal pail and paintbrush. The groundsman paced the distance from the goal line and painted the mud to mark the penalty spot. The spectators were so close to the touchline, they could almost have reached over the barrier and done the job for him. A far cry from the hallowed turf of Old Trafford, Daly scored.

Murph's signing of the Republic of Ireland international signalled an upturn in Derby's fortunes. Two wins and three draws marked the end of the season. Derby finished their campaign in 15th place, five spots clear of the relegation zone. Murph reflected with satisfaction on his achievement. When Clough rejected Derby's approach, the Rams sat at the bottom of the table. In his last 17 league games, Murph suffered only two defeats. He had done what the board had asked him to do. Longson acknowledged in his autobiography that what Murph lacked in experience in First Division management, he made up for with a nerve and skill, which astounded the veteran observer. Yet, when Murph returned from an end-of-season trip to Spain, the national newspapers speculated his job was up for grabs again. This time, Tommy Docherty appeared to be the great pretender to the Derby throne.

While the rumours circulated, Murph returned to Bisham

Abbey, on the opposite side of the flip chart, a student on an intensive two-week management course. Allen Wade had drawn up a two-year programme for managers handpicked by the FA. It intended to get managers to strip layers off themselves, to go on a 'voyage of self-analysis'. Two years earlier, the cohort included Bobby Robson, Graham Taylor and a man who would later offer Murph a lifeline, old-school Scotsman Jimmy Sirrel. The FA training centre's curriculum followed an imaginary club, Third Division strugglers Hamford Albion. Candidates had to apply for the vacant job, manage an unhappy squad, and sort out the club's finances.

Some parts of the course proved more relevant than others. The mythical club gained promotion in its first season. It presented the classmates with a new set of problems, managing success. Murph didn't have the luxury of that scenario in the outside world. He received no recognition for keeping Derby in the First Division. And this rankled him. Headlines about Brian Clough winning promotion for Nottingham Forest rubbed salt in the wounds. It didn't matter that it was a third-placed finish, grabbed with 51 points, the sixth lowest tally for a promoted side. Clough was only two and a half years into his contract, and the newspapers reflected his glory.

'Happy Clough confesses, it's just a miracle how I did it,' the headlines read.

Murph felt that fighting relegation was just as tough as chasing promotion, but far less glamorous. He took over a club struggling at the bottom of the table, when morale was low and internal problems were rife. Murph said he was paid to manage a football team. Unlike Clough, he wasn't a master of self-publicity. Maybe he could be as good as the fans' favourite, but he needed the board to give him the chance to prove it. As the summer dragged on, events took an unexpected turn. Fresh from Manchester United's FA Cup Final victory over Liverpool, Tommy Docherty's name hit the headlines. The press exposed the married father of four's affair with Mary Brown, the team physiotherapist's wife. The manager called it a personal matter and refused to resign, but the board disagreed and found him in breach of contract. Within days, the Glaswegian firebrand was on his way out of Old Trafford. And the football crows circled over Murph's head once again. Undeterred by the Doc's formidable reputation, Murph was bullish in his own defence.

'There's nothing Tommy Docherty can do for this club that I can't do,' Murph said to the press.

If the board of directors judged their manager by success and achievement, Murph said he'd had little time to display success, but he could already show his achievements. He had kept the club in the First Division, and with the likes of Gerry Daly was rebuilding the team. He had received a vote of confidence from the board. They were honest people and would stand by it. Whether Murph was canny or naive in his comments, he had no intention of quitting.

'I've fought them all off so far and I intend to be at Derby a lot longer yet,' he told the *Mirror Sport*.

Murph's fellow league managers feted the underdog's success. George Petchey, fresh from a Second Division relegation battle, spoke to Vic Railton from the *London Evening News*. The Leyton Orient manager would be toasting Murph and Derby County in the season ahead. He blamed Murph's situation on local politics and prejudice, rather than any fault of the manager himself.

'He stuck his ground. Good luck to him, he's the biggest victory for a long time.'

Even Railton, who had seen it all in football, said that a new contract was a notable victory for Murph and a considerable triumph for football itself. He suggested that football managers all over Britain would sleep a little sounder at night.

George Hardy returned well tanned from a Mediterranean cruise and confirmed Murph's position to the press. The only manager the chairman had wanted was Brian Clough. Since Clough had signed a four-year contract with Nottingham Forest, Murph's job was safe. Hardy assured the press that Derby had no interest in pursuing Tommy Docherty. Murph believed he could get on with the job in hand, throw off the stigma of being on a permanent trial and face the team and the forthcoming season with renewed authority. Docherty was on his way to Norway, on a £40,000 two-year contract with Lillestrøm SK. Or so everyone thought, including the Lillestrøm chairman.

The manager who replaced Docherty at Old Trafford was the same man who replaced him at Chelsea, Dave Sexton. A fellow Londoner, whom Murph admired; modest, full of integrity and a great motivator. Murph knew that Sexton instilled a sense of discipline in his Queens Park Rangers side. It explained why in only his second season in charge, QPR narrowly missed out on the First Division title. Murph's softly-softly approach kept Derby in the First Division and himself in a job, but at the start of the new campaign he was ready to follow Sexton's example and take a tougher stance on discipline.

'It's time the gloves came off,' he told Joe Lovejoy. 'Some people here won't know what's hit them next season. They've been having things too easy for too long.'

Murph finally felt he could walk around the club without wondering what people were thinking. His confidence mirrored the enhanced reputation of the town itself. In the close season, Derby was awarded city status as part of Queen Elizabeth II's Silver Jubilee celebrations. And when England defenders Roy McFarland and Colin Todd both signed new long-term contracts, Murph viewed it as a vote of confidence. The inexperienced manager had never suffered from a lack of belief in his technical ability, but he knew that team discipline, on and off the pitch, would be under scrutiny. It had probably cost Dave Mackay his job.

Under Murph's new regime, any player who accumulated over ten disciplinary points would see their wages cut. Any player suspended for reaching 20 points would get a fine for each match missed. Both Charlie George and Leighton James started the new campaign under suspension and lost a week's wages. Murph wanted to strike a happy medium between fear and discipline. He urged other managers to follow suit.

As the season gathered pace, Murph faced bigger problems than disciplinary issues. A series of injuries to key players and loss of form from others saw Derby propping up the First Division, only shielded by Newcastle from the lonely extremities at the foot of the table. County correspondent Gerald Mortimer described Murph 'like a man trying to run up the down escalator'. No matter how hard he was working, he couldn't seem to convert the effort into results. Derek Hales' goals had dried up since he joined the First Division. And as Murph prepared for a critical match at home to Leeds, the BBC reported on air that a managerial appointment was imminent. Stunned at the news that Tommy Docherty's name was linked with his job once again, Murph said he knew nothing about it. By a strange coincidence, ever since Brian Clough turned down a return to the Baseball Ground, Fleetwood Mac's *Rumours* had featured in the UK album charts!

Cold comfort for Murph. He had no option but to carry on preparing for the next game. Knowing that his job was on the line, he made a do-or-die decision, dropped his £300,000 striker from the starting line-up and gave a league debut to an 18-year-old from the reserve squad instead. A remarkable experiment and a career-changing decision for David Hunt, defender turned midfielder. A besuited Murph sat next to Hardy in the directors' box for the September fixture. Murph was oblivious that his 49-year-old Glaswegian adversary was sitting in the stands. In a pulsating display against their northern opponents, Archie Gemmill and Billy Hughes gifted their troubled manager a 2-0 lead at half-time. Murph took some comfort from knowing Derby were playing their best football of the season. Yet, before the final whistle blew on a 2-2 draw, his fate was sealed. After ten months of living on a perpetual knife edge, despite the promises and the public declarations of support, Murph's time was up. Hardy relieved him of his duties.

'Two points from ten,' was the chairman's brusque explanation.

The arrival of Tommy Docherty, a big-name manager, wouldn't do the chairman's reputation any harm. Yet the announcement unleashed the vitriol of the national press. Sportswriters across England savaged Derby for showing what they called 'the despicable side of football'. They believed that Murph and Gradi had done an honest job at a challenging time. The Derby board recruited them to keep the club in the First Division. They had done just that. John Sadler, 'the man who gives it to you straight' from *The Sun*, took aim at the Derby board,

'If Mrs Thatcher were to introduce a referendum on football this morning, Derby County would almost certainly be voted the nastiest club in the country.'

The chief sportswriter wrote that the Rams still only belonged in the First Division thanks to Murph's thick skin and perseverance. There was talk in the press that he would stay on as assistant manager, but neither Murph nor Docherty relished the idea. Within a week of arriving at the Baseball Ground, the new manager prepared to make wholesale changes. He offered Derek Hales on loan to any club which would take him and began a frantic round of transfers; 16 out and 14 in, within a year. The frenzy of transfer activity didn't pay off. Docherty managed a 12th-placed finish in his first season, and 19th in his second. If Murph was the inexperienced skipper who tried to steady the Rams' ship, Derby fans remember The Doc as the old captain who almost sank it.

Battered and bruised by the Derby experience, Murph began his search for a new job. First, he had to do 'the usual messy business' with his former chairman to receive compensation for the remainder of his contract. Murph worried that negotiations would drag on. He needn't have done. At a Derby reserve game against Nottingham Forest, he found help from an improbable benefactor, the ghost of Derby County, Brian Clough. Murph told John Wragg from the *Daily Express* how he happened to bump into the Forest manager who asked him how things were going. Murph explained his financial situation. Without hesitation, Clough took matters into his own hands. He hustled the out-of-work manager into a room, sat him down and summoned Hardy to join them. Sitting on the floor between the two men, Clough told the chairman he should do the right thing by his former manager. By the power of Clough, Hardy listened, and Murph received his compensation. Ol' Big 'Ead still wielded an unseen influence, long after he had left the Baseball Ground.

Murph later confided in Jeff Farmer, 'Nothing could be harder than the inferno I walked through at Derby.'

Yet he insisted that the ten traumatic months had not shattered his confidence. He still wanted to prove himself and show what he could do. The rookie manager had little time to dwell on disappointment. After only 48 hours out of work, Jimmy Sirrel restored Murph's faith in the football family. The legendary Scottish manager invited him to make the return trip to Nottingham and join him as coach at Second Division Notts County. Murph would soon learn that the Jimmy Sirrel school of management was as unusual as the man himself.

3

DOWN BUT NOT OUT

NOTTS COUNTY AND LINCOLN CITY

'Ye dinnae need to train with the balls, Colin, it's the balls that get you the f***ing sack. Make 'em run!'

Jimmy Sirrel barked his coaching suggestion to Murph, as he made his way across the pitch at Meadow Lane. The buck-toothed Glaswegian manager had returned to Notts County from Sheffield United for his second term in charge. In the six-year period to 1975, Sirrel had led County from a lowly Fourth Division club through two promotions to the Second Division. He rejoined a County side which faced a relegation scrap back to the Third. Sirrel appointed Murph to look after the reserve team and improve the standard of the youngsters moving into Meadow Lane. The two men had met on their weekly scouting trips, scouring non-league football for promising players. Murph admired his sharp-tongued eccentric boss. Former apprentices recall how the gaffer would come into the club after training, sit in the bath for hours on end and do his daily exercises, wearing a wetsuit as fragrant as his native River Clyde.

David Pleat recounts a story which Murph told him about working for Sirrel at County. One evening, the gaffer asked Murph to come into training the next day, wearing a collar and tie.

'Why's that boss?' he asked.

'I'll tell ye when I see ye.'

After a short training session the following morning, Sirrel told Murph they were getting in the car and driving all the way from Nottingham to Glasgow to watch a player at a little-known club. After a 300-mile journey they arrived at the ground. They had watched 25 minutes of the game when Sirrel turned to Murph and said, 'I've seen enough. We're off!'

Whether it was the player's gait or his attitude, there was something the gaffer didn't like. He drove the pair straight back down from Scotland to Nottingham. A 600-mile round trip.

'That's how eccentric, Jimmy Sirrel was,' Pleat told me, 'And he was Colin's mentor!'

Six months after he arrived at Notts County, Murph received his FA Coaching Licence. The FA's little red book was a permit to teach Association Football at all levels. The lessons that Murph learnt from Sirrel about football management were even more valuable. Murph survived the pressures of life at the Baseball Ground, but in the relative tranquillity of Meadow Lane, he learnt his trade. The wily gaffer, 22 years his senior, taught him that man management was the most valuable skill of all. A decade later, in conversation with David Spurdens from the *Daily Express*, Murph explained what it was like working with his former boss.

'I'd do the man a disservice to say it was an education. It was far more than that. It was a philosophy. A way of life.'

Sirrel was known to throw jugs of tea in the dressing room, and bark uncooperative answers to journalists on the hunt for a quote, yet he formed strong friendships with his players and management team. He was committed to nurturing the young-sters in his squad. Sirrel taught Murph if the gaffer earned the players' respect, they would try for him more than they would try for themselves. And if that happened, the boss was in with a fighting chance.

Howard Wilkinson held Sirrel in equally high regard. The two men had met at Lilleshall in the early 1970s, when Allen Wade invited Wilkinson to join his FA staff. In his first managerial role, Wilkinson took charge at County after Sirrel stepped aside to become general manager. The chairman of the LMA spoke with great admiration of his former colleague,

'When you talk about management in any sphere, you're talking about authenticity, sincerity, honesty, leadership, the ability to engage with people. To get them to understand the journey and to get them to understand their part in it. Jimmy Sirrel was that, but Colin was that also.'

Notts County first team squad at the start of the 1978/79 season. Centre front, manager Jimmy Sirrel. Standing on the second row, far left, trainer Jack Wheeler; far right, coach Colin Murphy. (PA Images / Alamy Stock Photo)

At the end of the first season of Murph's journey, Notts County finished in 15th place. One of seven clubs sitting above the relegation zone, implausibly separated only by goal difference. Twelve months after Murph joined the Magpies, Sirrel believed the management team was getting into its stride. But the old pro didn't know that events in the county town of Lincolnshire might turn his assistant's head. At the start of the 1978/79 winter of discontent a deep malaise permeated the whole country. Amid widespread national strike action, Third Division Lincoln City parted company with their deeply religious, deeply unsuccessful boss. The football hard man, Willie Bell, quit the club after ten months to become a soccer missionary with the Campus Crusade for Christ in America. He left Lincoln in an unholy mess. Bottom of the table; five points and nine goals from 14 games.

Murph received a call from Heneage Dove, local farmer and Lincoln City chairman, about the vacant position. Sirrel's right-hand man knew straight away he wanted to take the job. The decision to leave the gaffer took a little longer. Murph had to battle once again between allegiance and personal ambition. Just like Mackay, Sirrel had offered Murph a lifeline, and the younger man didn't want to let his mentor down. Working for a year alongside the seasoned professional at Notts County had given him five years' worth of experience. It was under Sirrel's guidance that Murph appreciated what management was all about. But in the battle between ambition and allegiance, ambition won. Despite having a young family, job security wasn't at the top of Murph's agenda. He would give up a secure position as Sirrel's number two to risk it all to become the boss again.

The Lincoln City job offered a step back up to the only job he had ever wanted, managing in the Football League. Sirrel wished his reserve team coach well; he admired his ambition. Although he said it was a matter of opinion whether Murph would be better off staying at Meadow Lane. Murph knew he was putting his career on the line, but he couldn't resist the challenge of rescuing Lincoln City from a disastrous season, sorting out the club and rebuilding for the season ahead. It was only the first of many gambles he would take in a 35-year career in the professional game. And he fancied the idea of moving the family to Lincoln.

'You can get a palace there for £20,000!' he said.

It would take time to get used to the setup at his new club. Derby and Notts County boasted an army of paid helpers. Lincoln City relied on volunteers. When Murph took up the job at Sincil Bank, he sat in his cubbyhole, so small you could barely call it an office, lodged under the old wooden stand. His signed contract lay in an envelope on the desk in front of him. As Murph reflected on the mammoth task ahead, Chris Ashton, a young teacher and Lincoln City volunteer, walked in to speak to the manager. Ashton remembers the day as if it were yesterday, happy memories of a long-term association with the City boss. The volunteer shook the snow from his boots and Murph handed him the contract to take to Gilbert Blades' office, a 20-minute walk to the Glory Hole in Lincoln. The boss put his hand in his wallet and pulled out an old green one-pound note,

'That's for going up there for me.'

Ashton delivered the contract to the office of solicitor and Lincoln City director Blades, but he didn't spend the oncer. He kept it as a keepsake for years.

At his first game in charge since his brutal departure from Derby County, Murph arrived in the visitors' dressing room at Hillsborough to find a pile of good luck telegrams waiting for him on the table. He might have hoped for a message from George Hardy, but Murph was sanguine that managers rarely won battles with chairmen. He was keen to move on. Heneage Dove, chairman of a club two divisions below Derby in the Football League, appreciated what he had found, a manager with unbounded enthusiasm and First Division experience. It impressed him that Murph only asked for a short-term contract and limited compensation if he didn't succeed. And Murph appreciated that the board would give him the freedom he needed to get on with the job.

The Lincoln City players were under no illusions when they reported for training on his first day in charge. The holiday was over. He was going to get them fit and organised and if they wouldn't do it willingly, they would do it the hard way, training morning and afternoon. Murph's experience at Derby had toughened him up. Brian Clough haunted the Baseball Ground, and when Murph arrived at City, the spectre of Graham Taylor still hovered over Sincil Bank.

Taylor had left for Elton John's Watford 16 months before, and two City managers had been and gone since then. Taylor was a man who achieved so much for both the club and the city. The job appeared to have frightened people off. But Murph wasn't afraid of comparisons. He vowed to organise the team like his famous predecessor had and embrace the city in the same way too. After that, the team would play his way, because if he didn't succeed at Lincoln City, failure would finish him. Murph not only needed to rebuild his career but the structure of a club which had collapsed since Taylor won the Fourth Division title in such style. Seventy-four points and 111 goals in one season. It was quite an inheritance, but Murph felt ready for the challenge.

At his first team talk in the Sincil Bank dressing room, he looked at each of the players in turn.

'I don't know what's been going on at this club, but if Phil Neale can't make it into the team, something's not bloody right.'

Neale, the Worcestershire County Cricket Club middle-order batsman and Lincoln City full-back, previously suspended by Willie Bell, breathed a sigh of relief. He'd got the approval of the gaffer, or at least semi-approval.

'But you can shave that bloody beard off,' Murph said. 'I never trust a bloke with a beard!'

Neale had grown the facial hair during a dispute with the outgoing manager; a minor act of rebellion from the clean-cut defender. He had signed for Lincoln City after Graham Taylor's father, a sports journalist for the *Scunthorpe Evening Telegraph*, spotted his potential. Taylor didn't believe the club should penalise Neale for his talent at two sports. Although the cricket and football seasons overlapped, the manager applied a general rule: if the Imps were fighting promotion, Neale would stay to see it through. If Worcestershire were at a crucial stage of the season, the defender would delay his return for pre-season training. Sometimes it clashed, but mainly it worked, until Willie Bell, a straight-talking Scot, took over as manager.

He suspended Neale for his delayed start to the season and told the press he wasn't fit enough for the reserves. Bell made him do extra training, running up and down the South Common every afternoon. The talented sportsman was about to walk away from football, but kept in close contact with Taylor, who advised him to sit tight. His former manager's gut feeling was right. Neale kept his place in the first team, and Bell jumped before he was pushed.

Skipper no.14 Dennis Leigh shakes hands with the new gaffer, Colin Murphy, when he takes over Lincoln City, in November 1978. A bearded Phil Neale, in the striped shirt, and fellow teammates look on. (Image courtesy of the Lincolnshire Echo*)*

When Murph arrived at Sincil Bank, he faced a more complex set of challenges than whether Neale could juggle two sporting careers. The club was poles apart from First Division Derby County. Murph could no longer choose from 15 or 16 first team players and decide which three of ten apprentices to retain. City boasted a first team squad of 12 players. The club was losing money, and apprentices were scarce.

Managing in the lower divisions was a much more hands-on affair. At Derby, Murph managed a team, but at Lincoln he would have to manage a club. The transition would challenge him. He needed more patience in explaining what he wanted from players, more involvement with the Supporters' Club, more skill when dealing in the transfer market. And he had very little time. By mid-November, City were languishing at the bottom of the Third Division, five points adrift from the rest of the field. They boasted the worst playing record in the Football League.

After landing the number one spot, Murph called up his former flatmate, Lennie Lawrence, with the offer of a job. In the musical chairs of football management, Malcolm Allison had given up his post at Plymouth Argyle for an ill-fated return to Manchester City. This left Allison's number two without a job. Lennie had relished his brief spell as caretaker manager before 'Big Mal' arrived and was desperate to stay in the professional game. Murph's job offer couldn't have come at a better time. The City boss said he wanted Lennie to join him, but he didn't specify the role. Lennie thought he was going as Murph's assistant. It turned out he'd accepted the job of reserve and youth team coach.

'I went there without really knowing that,' Lennie told me, 'but in fairness he was right. I thought I was big-time, but I wasn't ready.'

Lennie recalls that when he arrived at Sincil Bank, his old pal Murph had picked up some of Jimmy Sirrel's unusual habits. Murph ran around Sincil Bank at breakneck speed, and Lennie had to remind him to eat. Murph modelled himself on his former boss, who ate his breakfast cereal the night before. It saved him time in the morning.

'It's good enough for Jimmy!' Murph laughed as he turned down another offer of a solid meal.

Bert Loxley, former trainer, player, manager and club physio, in his 15th year at Sincil Bank, completed Murph's management team. The gaffer described Loxley as a stalwart of the club, like Gordon Guthrie at Derby, and Jack Wheeler at Notts County. Murph was ready to assess the strengths and weaknesses of his players, but poor weather brought the show to a halt. At the start of the coldest winter in 16 years, four cancelled away games destroyed continuity, and goalkeeper Peter Grotier picked up an injury. Lodged at the bottom of the Third Division, Murph found out who his First Division friends were. Ipswich manager Bobby Robson offered goalkeeper Laurie Sivell on a six-week loan. Sivell's first of only two appearances brought City face to face with Graham Taylor's Watford. An unhappy meeting for Murph's first encounter with arguably the Imps' most successful manager. City slumped 2-0 away from home.

Behind the scenes, Murph worked well with Lennie, but he didn't always see eye to eye with his reserve team coach.

'I was a purist,' Lennie admits, 'and we clashed a bit. I didn't always agree with his coaching methods. And at times I was reluctant to do what he said.'

Lennie recalls how in the middle of winter, Murph encouraged the players to run around on an unplayable pitch, throwing snowballs, larking around in the snow. It offended Lennie's coaching principles. He couldn't see the point of it.

'He's mad. Do you think it helps?' he asked striker Gordon Hobson.

'Yeah, I think it does,' the player said.

Lennie realised that right from the start, the players 'got' Murph, and they 'got' his motivational methods. And for that reason, they would play for him. But by the middle of March, with 18 games left in the season, the Imps faced almost certain relegation. Murph was clinging on to his track record. Three times he had joined clubs which were struggling, and three times they survived the drop. But with successive drubbings away from home, 6-0 to Swindon, 5-1 to Chester and 4-1 to Walsall, Murph accepted the inevitable. The team wasn't good enough to avoid relegation. Two months later, propping up the table with a meagre 25 points, Lincoln City dive-bombed out of the Third Division.

Despite Colin Murphy's punishing training schedules in the 1978/79 season, Lincoln City couldn't avoid the drop. Colin leads the pack ahead of Mick Smith (no.19), Brendan Guest (no.7), John Fleming (no.6), Phil Hubbard (no.4), Terry Cooper (no.5), Alan Harding (no.16), Dennis Leigh (no.14) and Alan Jones (no.8). (Image courtesy of the Lincolnshire Echo)

Murph had already made a show of commitment to the City fans and tied his long-term future to the club. He moved Judith and his young family from their home in Castle Donington to the Lincolnshire village of Thorpe-On-The-Hill. Despite relegation to the bottom tier of the Football League, the Imps' faithful shared his optimism. After three years in the Third Division, they no longer saw themselves as a Fourth Division club. As soon as the season finished, the fans inundated Lincoln bookmaker Jim Hicks with enquiries about the odds for them going straight back up. He offered 8-1 for the championship, and only 2-1 for a place in the top four. The end-of-season odds reflected that only a handful of players remained from Taylor's championship-winning side.

Murph had set out to change the ageing but popular team and made no apologies for wielding the axe. Taylor did the same in the winter of 1972, when the 28-year-old former Imp succeeded David Herd as manager. Some of Taylor's decisions were unpopular, but the fans soon forgave him when they saw results. Apart from one or two players, Murph felt the team lacked the talent to survive. Twelve players departed company on free transfers. It wasn't just the squad Murph wanted to change, but the image of the club. He said he would promote discipline and integrity as his key values. And he would do it with a young side.

Faced with the wholesale transformation of a football team, Murph knew he hadn't accepted the job to make himself popular. He described himself as a demolition expert knocking down unwanted chimneys. He intended to rebuild a team with players who had pride and conviction in their performances, young signings hungry for success. One player survived the cull: the now beard-less Phil Neale. Murph, useful with the bat in his younger days, supported Neale's dual roles with Worcestershire and Lincoln City. The university-educated, Russian-speaking defender appreciated the gaffer's continued support.

Brian Clough faced a similar situation a decade earlier, with Ian Buxton, the Derby County inside-forward and Derbyshire all-rounder. But Clough was less accommodating than Murph. Anton Rippon, author, columnist and aficionado of all things Derby County, reported in the *Derby Evening Telegraph* that when the player didn't arrive back for the first day of pre-season training, the manager told him he would never play first team football again. Not one to miss a good selling opportunity,

Clough picked Buxton for the next game. Derby won 3-1, Buxton scored, and Clough sold him to Luton Town for five times his original price tag, as a valuable member of the first team squad!

In a similar stroke of good fortune, six months after he arrived at Sincil Bank, Murph approached the board of directors for an extension to his short-term contract. He asked for one year. They gave him two. Chairman Dove cited Murph's work ethic and his honest approach as the reasons for extending the agreement. Murph welcomed the vote of confidence. He felt responsible for the young players he had brought to the club and gushed to the press that the directors had given him the freedom to get on with the job. Murph needed to savour this glorious honeymoon period. He wouldn't always enjoy such a positive relationship with the Lincoln City board. But the small-club setup where he controlled everything suited him. He supervised the first team training, made new signings, watched the reserve team play.

He wanted to assess young players; wanted them to know that he was interested in their development. He attended schoolboy trials to run his eye over future apprentices, hoping to get their first foot on the professional ladder. Murph encouraged Lennie to play an inexperienced team in the reserves, to give a handful of schoolboys the chance to play games in the Northern Intermediate League. Using the same principle he had applied in the Central League at Derby, he valued player development over results. Lennie acknowledges he didn't always agree with his boss, 'I didn't appreciate some of his managerial quirks and mannerisms, but it was exactly what Lincoln needed at the time.'

Murph recognised that his primary job was to get the team out of the Fourth Division, and if he achieved that, the fans would forgive everything else.

'If we go up, people will no doubt say I am a good manager. But I will still be the same manager I am today,' Murph said.

Of course, he wanted promotion, but he wanted to bring on the youngsters as well.

At First Division level, you could spend money on a player

and know he would perform for you. Three tiers lower down, you couldn't be so sure. With severe constraints on capital, Murph and Lennie needed to be more inventive in the transfer market. They scoured non-league to find players who were hungry and had something to prove. A young Jamaican striker from Southern League Stourbridge caught their eye. With 36 goals to his name, Tony Cunningham was creating more than a little interest from professional clubs. But at 21 years old, he didn't see Fourth Division Lincoln City as the pinnacle of his aspirations. He rejected City's offer of a trial.

Cunningham told me how a chance encounter caused him to reconsider. As he was waiting to meet the Stourbridge team coach in a hotel car park on the M6, he bumped into former Wolverhampton schoolmate, Derek Statham, with his West Bromwich Albion teammates. The England U21 player introduced Cunningham to his namesake, the legendary winger and style icon, Laurie Cunningham. They started chatting. Laurie questioned why Tony would turn down the chance of a full-time contract and told him if he received an offer from a professional club, he should take it. In the summer of 1979, they both made history. Laurie Cunningham became the first British player to transfer to Real Madrid for £950,000, and Tony became the first black player to sign for Lincoln. His £20,000 transfer fee set a non-league record at the time.

Still keen to expand his team, Murph sent Lennie on a scouting mission, a Thursday night trip to Stafford Rangers. The England non-league team was playing its first international semi-professional tournament at Marston Road. The gaffer gave strict instructions for Lennie to watch a promising centre-half from Nuneaton Borough.

'Don't come back and tell me he can't play on the ball. Just come back and tell me if he can defend.'

Lennie reported back, 'He's not the greatest on the ball, but he's a bloody good defender.'

Satisfied with his hunch, three days later, Murph drove to

watch Trevor Peake in his second outing for the England C team, against the Netherlands. He realised he was watching the best centre-half in non-league football. Peake had delayed joining a league club in favour of completing his trade apprenticeship. With transfer fees beyond the reach of many clubs, more part-time players were progressing to the Football League.

Peake was ready to sign for Northampton Town in the close season, but Murph invited him to Sincil Bank for talks. The manager outlined in detail what he expected from his centre-halves.

'He seemed to have a plan,' Peake recalls over 40 years later. 'He was confident we could bounce straight back. He said all the right things.'

Peake took his dad to the meeting for moral support, and impressed by the manager's thoroughness and vision, the 22-year-old signed professional forms the next day. A £15,000 fee from the Southern League made him the second highest non-league transfer after Tony Cunningham. Peake had to take a pay cut from working on the factory floor and gave himself two years to make it work. Four years later, he was playing for Coventry City in the First Division. The gamble paid off.

Murph recognised it was easy to spend money, but not so easy to get value for money. To do that, he needed to shimmy his way around the transfer market. Murph knew how to find a player, and he wasn't afraid of putting in the legwork to do it. Every night he was on the road, scouring the non-league circuit, putting 200,000 miles on the clock of his trademark white Mercedes. He also needed patience. Murph and Lawrence tracked Cunningham for three months before signing him in a meeting at midnight.

'No one's heard of him. I want someone who's got something to prove. Just like I've got something to prove,' Murph confided to sports journalist Mike Fennell.

Murph liked a player with Cunningham's profile: strong and fast, but with a rawness about him. He would spend countless hours on the practice ground with his new signing.

'Lay that ball off. Make that run. You've got to be in the area to damage them.'

Murph felt that Cunningham lacked the natural skill of striker Mick Harford, but he made up for it with his pace and strength. Murph liked that. And he liked to mould his young players. The Lincoln board supported their manager's dealings in the transfer market, determined to assemble a team which could take City back into the Third Division. Chairman Dove insisted that balancing the books would have to come later. He couldn't fault his new manager's commitment and told the press that Murph had barely stopped to eat, breathe or sleep, since he joined the club.

As the team was taking shape, Murph took an uncompromising approach to pre-season training. New signings Tony Cunningham, Trevor Peake and David Carr all received a baptism of fire when they trained with their teammates for the first time. For four intensive days, the 'Death or Glory' boys from the 17th/21st Lancers put the Imps through their paces. The team's initiation into army life at Bovington Camp included early mornings, cold showers, and clambering over 12ft walls on the army assault course. Murph believed that teamwork formed the backbone of all successful sides.

Dave Mackay had taken his First Division stars to army camps when he was in charge at Derby County, and Murph recognised the benefits of camaraderie as well as discipline. Even if Lincoln couldn't be big buyers, he would do his best to develop a collective competitiveness and a sense of team spirit.

To boost their chances of an early return to the Third Division, Murph extended his coaching team. He turned to the considerable experience of a man who had felt the golden touch of Brian Clough. John Sheridan, an experienced defender with Notts County, transferred to Hartlepools United, before the club changed its name, and after Clough took over as manager. Sheridan followed the boss as coach to Derby, Brighton and Hove Albion, and Nottingham Forest, and arrived at Sincil Bank fresh

from a spell as the national coach to Qatar. Murph enjoyed the
Clough connection, but over time regretted his decision to bring
Sheridan to Lincoln. Forty years later, in one of many conversations we had about his career, Murph described his former
assistant as a 'poor signing'; a coach who failed to develop a strong
relationship with the players.

Murph built his new team around Harford and Cunningham. Most teams played with a big centre-half and a smaller
covering defender, but Murph put his two powerhouses up front.
Both over six feet tall, impressive climbers and headers of the ball,
Cunningham offered pace and Harford brought control. If their
teammates gave them the service they needed, they could challenge any opposition. Murph believed that it was the front men
who destroyed teams. He likened Harford and Cunningham to
Radford and Kennedy, who hunted as a pair when Arsenal did the
Double back in 1971.

As he bedded in the team, Murph soon learnt that victory
could bring as much criticism as defeat. A bad-tempered game
against Tranmere Rovers in late September 1979 saw Lincoln win
3-0 at home and score two penalties. When the last goal went in,
Murph flicked the Vs towards the Tranmere dugout. He avoided a
caution, but not the wrath of an enraged Lincoln fan who fired
off a letter to the *Lincolnshire Echo* demanding a printed apology.
Murph refused to take the criticism lying down. Instead, he gave
the complainant a lecture in philosophy.

According to Murph, the fan was mixing up moral attitude
and moral behaviour; a moral attitude doesn't bring about moral
behaviour. Murph explained that he fined the fans' favourite
Gordon Hobson £50 for taking a dive and getting an opponent
booked at Walsall the week before. He criticised the pre-meditated
immoral behaviour, but his own action was different, not
dishonest or cheating. He was celebrating the third goal, which he
described as 'a triumph for football'. Murph offered a lukewarm
apology if he'd upset anyone but suggested that the disgruntled
fan might have done better to write a word of praise for the

team's performance: two penalties gained by good attacking football.

Only three months after Peake's arrival, Murph expressed regret that the strong man of City's defence wasn't already rubbing shoulders with the likes of Derby's Roy McFarland in the First Division. But he brought Peake to the club to teach him, and he wouldn't let him go till the time was right for both the player and the club. Murph was looking to buy another Peake or Cunningham, a player he could work on and bring through.

Surviving in the Fourth Division was like walking a tightrope, balancing the strength of the team with the financial needs of the club. Murph knew that First Division sides were sending their scouts to City games. It was a double-edged sword; positive confirmation that he was making the right signings, but unsettling for the players. He realised that no Fourth Division club could exist on gates alone; at some point they would all have to sell to survive.

Murph committed City to a policy of young players. He found them easier to coach and motivate; they displayed greater ambition and fewer vices. But he also needed another older player to organise things out on the park. He found the perfect combination of youth and experience in 23-year-old Derek Bell, a proven goalscorer with Barnsley and a runner who would break down the left-hand side of the pitch. By December, Murph considered City as one of the most skilled teams in the Fourth Division, but when they struggled in two or three games against more physical sides, he saw the reality of playing in the lower league. If they played too much attractive football and weren't physical enough, they wouldn't get off the bottom rung. Looking to play a more physical game, Murph signed full-back Trevor Thompson from Newport County. The boss was unconcerned that he brought a reputation for 'over-robust tackling' along with him.

When Murph started talking about selling City players for six-figure sums, nobody believed him; Lincoln was not that kind of club. But they sat up and took notice when he signed a deal to sell his 21-year-old central midfielder, Glenn Cockerill, to Swindon

Town. Cockerill became only the fourth player to move from a Fourth Division club for a fee of over £100,000. It was too good an offer to refuse, but Murph was sorry to see Cockerill go. He felt sure he could have fixed him up with a club in a higher division. In fact, the move didn't work out and Murph liked the midfielder so much, he brought him back to Sincil Bank 18 months later. Challenged at a shareholder meeting before Christmas, when he would stop dealing in the transfer market, Murph said, 'I'll stop when I've got a good enough team to keep me in a job!'

He didn't know how long it would take to build a team, but it could take twice as long as it did to ruin one. It all depended on how much cash was available, or if the talent was homegrown. At the end of January, he signed midfielder George Shipley from Southampton for a club record fee of £38,000. His advice to the former First Division player, 'George, you don't pass the ball to him, you just loan it. You're like a bank manager. You loan it, because you want it back!'

In the 15 months since Murph took over, 17 players had left the club and 11 players had joined. City were fielding a trans-formed team, including eight players under the age of 22. Murph prided himself on promoting the youngsters. He played Phil Turner from the youth team for his debut against Wigan; a 17-year-old central midfielder pitted against one of the strongest teams in the division. The Imps won 4-0. Murph explained his theory on what to look for in a young player: enthusiasm, tech-nical ability and physique. It helped if the youngster was clean-cut and had a decent family too. Although Murph wrote in his news-paper column, 'That's not to say that if I saw a complete rascal who had some football talent, I would turn him down!'

The Manager's View in the *Lincolnshire Echo* became Murph's mouthpiece; a weekly ramble around all things football, and at times, a chance to vent his frustration. He complained that defensive tactics from the opposition ruined the game for teams who wanted to play football. Following a dreary 0-0 draw at home against Northampton Town, Murph accused the Cobblers' manager, Clive Walker, of playing eight men in defence. He criticised Tranmere Rovers for playing a sweeper at home. If defensive tactics stifled attractive attacking styles of football, it would destroy the game for their fans.

Murph knew that in a rural community you had to work harder to get supporters through the turnstiles. Statistics showed that a club operating on five per cent of the population would be in reasonable shape. With gates averaging almost 4,000, Lincoln were there or thereabouts. But they had to avoid complacency. The club needed to come up with something new to engage the fans.

Murph responded by sending his football team out into the community to drum up support. Players paid 'get to know you' visits to local factories, toured the shop floor and chatted with staff. Murph presented fundraising cheques and handed out prizes at pub darts competitions, cricket clubs and village halls. Even Murph's wife Judith wasn't spared the call to arms. The 26-year-old mother of two smiled for the camera, as she bought a sponge cake at the Aubourn Over 60s Club coffee evening, from ladies unlikely ever to set foot in Sincil Bank.

Murph left no community stone unturned. Ruston's Gas Turbine works hosted a Maurice Burton Mastermind special. The local *Lincolnshire Echo* journalist turned quiz compiler pitted the Lincoln players against the Waterside South workforce. Ruston's edged it with a tiebreaker, but Mick Harford proved to be City's top scorer, both on and off the pitch. Murph invited Burton into the football fold, and in return the journalist acknowledged Murph as the saviour of the Imps. It was Murph's team that they were watching each week.

'Not always with the confidence that they would win,' Burton wrote, 'but certainly knowing that the team wore the club colours with ambition and pride.'

With a net surplus in the transfer market, the board appreciated the manager's progress. He had put together a team out of thin air and re-formed a club with no cash. Murph objected to being called a wheeler dealer, he wanted to show his true skills, coaching and organising the team. His aim was to build a team fit for the Third Division, not just to win promotion from the Fourth. He wanted a team which could look towards the second tier with some hope of success. And help him fulfil his dream of returning to management at a higher level.

Murph became a champion for the little clubs of the Fourth Division. When Ted Croker, secretary of the FA, proposed controversial changes to the league structure, Murph didn't hold back with his criticism. He rejected the call to limit entry to the top two divisions, and scrap full-time professionals in the Fourth. He abhorred the idea of running regionalised mini leagues to replace the bottom two tiers of the Football League. He believed that players, managers and supporters alike, needed the incentive of playing at the highest level. If you took away the chance of promotion, you would stifle enthusiasm and ambition. Under the new proposals, Graham Taylor's Watford wouldn't be on course to leapfrog from the Fourth to the Second Divisions in three consecutive seasons. As his parting shot, Murph told Maurice Burton that if Croker had made his suggestion in Lincoln, 'I think someone would have strung him up from the cathedral belfry!'

Murph believed that Fourth Division outfits had to decide for themselves if they were going to be a 'Mickey Mouse club' or a proper part of the Football League. The organisation demanded full-time professionals, floodlights, groundsmen and decent training facilities. If lower-league clubs couldn't fund this from revenue, they should make way for other clubs which could. Murph saw City as the exemplar of a Fourth Division side. They were installing new floodlights, building a new gymnasium, had appointed a new groundsman. And the manager, as luck would have it, had signed a further 12-month extension to his two-year contract, a commitment to the club until May 1982.

By March 1980, Murph was developing a settled line-up. City were pushing to get among the promotion challengers, when disaster struck. Mick Harford, top scorer with 14 league goals, faced a two-month recovery from a cartilage operation. Murph tried to put a positive spin on the crushing news. It would give another player the chance to step up and prove himself. Murph concentrated on what he did best, strengthening his squad.

He had his eye on a centre-half from Northern Premier League Boston United. With Lennie at the wheel of Murph's Mercedes, they made a three-hour journey down to Dulwich Hamlet on a Tuesday night, to watch the FA Trophy quarter-final replay. Boston won 2-0 and Murph knew he had found a player who would complement Trevor Peake in his back four. The next morning the gaffer put a call through to Sheffield Newspapers, where Steve Thompson, Boston's no-nonsense hard man, was selling advertising space. Thompson remembers the phone call well.

'Steven,' Murph said, 'I'm going to change your life. But what's that f***ing noise I can hear in the background?'

'I'm in the classified department. It's full of telephones.'

'It's no good, we need to speak in private. Call me back and make sure it's from a phone box.'

In an age of recruitment, five years before Vodafone launched their first mobile phone in the UK, Thompson went to a Sheffield city centre phone box armed with a pocketful of 10p pieces. As he fed the payphone, Murph told him, 'I'm going to make you into a football player. You've got all the ingredients, but you need to stop getting sent off.'

Murph would still be saying that to him, two years later, at a promotion-deciding game against Fulham.

Thompson signed for Lincoln at the end of the season, and Murph introduced his confident central defender to the dressing room.

'This is Steven Thompson. He's got more f***ing disciplinary points than we've got league points!'

The disciplinary record of his new medallion-wearing signing didn't worry Murph. In the right areas of the pitch, he loved players who were tough and uncompromising and stood their ground. With his latest addition, Murph reached a milestone; 30 transfer deals in 18 months.

Cunningham slotted home four goals during Harford's absence through injury, but it still wasn't enough. They had left their promotion push too late. Murph hadn't achieved what he set out to do in his first full season in charge. Despite scoring nine goals in the last two games including a hat-trick for Gordon Hobson, Lincoln finished the season in 7th place. Rebuilding the team had taken longer than Murph hoped, but he had put together a group of players with the right attitude and drive.

Trevor Peake remembers the reaction of the young squad, 'We were disappointed, obviously. We wanted to get promoted, but we were clever enough to recognise it was a transitional period. We were still learning as a group. There was no bad feeling towards Colin.'

Murph signed off The Manager's View, his last of the season, on an optimistic note, 'We have fitted together in a nice little unit with a bright future for us all.'

One question remained. Would that bright future include promotion at the second attempt?

4

THE SKY'S THE LIMIT

LINCOLN CITY

Murph rubbed his hands with delight at the League Cup first-round draw. Lincoln City faced Third Division Hull City at the start of the 1980/81 season. The Tigers had been active in the transfer market, trying to recover their Second Division status, and no one gave Murph's young upstarts a chance. But they sat up and took notice when the Imps handed out a 5-0 thrashing to their opponents in the higher tier. A hat-trick for Mick Harford, and another brace in the return leg at Boothferry Park. Seven goals from City and two clean sheets in four days. The gaffer had published his statement of intent. Yet Murph knew a season and a career can turn in an instant.

In the fourth league game of the season, summer signing Colin Boulton, Derby County's championship-winning goalkeeper under Brian Clough and Dave Mackay, broke his leg so badly it ended his career. Murph took a chance and plucked David Felgate from the relative obscurity of Bolton Wanderers' reserves. It was a good hunch. The player who produced three clean sheets in his first four games earned an international cap for Wales within three years.

Before a top of the table clash at home to Aldershot in mid-September, 4,446 voices of local support cheered Murph as he stepped on to the pitch. The proud recipient of the Fourth Division Manager of the Month award, Murph dedicated the honour to the 'ability, application and discipline' of his players. He didn't mention if he would share the prize; a gallon bottle of Bell's whisky, 4.5 litres in new money.

Colin Murphy receives the Fourth Division Manager of the Month award for September 1980. (Image courtesy of Lincoln City Football Club)

Harford, the Player of the Month, took home a *Match Weekly* plaque and a cheque for £100. And at the end of the game, the knowledge that the 1-0 result was City's first home defeat in 26 league games. With two points lost in the race for promotion, Murph warned against overconfidence and complacency from his young players. Only Phil Neale, the club's longest serving player at the age of 26, had fought a previous promotion battle.

The energy of Murph's inexperienced team excited him. And Third Division Chesterfield saw something they liked in the Imps' spirited manager. The Spireites came in for Murph's services in their push for promotion. He turned the job down. The City players had placed their future in his hands, and he intended to repay it with his loyalty. The team returned the faith with a comprehensive 8-0 thrashing of Northampton Town, including four goals for Gordon Hobson. The player's hat-trick at Torquay at the end of the previous season had persuaded the gaffer to play him in a central striking role. Murph's priority was to keep a solid squad; if competition existed for first team places, every player would have to up their game.

With Bell and Cunningham snapping at Harford and Hobson's heels, Murph was still on the lookout for new recruits from non-league. He was no stranger to standing outside mines, factories and foundries, knee deep in snow if needed, in search of his next signing. Murph told sportswriter Tony Hudd that only a few years earlier, any young miner would have jumped at the chance of becoming a professional footballer. With a relative leap in wages, he found it difficult to tempt them with an offer of £130 a week to appear in the Football League.

There couldn't have been a better time to join the Imps. After 23 games, only First Division Liverpool had scored more than Lincoln's 42 goals. And with 13 goals against, only Ipswich had conceded fewer. Lincoln were sitting a single point behind top-of-the-table Southend. A catch me if you can battle, which would occupy copy editors for the rest of the season.

Despite the team's success, Murph still had to wrestle his local critics. In his first season in charge, the club made a loss of £90,000. A year later, the deficit had reduced by only £10,000. Murph didn't pull any punches. In The Manager's View he blamed the losses on his predecessors' bungling and inefficiency; overspending in the transfer market and overpaying players for the division they were in. To get the team to the top of the league would be one thing but achieving financial stability would take much longer.

Fourth Division clubs were forced to be sellers, not buyers. It wasn't what Murph wanted, but both he and the fans had to face reality. In the 1979/80 season, Lincoln secured total home league attendances of only 85,000. Murph had clawed this back to almost 58,000 at the halfway point in the new campaign. If the fans wanted to criticise his success, Murph warned they should look for another manager.

'If ever I elect to leave this club,' he wrote, 'I will give one promise. It will stand up on the pitch, it will stand up at the bank and any new manager will have what we call in football, "A nice little job".'

Five years after Heneage Dove took over as chair, he stepped down at the annual shareholders' meeting, and passed the hot seat to a younger man: impeccably groomed local potato magnate Dennis Houlston. Murph described his relationship with Dove in The Manager's View.

It 'certainly had plenty of argument in it, but at times was almost completely harmonious ... without a shadow of a doubt, we agreed on certain things concerned with the club, though possibly we often disagreed about the means of achieving them'.

Murph was at his diplomatic best dealing with his former paymaster, but he wouldn't always be so conciliatory with future chairmen.

The newly appointed chair knew that Lincoln City owned a ground and a team which were increasing in value. But even to compete in the Fourth Division, they couldn't take immediate benefit from either asset. The outgoing chair painted a bleak financial picture. Murph's squad, with a conservative value of £500,000 matched Taylor's team from 1975; their league position, their young players and the quality of football played. But there was a gaping chasm opening up in the finances of the club.

Within five years, wages had more than doubled. With the country deep in recession and no signs of improvement, Lincoln couldn't rely on increased gates to solve their financial problems. The stark reality of a growing deficit forced Murph to conjure up an end-of-year bonus for the club. Knowing he had to balance the books, he called Peake and Harford into his office. Several clubs had shown an interest in Murph's skipper and leading striker.

'One of you will have to go,' he told the pair.

Murph was honest with both players. They knew which clubs had expressed an interest, and the stage of negotiations. Reluctantly, the gaffer took a decision which would devastate the fans.

Many of them saw the big-money sale of Glenn Cockerill as a one-off transaction. They didn't expect that only three years after he signed for Lincoln, another of the Imps' favourites would leave Sincil Bank.

On a frozen December morning, Murph took an early train from Newark with his prolific goalscorer, Mick Harford, to talk terms with Newcastle United. The 21-year-old striker had scored 15 goals in five months, three hat-tricks in his City career, one in a 5-0 drubbing of Torquay United only a month before. Harford arrived at Sincil Bank from Lambton Street Boys' Club as a talented right-half. Under Murph's guidance he had developed into a formidable centre-forward and done no harm to his transfer value in the process.

Harford's sale to Newcastle set a new Fourth Division record; a £180,000 fee which would drop into the black hole of the club's operating costs. Trevor Peake stayed at Sincil Bank to see the campaign through and pick up the Player of the Season award for the second year running. He didn't have any regrets when we spoke four decades later.

'Mick had started the season well, and I was just happy with how the team were performing, enjoying my life as a footballer. I'd worked in a factory from 16 to 21.'

Murph recognised the irony of his success. If he did his job well, and helped players to develop their skills and understanding, he would continue to lose them to the higher leagues. He didn't want to sell Harford, but as a 'responsible football manager' he knew he had no choice. In an interview with sports journalist, Dave Spurdens, several months later, Murph said, 'It hurt to part with him, but at the same time, it would have hurt even more if the club had folded under the strain of high interest rates.'

Nineteen months into Margaret Thatcher's 11-year tenure as prime minister, bank rates stood at 14 per cent. By the end of 1980, inflation had soared to over 16 per cent. By helping the club's finances, Murph made his own job harder. But he still saw enough strength and character in the team to push for promotion.

After a lean spell in front of goal, the fans might have forgotten that Tony Cunningham scored 15 league and cup goals in the previous season. The athletic forward reminded them with an emphatic man of the match performance in his next home game against Mansfield Town. A hint of confidence that alongside Hobson and Bell, he could fill Harford's shoes. Although City benefited from a rising market with the sale of their 'head waiter' the bumper transfer fee exposed a general malaise. As football entered a new decade, every manager in the Football League bemoaned a trilogy of woes: inflated transfer fees, the scourge of hooliganism and falling gates. For the most part, transfers were no longer cash transactions. Murph argued that if all fees had to be paid in cash within seven days, some sanity would return to the market.

Lincoln were the only Fourth Division team not to lose a league fixture in December. Yet Murph was more impressed with the team's character than its results. They battled the psychological effect of losing Harford with greater positivity than when they lost Cockerill the season before. The Kent Messenger Group's chief football writer, Tony Hudd, asked Murph what had changed. The manager flicked through the well-thumbed dictionary he kept on his desk. He stopped at 'team spirit' and read out the definition, 'The willingness to act for group rather than individual benefit.'

Steve Thompson told me of the strong bonds which were formed within the squad.

'I became very good friends with Trevor Peake and Tony Cunningham. We were three working lads who had come into football. We trained together. We went out together. We were like the three amigos.'

Murph had built an inexperienced team which would fight for each other. The defence was under extra pressure without Harford up front. They knew if they conceded a goal, they would struggle to bounce back with two to win, but the gaffer gave them confidence and renewed determination. Murph treated each player as an individual; some had to be worked hard, others left alone. But they all had one thing in common; at three o'clock on a Saturday afternoon, they controlled his destiny. He remembered Jimmy Sirrel's advice: the most important reward for any manager was the players' respect.

Murph looked back on the year with satisfaction. He felt confident he had earned the ultimate prize. With an effective defence and attractive attack, Lincoln was producing exciting football. Murph believed the game should be played in the penalty boxes; do well in your opponents' box, make no mistakes in your own, and you would win matches. He recalled Jimmy Sirrel's pithy catchphrase, 'If ye dinnae score, ye dinnae win.'

The City boss encouraged his full-backs and midfielders to get forward to put pressure on the opposition, to produce attacking play. He would get no satisfaction from fielding a successful team, still playing in the Fourth Division. Lincoln needed to strive for promotion from the Third. And maybe they could dare to do a Grimsby, like former City boss George Kerr, and leapfrog from the Fourth to the Second Division in consecutive seasons.

'If we aim for the sky, we might get halfway there,' Murph wrote in The Manager's View, 'and that in itself would be a big achievement.'

Murph's passion and long-term vision brought a new year's gift from the board; an extension to his contract until May 1984. Houlston announced the offer without Murph by his side. His manager was standing in front of an FA Disciplinary Commission with suspended skipper Trevor Peake. Murph accepted the contract extension. And in his weekly newspaper column, he philosophised on the nature of ambition, achievement, and success. In the world of football management, he saw two options. You could change jobs every couple of years, achieve, move on and repeat; advance your own career, but miss out on the reward of watching a player develop. Or you could take the long-term view, bring in a lad on schoolboy forms, sign him as an apprentice, make him into a professional, and see the programme through. Murph preferred the latter, while retaining an option on utopia, taking a club from the Fourth Division through to the First.

He believed the biggest achievement in life was to leave something behind. If he left City in three years' time, he wanted to leave a legacy of a new gymnasium, a few good quality players and Second Division football. He might have to settle for two out of three.

Murph appreciated the heavy responsibility which lay on the shoulders of his inexperienced team. They faced a tough challenge; battling promotion and trying to tempt recession-hit supporters back through the turnstiles. Inevitably, at times, tempers frayed. Almost 40 years after the event, Steve Thompson still remembers an argument which broke out at a snow-covered Sincil Bank. Playing a game of five-a-side in the car park, Murph's assistant, John Sheridan, tripped Tony Cunningham up on the tarmac. The player picked himself up and rubbed the skin from his hands. Cunningham, unafraid of sticking up for himself, squared up to the old-school coach. Sheridan turned round, made a wise crack, and tripped up the 6ft 2in striker again. Cunningham swung a punch and hit the gaffer's number two, who scrambled to his feet.

'I've never been knocked down in all my years in football!' Sheridan said.

Cunningham swung for him again. Tommo laughs at the memory.

'We're all looking at Colin, thinking what the hell's he gonna do?'

Murph's response?

'John, I'd go for the best of three!'

When I met Cunningham at his office in Lincoln, I reminded him of the car park incident, curious whether the story might have improved with age.

'I heard you decked him twice,' I ventured.

'He's probably right there. I think I held him by his throat or something.'

And after a moment's hesitation, the former striker turned defence lawyer said, 'But I can assure you, John didn't cross me again!'

Murph liked a good scrap. In team talks before a game, Tommo remembers how the gaffer would run through the opposition team list,

'Steven, that one likes a drink. He'll have been p***ed on Friday night. When you get a chance, give him a f***ing whack!'

A far cry from the unpolluted diet of the modern era. Murph recognised that the squad needed to let off steam, but he believed in the ethos of bringing on junior players and giving them 'the right habits' to have the best chance to succeed. A youth development programme had to be a vital component of the club. Any club which shirked its responsibilities to its youth policy had no future. The challenge was to run a programme at a profit over several years. Lincoln had five lads from Sheffield in their ranks: Gordon Hobson, Phil Turner, Stuart Hibberd and Wayne Biggins, all signed from junior football for a song. The fifth, Steve Thompson, a bargain at £15,000, formed the bedrock of the defence with Trevor Peake.

While Murph praised team morale after Harford moved to Newcastle, it was difficult to deny the impact of the towering playmaker's departure on the club's results. Although City enjoyed a run of 12 unbeaten games in the league, they included seven draws and only 14 goals. Harford hadn't just been a goalscorer but a match winner too. Hobson, Harford's great football friend and rival, found his goal tally falter at 15. Murph relied on Felgate, who conceded only seven goals in a dozen matches. And somewhat out of character, the manager recognised the positive contribution of the referees.

Earlier in the season, the press devoted column inches to the relationship between officials, players and the governing bodies, regarding the role of red and yellow cards; a system introduced for the 1970 World Cup. The FA had waited six years to join the disciplinary party, but only five years later, the English Football League abolished its use. The FA blamed 'demonstrative referees'. It appeared that the power of the red card encouraged officials to show off. Murph said he disagreed with getting rid of the disciplinary system; it made it easier for everyone to know what was going on. But as the season developed, he changed his mind. Relationships between players, officials and managers seemed to have improved.

Murph believed the referees played a part in City's success by enhancing the quality of play. Yet six years later, the Football League changed their minds again and reintroduced the disciplinary system. In an ironic twist, the first recipient of a red card in the 1987/88 season was ex-Lincoln ace Harford, playing against Murph's old club Derby County.

As the transfer deadline approached in March 1981, the economic recession dampened the usual level of activity. Murph predicted there would be salary shocks in store. The freedom of contract rules introduced four years earlier allowed players to move clubs after their contract had expired. It was difficult to know who benefited more, the individuals or their employers. The Professional Footballers' Association (PFA), the world's oldest professional sporting trade union, lobbied for a limit on transfer fees. They predicted that 500 league players would be out of work at the end of the season.

Government policy was getting inflation under control with high interest rates, but at the expense of rising unemployment. Six thousand people a day were joining the dole queue. In the professional football arena, managers could pick the players they wanted, and decide how much they were prepared to pay.

Murph looked at his team of largely homegrown talent and non-league purchases with an element of pride. He took it as a compliment that Southend's manager, Dave Smith, was constantly looking over his shoulder at Murph's inexperienced City side. The day before the Blues' fixture against Scunthorpe, 14 members of the Southend squad turned up with their manager to watch Lincoln play. As the challenge for the title heated up, so too did the gamesmanship. Faced with their top-of-the-table clash in Essex the following week, Murph chose not to play the usual Friday night fixture and opted for a Saturday afternoon kick-off instead. He didn't want to play the more experienced Roots Hall team under floodlights and intended to take as much travelling support as he could. Southend got their revenge and charged the Lincoln fans £4 for a standing ticket which cost the home support £2.

After a hard-fought 0-0 battle, where tension on the pitch spilt over on to the terraces, the Lincoln team acknowledged the 2,500 travelling supporters. Relieved smiles spread across the Lincoln City dressing room. Two points behind Southend. A game in hand. A goal difference of three to recover in the remaining five games. City were still well placed for a title challenge. Until they took their travelling support to Mansfield Town. Two goals down and two points lost. Lincoln took a tumble in the race for the championship.

Murph appeared to have anticipated the backlash. In The Manager's View published in the *Lincolnshire Echo* the same day, he lobbed a well-timed grenade.

'What is a supporter, what is a cynic, what is success?' he asked.

Murph's 1,000-word essay, a third-person reflection on 'a national basis' couldn't hide the irritation of this particular manager. He wrote a thinly disguised attack on cynics who criticised rather than championed the team. The manager may well have been frustrated by selling his best player, yet he carried on with a less experienced side and found a different form of success. Murph suggested this manager could 'put his head on the pillow at night and know he was beyond reproach'.

Criticism of the lack of variety in the team's style of play was a minor distraction from chasing promotion. At home to Port Vale, one goal scored, two points gained. Lincoln fans had already done the maths. Three games to go before the end of the season, City were still challenging for the title spot. But whatever happened, they'd be climbing out of the Fourth Division on 4 May.

Promotion at the second attempt; Murph had chance to breathe. And the contributors to the Lincoln City match magazine took a collective bow. *Birmingham Evening Mail* allotted them the Fourth Division Programme of the Year award. Murph's manager's notes, Colin Murphy writes, were feted for the first time. It was only the start of Murph's literary career. There would be more high-profile awards to come.

The team made the 220-mile journey to their Bournemouth fixture, feeling distinctly more relaxed. And the gaffer was learning to delegate. He left his reserve team coach in Lincoln with strict instructions.

'Lennie, this is what I want you to do. Take David Hughes with you and go and get that little winger from Scunthorpe.'

Murph had another deal up his sleeve, swapping Hughes, a midfielder he'd inherited from Willie Bell, for the 'little winger' in question, Steve Cammack. The Scunthorpe player was reluctant to leave the Iron, and the club was reluctant to sell him, but with £140,000 of debts hanging over them, they had little choice. In an era before footballers had agents and managers had mobile phones, Lennie remembers sitting in his car outside The Old Show Ground with papers in hand. He had to find a phone box and register with the Football League by five o'clock.

'What about the directors?' Lennie asked Murph. 'Do they know about this?'

'Nah, just do it!' the gaffer said.

With his transfer deals done, Murph savoured the last home game of the season. After a blinding diving header from Tony Cunningham, the final whistle blew on a 1-0 victory over Darlington. Hundreds of fans invaded the pitch, desperate to celebrate their team's hard-won promotion. Murph appeared in the directors' box, spraying a bottle of champagne, and wearing a grin as broad as the Railway End terrace. He had achieved what he set out to do. In dogged pursuit of champions, Southend, Lincoln hadn't dropped out of the top two since the end of August.

Maurice Burton caught up with Dennis Houlston after the last home victory of the season. The impeccably dressed chairman, who looked more like a film star than a potato farmer, reflected on what his manager had achieved in two and a half years in charge. A restructured team with mostly young players, two record-breaking Fourth Division transfers and a promotion to boot. At one stage in the season, Murph's first team, Sheridan's reserve team and Lennie's juniors all topped their respective leagues. The strength of Murph's management team supported his ambitions. He had taken the Imps out of the Fourth Division for only the second time in 19 years, with a young and improving side, built and developed from the sale of its own players. Hobson had emerged from Harford's shadow and scored 21 goals. The manager was enjoying an uneasy peace with the Lincoln City board. What could possibly go wrong?

With proceeds from the Mick Harford sale, City were in a stronger position than champions Southend. The Blues stepped up to the Third Division, trailing a £250,000 deficit behind them. Promotion came at a price. Even ignoring wage demands, the Imps faced a significant hike in operating costs with no immediate increase in revenue. City's away games at Plymouth, Portsmouth, Exeter and Carlisle would all require overnight stays.

Murph didn't waste the summer worrying about the cost of success. On the premise of a family holiday, he took a flight to Fiji for the whole of July. He just happened to have contacted Allen Wade, the FA's director of coaching, offering the Fiji Football Association (FFA) his services. With less than a week's notice, the FFA decided to send a team to the inaugural competition of the South Pacific Mini (SPM) Games; a 1,600-mile trek to the Solomon Islands. Never one to shy away from a challenge, Murph had only two days to give simple and swift training to the hastily cobbled together team. He smiled for a photo opportunity with the national team coach.

'There's no time for any real tactical stuff,' he told the *Fiji Sun*. 'They'll get confused.'

It was a mutually beneficial arrangement. The amateur FFA received pro-bono advice from a professional English football coach. The local Fijian press reported with enthusiasm that Murph was a coaching badge holder, recognised by FIFA. And rather less accurately, that he played for First Division Newcastle United in the 1960s. If the district associations used his services, they paid for Murph's travel and accommodation. Even on holiday, Murph couldn't resist brokering a deal. He wrote a report for the FFA on how to develop football through coaching schemes at the national level. Fiji fared better at the SPM Games than Western Samoa, who endured a minus 45 goal difference after only six games.

At the end of his stay, Murph batted away suggestions he might make the arrangement with the FFA more permanent. He had a three-year contract at Lincoln to fulfil. But the idea of working abroad offered a certain attraction. In four years' time, after an unexpected change of circumstances, he might be tempted by sunnier climes.

Murph returned from Fiji to a new points system in the Football League. Three points for a win instead of two; a move designed to promote attacking football. Murph suggested a more radical approach to enhance the game, restructuring players' wages in line with results. The psychology of players fascinated him. He wondered how their attitude would change if they received more money for an away win or an away draw, than a home draw. Would it make the game more interesting for their supporters and stem the tide of falling gates?

Four games into the new season, Murph faced more pressing concerns than a hypothetical change to the wage structure. With his defensive duo Thompson and Peake on crutches with a stress fracture and damaged ligaments, deputy Phil Turner joined the hobbling pair in plaster. Facing a League Cup game against First Division newcomers Notts County, Murph took a risk and brought his injured skipper back. The gamble paid off. After nine missed games, Peake scored the equaliser. Murph was pleased to have Glenn Cockerill back in the team, re-signed from Swindon Town at the start of the season. The gaffer looked forward to taking the Imps back to Meadow Lane for the second leg. County was still a well-run club under his mentor, Jimmy Sirrel, and Murph saw Lincoln as 'Notts County Mark 2' operating at a lower level.

Murph's success against higher opposition didn't go unnoticed. He emerged as favourite to replace Richie Morgan at struggling Second Division Cardiff City. Mindful that Watford had tempted Graham Taylor away from the Bank with disastrous consequences, Lincoln City's board of directors didn't want history to repeat itself. Dennis Houlston, described by Maurice Burton as 'a man who usually gets what he wants', made an unexpected announcement. An updated contract would secure Murph's services at least until May 1985. The manager wouldn't walk away from a team he built himself. He wanted to stay to reap the benefit. Murph appreciated that Houlston and the board of directors backed his plans, a welcome change from the odd stormy altercation with the previous chair.

Murph celebrated his new contract with a third defeat in a row. There was still much to do.

The gaffer took the second-leg result against County in his stride. He allowed City's physio Bert Loxley, a former County player, to revel in the 3-2 victory. The boss was more interested in the third-round draw, a chance to pit himself for a second time against Graham Taylor's Watford. Undeterred by the commitment of their Second Division opponents (five of Taylor's players had needed stitches in the previous three games), Lincoln held Watford to a first-leg draw. In the replay, despite two goals from Tony Cunningham, Lincoln lost 3-2. In the changing room after the game, Murph ripped into Steve Thompson about covering Watford's hero, Luther Blissett.

As Murph stormed out of the room, Tommo turned to Peake

on the dressing room bench, and asked, 'Peakey, was I marking Blissett?'

'No.'

'F***ing hell, he's just ripped into me, I'm not having it.'

'Tommo. Don't do it, you know what you're like, don't do it!'

Thompson wasn't listening. The red mist had descended. He strode across to the boss's office, where Murph took one look at his raging centre-half and put his hand under the desk.

Psshhhhh. The sweet sound of release. Murph stretched out his arm and handed Thompson a bottle of beer.

'Right, Steven, what do you want to say?'

Tommo took the bottle in stunned disbelief. For once, Murph's garrulous centre-half was lost for words.

'Shall we talk about it tomorrow, Steven? And by the way, drink the beer before you go back into the dressing room.'

High expectations in the 1981/82 season. Chris Ashton, far left, from the Lincoln City Supporters' Club, and Maurice Burton, second left, from the Lincolnshire Echo, *join Colin Murphy and the first team on the away bus. (Image courtesy of the* Lincolnshire Echo)

November brought two more causes for celebration; England qualified for the 1982 World Cup finals in Spain, and popular Yorkshireman John Pickering took over from Sheridan as Murph's number two. The gaffer hoped that Pickering's coaching expertise would help develop the squad; the former Blackburn Rovers manager had a great deal of experience. Lennie Lawrence, Murph's youth team coach, recalls he didn't welcome Pickering's arrival as much as he might. Lennie still thought he should have been in line for the assistant manager's job, but his relationship with Murph's new number two extended well beyond their respective roles at Sincil Bank. Over a decade later, when Lennie arrived as manager at Middlesbrough, he promoted Pickering, 'a terrific coach' to the role of his assistant manager. The duo found immediate success, achieving promotion at the first attempt to the Premier League.

With Pickering on board, fitness dominated Murph's game plan, running up and down the South Common and patterns of play. The coach from Stockton-on-Tees quickly earned the team's respect and became the conduit between Murph and his players. They knew who the boss was, but they went to his number two if they wanted to know what the boss thought.

Trevor Peake remembers Pickering with obvious fondness.

'He was an ex-player, a centre-half so he passed a lot of things on to me. How to cope in certain situations, starting distances, things like that. He would spend a lot of time with the back four, trying to make us better players, solid as a group. Because he'd played the game for years and was more experienced, he could understand what we were thinking ... before we even thought it! I had the greatest respect for John as well as for Colin.'

Pickering slotted in perfectly alongside Murph, in the 'firm but fair' category, and Peake believes they got the balance just right.

With the new indoor gym just a short pass from Sincil Bank, Pickering could put on all the training sessions he wanted; eight v eight, five v five, two and a half days a week. On Thursdays and

Fridays, Colin took over; 11 v 11, corners and free kicks. Like his mentor Jimmy Sirrel, Murph organised a lot of practice games. He didn't have time for five-a-sides. He wanted to educate his players, improve their positional play and see what made them tick. Steve Thompson remembers turning up at a gym session one day where there were 20 or so players and 15 footballs.

'Right, you lot, grab a ball,' the gaffer said, 'and volley it as hard as you can at anyone you don't like.'

The players obliged, smashing balls at their least favourite teammates.

'That's useful,' Murph muttered, and left.

The psychology of football and the power of group dynamics fascinated Murph. Thompson recalls the boss's tactics.

'He liked to get into players' brains. He liked to get into the psychology side of things. In them days I don't think too many managers did that. He liked to know the ins and outs, what your parents did. He seemed to know everything about you. "Steven, have you been out for a drink last night?" He always kept you on your toes. He knew everything.'

Murph also wanted his players to train as they played. He loved the physical side of football, and although he hadn't progressed beyond non-league as a player, he had shown no fear. Murph believed that success would come from keeping the players on their toes. He taught the team to 'Expect the unexpected.'

In the winter of 1981/82, wild weather plunged the football season into disarray. Reminiscent of the Big Freeze almost two decades before, snow swept across the country and ravaged the fixtures list. Out of 193 league games scheduled for the four weeks from mid-December, only 40 took place. City's away defeat against Reading on 5 December would be their last league game for six weeks. Faced with a backlog of fixtures, Murph organised a friendly against Luton Town, midway through the Hatters' Second Division championship-winning season. In the floodlit match at Sincil Bank, deep fog descended over the ground. Only six minutes into the second half it was abandoned with a goalless draw. The players expected to head home and come into training the next day, but Murph had other ideas.

'Right, you lot, get changed into your training gear, we're heading up the South Park.'

They couldn't see five yards in front of their noses, and Murph was taking them running up the common. The players questioned his sanity. As they left the ground and crossed the road, the gaffer tripped up over a paving slab, fell headfirst and scraped the skin off his hands. He rubbed his palms vigorously, but carried on running, determined that no one would know he was hurt.

All geared up for the 1981/82 season. Lincoln City's management team, from left to right: manager Colin Murphy, assistant manager John Pickering, reserve team coach Lennie Lawrence and physio Bert Loxley. (Photograph from the Murphy family collection)

The lost revenue from home fixtures that winter had a crippling effect on clubs throughout the Football League. But ever the optimist, Murph pointed out that their League Cup matches against Hull City, Notts County, and Watford had attracted total crowds of over 38,000. And the unscheduled break gave Pickering the chance to get to know the squad. With three points for a win, a couple of victories could quickly improve their league position.

The boss was right. By the middle of March, with 11 unbeaten league games under his belt, there was everything to play for in the last third of the season. In the Colin Murphy writes section of the matchday programme against Oxford United, the gaffer gave an upbeat message to the fans, 'The vital ingredients of teamwork, spirit, organisation, together with the principle of developing "your own" which in itself engenders healthy, competitive club situations, certainly appear to be overtaking our more affluent counterparts. Can we keep this up? When will Lincoln "crack"? These seem to be the topics of conversation as one travels around the circuit. Well, most certainly the players "have the bit between their teeth" the confidence of the management, and I am sure they will not relent without one extreme fight.'

Murph fielded the fittest team in the league. Tommo remembers the regime.

'You knew what you were doing attacking, what you were doing defending. Preparation was everything.'

Murph didn't hold back in his team talks.

'Why the f*** when the ball went over there, Steven, did you go over there?'

'Well, I thought ...'

'Let me stop you there, Steven. If you start thinking, we're all f***ed!'

By 20 March 1982, Murph reached a significant milestone; Lincoln sat third in the Third Division; their highest Football League position for 20 years. Yet the success coincided with a smorgasbord of problems; Shipley on suspension, Peake with a niggling calf injury, and Thompson due to face the FA Disciplinary Commission after totting up 22 penalty points. Murph would need the rest of his team to dig deep. Not every player was up for the fight. Steve Cammack took the earliest opportunity to beat a hasty retreat. Signed by Lennie on Murph's instructions,

Scunthorpe's top goalscorer had first met the gaffer at Sincil Bank. The relationship got off to a poor start, when the new arrival placed his hands on the furniture.

'Get your f***ing hands off the table!' Murph barked. 'That's my desk.'

Cammack didn't forget their opening exchange. It resurfaced in an interview he gave to Max Bell, author of *Scunthorpe United 20 Legends*, almost four decades later. The Iron's all-time top goalscorer had nothing positive to say about his Lincoln boss. After only six months playing on the wing at Sincil Bank, Cammack snatched a transfer back to Scunthorpe United. He didn't enjoy playing wide right any more than he liked his manager's attitude. Speaking to the *Grimsby Telegraph* in the late summer of 2020, Cammack didn't hold back, 'Colin Murphy was a complete and utter arsehole. I'm not being funny. Playing for Lincoln was a shocking experience.'

Unhappy at Murph playing him out of position, a chance encounter with Cammack's former chairman smoothed the player's return to his former club. He swapped six goals in 18 appearances for Lincoln to pick up the Fourth Division golden boot a season later. Proof that it was either easier to score 25 goals in a lower league, or that Murph didn't always get his team selection right.

Called to a FA disciplinary meeting with Thompson at the end of March, Murph told the player to meet him at Newark station. Tommo remembers his surprise at the boss's generosity, full English breakfast, sandwiches, cups of coffee at King's Cross. When they arrived at the FA Headquarters in the stuccoed splendour of 16 Lancaster Gate, Murph told his bruising centre-half, 'Don't open your mouth, leave all the talking to me.'

In front of the disciplinary hearing, Murph wove an eloquent tale of misery and regret.

'Gentlemen, I've rescued this boy from a broken marriage. He's had a terrible upbringing. A dreadful disciplinary record at

Boston. I've transformed him, made him into a player. He is very, very remorseful.'

Thompson, sporting a black eye from a collision at Exeter, shot his boss a glance. Terrible upbringing? What was the gaffer on about, he'd grown up in a loving home with his mum and dad? They left the room while the committee took time to deliberate. Murph turned to Tommo.

'Steven, don't say a f***ing word!'

With less than two months left of the promotion-chasing season, Murph would do anything to ensure that Tommo could play a vital role in the campaign. The disciplinary meeting reconvened. The committee praised Murph's contribution to Thompson's redemption, but despite the manager's eloquent performance, they handed his centre-half a two-match ban. Murph assured the committee he would mete out additional punishment, 'I'll fine him two weeks' wages. And all expenses incurred on this trip.'

Arriving back at King's Cross, Murph asked Tommo, 'Fancy a bite to eat?'

'No, thanks, cos I'm going to pay for it all, aren't I?'

Two full English. Four coffees. Two sandwiches. A small price to pay for a two-match suspension served well before the last push of the season. Tommo would be available to play in a season-defining game against Fulham. A match he might wish to forget.

Before deadline day, Murph signed three free transfers, to insure against injuries and suspensions. In a pas de deux with Cammack, Hughes returned from Scunthorpe where he'd slotted in at left-back. He was well placed to cover for Phil Neale if the cricket season beckoned. And John Ward, from Taylor's promotion-winning team of 1976, would replace Hobson, Cockerill or Cunningham if needed. With David Rodgers, from Torquay United, on hand for the suspended Tommo, Murph had all bases covered.

Twelve games to go. Murph had proved without doubt that Lincoln could develop their own players and still achieve success.

Twenty-year-old Stuart Hibberd, a former City youth player, had displayed nerves of steel, with two penalties scored at Exeter in the space of a minute. Delighted with the Imps' surge from behind, late in the season, on 27 March, Murph shouted with full caps joy from The Manager's View, 'WE ARE TOP of the league'. The team held a fragile grip at the top of the table for another week, and the doubters were coming back to Sincil Bank. A crowd of 8,243 filed through the turnstiles to watch City beat Huddersfield Town; more than double the home gate on the first day of the season.

Six wins and three draws in March earned Murph the Third Division Manager of the Month award, the third time he had picked up an award in his management career. Delighted with the recognition, it made him even more determined that City would be in the fight to the last game of the season. As the pressure increased, Murph knew fear might creep into the push for promotion. In his weekly newspaper column, he acknowledged the merits of mediocrity. It kept everybody happy, but hopeful. But he vowed not to give in to fear and change his tactics. He would continue to play three strikers both home and away; attacking football determined to win every game.

With only one defeat in their previous 19 games, City travelled away to Swindon. The Robins dealt them a crushing blow; a scrambled goal scored by the home team and three points lost for the visiting side. There were 30 Third Division matches still to play among the season's hopefuls. Five contenders for three promotion places. One thing was certain. The season would go to the wire.

Almost 40 years later, Phil Neale still holds a debt of gratitude to his former boss. As the end of the season approached, Lincoln's left-back faced a headache of sporting success. His first game in charge as the newly appointed captain of Worcestershire would be at Headingley on 8 May. The same Saturday that City would play the next game in their promotion push at Chester. During a three-day County Championship game before the Headingley fixture, the City board told Murph to send Neale a telegram. The directors expected the player to turn out at Chester at three o'clock on the Saturday afternoon. The gaffer felt sympathetic to his player's dilemma, but the directors gave him no choice. Neale still earned more money playing Third Division football than he did as captain of a county side. His hands were tied.

He turned up at Headingley for the start of the limited-overs game against Yorkshire, left himself out of the team and dashed to Chester to put on the number three shirt. At the mercy of an M62 diversion and heavy traffic, Neale arrived at the ground with only half an hour to spare, just in time for Murph to register his name on the team sheet. The Imps beat league stragglers Chester 2-1, and Worcestershire won by two wickets. Neale had got away with it, but Murph recognised the increasing difficulty his full-back would face juggling two professional sporting careers. He later took the player to one side and handed him a typewritten letter. If there were ever another clash of key fixtures, cricket would take priority over football. He sealed the letter in an envelope and said to Neale, 'Keep it safe. I hope you never have to use it.'

Neale knew the letter could rebound on Murph if he ever needed it. He appreciated the boss's loyalty.

After the Chester fixture, City took a break from their Third Division schedule while promotion rivals Carlisle, Fulham and Burnley caught up on games in hand. The Football League pushed the Imps' final game against Fulham, back to 18 May. A crunch fixture in the season; Fulham would go up if they managed a draw. And City needed three points to secure promotion in third place.

Over 8,000 City supporters travelled to Craven Cottage to watch the greatest battle of the season. A total of 20,398 fans piled into the ground. In an edgy start to the game, Fulham struggled to cope with the City frontline. At half-time they left the pitch with a 0-0 stalemate. The match exploded in the second half. Dean Coney launched a promising attack for Fulham and reached the edge of the penalty box. Steve Thompson mowed into him like a bulldozer, making no obvious attempt to get the ball. Coney went down. No hesitation from the referee; a red card for Tommo's second bookable offence. With shoulders hunched, Tommo left the pitch. Murph put his arm around his centre-back in the dugout.

'Steven, you were f***ing unlucky.'

Fulham responded with a free-kick routine they'd used to impressive effect throughout the season. Tony Gale lofted the ball and Roger Brown headed it home.

In the 57th minute, Lincoln were 1-0 down.

'F**k me, Steven!' Murph shouted, whacking his centre-half across the head.

City launched everything at Fulham, and David Carr clawed a goal back. For the last 20 minutes City piled on the pressure. They needed one more goal to go up. Sean O'Driscoll made a goal-line clearance, but the Imps couldn't break their way through. As the final whistle blew, the league table told an agonising story. Fulham on 78 points, Lincoln and Carlisle on 77. Lincoln had a better goal difference, but Carlisle held the trump card, a game in hand.

Three points to play for, on the last day of the extended season. The Imps faced a torturous 24-hour wait to see if bottom placed Chester could beat title-chasing Carlisle at Sealand Road. Senior City players wept in the visitors' dressing room after the game. The odds were stacked against them. Chester had won only two games at home all season and sat 14 points adrift of the pack.

City had given everything they had in their contest at Craven Cottage. Roger Brown who battled with Tony Cunningham throughout the match, said, 'Sometimes when you play hard against somebody, they'll hide a bit, go away. He [Cunningham] didn't. He kept coming back for more.'

Brown recalled the momentous game for Throwback Thursday, the club's history series on Fulham's website. The record goalscoring Fulham defender missed the celebrations on the Cottage balcony after the match. He needed 12 stitches above his eye and six in his cheek where Cunningham had left his mark. Tommo, Lincoln City's Player of the Season, has his own memory of the fateful fixture.

'I still maintain to this day it wasn't a sending off.'

Chairman Dennis Houlston didn't wait to find out the result of the Chester match. Fifteen minutes after the Fulham game, he shocked his board members by handing in his resignation. After 20 months in charge, he blamed the lack of support from most of his fellow directors. A shell-shocked vice-chairman Heneage Dove travelled back to Lincoln on the players' coach. When Houlston took the chair, Maurice Burton had suggested the personal ambition of the potato mogul was to be associated with a promotion-winning side. Burton had called it right.

Twenty-four hours later, as expected by the run of form, Chester lost 1-0 to Carlisle. Burnley and Carlisle had 80 points, Fulham 78, and Lincoln 77. Five years before the play-offs were introduced into the vocabulary of the Football League, a single point sealed City's Third Division fate. Murph felt the gut-wrenching agony of disappointment and regret. If City had gained promotion, he knew they would still be a Third Division outfit playing in a higher tier, but he would have taken his chances.

After almost three and a half years at Sincil Bank, Lennie Lawrence recognised his time was up. The directors had decided to remove the youth team from the Northern Intermediate League, a competition they had joined under Graham Taylor. As a cost-cutting measure, the youth policy was being wound down.

'In football,' Lennie told me, 'You've always got to have one eye on an exit strategy.'

It was time to move on. He started to negotiate an exit deal from the club when a chance visit to his local newsagents transformed the course of his footballing career. A habitual *Daily Mail* reader, he had to settle for buying the *Daily Express*. A job advert caught his eye: reserve team coach at Charlton Athletic. Lawrence wasted no time. He met manager Ken Craggs in London and accepted the job there and then. Six months later when Craggs got the sack, the board put Lennie in temporary charge. A job which turned out to be anything but temporary; he stayed at The Valley for the best part of nine years and gave the Addicks their first promotion into the First Division for almost three decades.

Thirty-five years after leaving Lincoln City, Lennie still speaks warmly of Murph's contribution to setting him on the path of his long-term career. He admits that when he arrived at Lincoln from Plymouth, he thought he knew it all.

'What Murph taught me was about man management and running every aspect of a club. He had an eye for a player as good as I've ever known. He had motivational skills. A bit off the wall. He was a good coach, and he was a good tactician, but boy could he motivate them. That's what he taught me. So, when I got the chance, I was ready. If I hadn't had that time at Lincoln, I don't think I would have lasted in the game.'

Even today, Lennie will define people by their answer to the question, 'Are you a manager who can coach, or a coach who can manage?'

He has no doubts about Murph, 'He was a manager who could coach. And I was the same at Charlton, because I'd learnt it off him. He wanted to manage everything. He had a say in the recruitment. He wanted to sign all the cash chits, he wanted to know all the ins and outs. He'd paint the ground in the summer. He was into absolutely every aspect. It was before the era of the chief executive. Murph ran everything.'

Lennie's departure gave way to a tumultuous summer. The club's profit and loss account for the year reported a net loss of over £250,000. The wage bill was more than twice the income from gate receipts. When director Gilbert Blades stepped up to the chair, the club was teetering on the brink of liquidation. The board had very little time to respond. A radical rethink was required. A quick decision defied the slow process of local government. Lincoln City Council intervened to save the club. By just one vote, they passed a motion to purchase the freehold of the land at Sincil Bank. The £225,000 asset would be held for the benefit of the community and leased back to the football club.

And at the start of the new season, with no money in the coffers, Murph faced one of the biggest challenges of his career. He knew he would have to pick himself up, take his contracted players and start all over again. And try to forget how frustratingly close they had come to taking the club back into the Second Division, for the first time since 1961. He couldn't predict the battle that lay ahead.

5

CODE OF SILENCE

LINCOLN CITY

They didn't have to carry too many chairs on to the pitch for the annual team photo at Sincil Bank. It had been a lean summer in the run up to the club's centenary season. Murph was left with a skeleton squad of only 15 players and four apprentices. Despite the well-curated smiles of the board of directors, Murph knew there were cutbacks in store. A wage dispute with the players had kicked off the start of the season. In a *Central News* report, chairman Gilbert Blades gave his stark response.

'It's either solved by sensible negotiations ... or you just go bust.'

In a national recession with local unemployment running at 13 per cent, the Lincoln City board proposed a 45 per cent cut in players' bonuses. The players fought back. Tradition dictated that clubs which stayed in the same division transferred their wage and incentives structure into the new season. David Carr, the softly spoken PFA representative, an ever-present member of Murph's team, stood up for his fellow players. They didn't want to strike. They wanted the board to honour the gentlemen's agreements they made when the players signed their contracts. The argument rumbled on. And the need to reduce expenses forced Murph into the transfer market again. There was an obvious target. Lincoln's joint-top goalscorer from the previous season, Murph's towering striker, Tony Cunningham.

Murph valued Cunningham as the type of player who created as many assists, as he scored goals. He would miss his striker's strength and pace, but when Second Division Barnsley came in for him, Murph felt he had no choice. He made his third major transfer out. A boost of £80,000 to the Imps' war chest. The club was selling to survive.

A difficult start to the 1982/83 season, but Colin's not ready to throw in the towel just yet. (Image courtesy of Lincoln City Football Club)

It was a downbeat Murph who wrote in The Manager's View in early September, 'History has proved that promotion has always been gained by squads, and not teams.'

To combat the economic disaster facing many clubs, the FA extended the loan system to five players in a season. Murph took Seamus Heath, a utility defender, on loan from Luton Town. Against the odds, Murph's depleted team won six out of their first seven league games. But with the perfect storm of a national recession and dwindling gates, they were swimming against a Third

Division tide. They couldn't sustain a club on transfer deals alone, with average home gates of little above 4,000. Penny-pinching and unpopular measures came in; complimentary tickets went out. Murph was managing a successful side, but the club was on the breadline.

With average basic wages of £180 a week, players could earn up to an extra £120 a week in performance-related bonuses. At the annual shareholders' meeting, financial director Heneage Dove explained the far-reaching impact of failing to gain promotion to the Second Division. An £80,000 insurance policy, taken out in the event of promotion, would have paid the players' bonuses. With the help of arbitration, the players agreed an eight per cent wage cut to support the club's financial future. Yet only two months into the season, Murph hit crisis point. Striker Gordon Hobson joined Derek Bell on the injured list.

Saturday, 2 October 1982 is a memorable date for any veteran Imps supporter. Lincoln travelled away to Newport County. Murph told Maurice Burton before the game that he had an unorthodox idea for Hobson's replacement. The *Lincolnshire Echo* reporter thought Murph was joking until he got off the bus at Somerton Park.

The matchday team sheet looked predictable enough:

1. Felgate
2. Carr
3. Neale
4. Cockerill
5. Peake
6. Thompson
7. Hibberd
8. Turner
9. The journalist stopped short.

9. Naylor

Naylor? Had Murph gone mad? Stuart Naylor, reserve team goalkeeper, was playing up front. With only one outfield substitution allowed in a competitive match, Murph stunned the travelling support with his makeshift number nine. But Murph knew what he was doing. When Naylor made a four-hour Saturday morning dash from his home in Wetherby to Newport, the manager flicked a metaphorical V sign at the board. His not very subtle message, if you don't give me enough outfield players to fight for promotion, what the hell do you expect? Naylor took to the pitch, and Murph gave his stand-in centre-forward one piece of advice.

'Don't go back and defend like a goalie. You'll f***ing catch it and give away a pen.'

Naylor didn't concede a penalty, but Lincoln went down 1-0 to a goal from ex-Imp Tommy Tynan. The boss got ready to weather the storm. He wasn't worried. He'd lost the game but felt sure he'd scored a moral victory. City still sat at the top of the table. The newspapers latched on to the goalie up front story. And column inches guaranteed extra pressure on the board.

Desperate to keep up momentum and expand his dwindling team, Murph liked the look of a right-back at Blackpool, Gordon Simmonite. The defender had played in the England non-league team with Trevor Peake. Simmonite remembers when Steve Thompson, an old teammate from Boston days, gave him the nod.

'Murph's going to ring you,' Tommo said, 'but go somewhere no one can hear you. It's got to be kept secret.'

Simmonite didn't know quite what to expect from the 007 agent routine but met Murph at Sincil Bank in the players' bar. The manager put his head round the door. Simmo waved at him, and Murph walked straight back out. The player waited, but Murph didn't reappear. Tommo said he'd find out what the gaffer wanted. He reported back.

'He's not going to speak to you.'

'Why not?'

'Cos you're wearing jeans!'

When I met Simmonite and Colin's son, Ben, they laughed at the story.

'He was funny like that, wasn't he?' Ben said, 'I probably didn't wear a pair of jeans until I was 19. It stayed in my head; you just don't wear them.'

Simmonite agreed.

'It was his standards, but also his way of saying, you conform, whatever.'

The next time Murph and Simmonite met, the popular defender travelled to Lincoln for the first leg of the League Cup fixture against West Ham. In the 1982/83 season the League Cup became the first major English competition to secure a sponsorship deal. For the next four seasons, with the Milk Marketing Board as its unlikely sponsor, the League Cup was known as the Milk Cup.

Simmo joined 13,898 fans who filled Sincil Bank to the rafters for the electrifying game against West Ham. In front of the biggest home crowd for six years, City held the First Division side to a 1-1 draw, and Simmonite agreed terms. The £500,000 West Ham goalkeeper, Phil Parkes, who made three stunning saves in the second half, cost more than the entire Lincoln City team. Murph put his success down to not overfeeding the players. He had four packets of plain biscuits delivered for the pre-match meal.

'I want to keep them hungry for success!' he quipped to the waiting press.

In Simmonite's first game for the Imps at home to Millwall, City put three goals past captain Sam Allardyce and Millwall's defence. They won 3-1 and sat on top of the Third Division with a 100 per cent home record. The *Match of the Day* film crew reported from Sincil Bank and Glenn Cockerill produced a masterclass for Jimmy Hill's weekly skills spot.

Murph praised his central midfielder, 'Well, he's quick and he's strong ... The boy just loves playing football ... We sold him for 100, bought him back for 40, so look up Glenn you might be down the road again shortly!'

The interviewer asked Murph if Lincoln achieved promotion, how they might survive in the Second Division.

'I might be out of work by Christmas!' he laughed.

Then, in a thinly veiled criticism of the Lincoln City board, Murph pointed out he had done just about as much as he could on fresh air. If the club got promotion, players would need pay rises and he would have to make a couple more signings. Murph looked theatricality to the heavens for an answer where the players might come from.

'I don't know. I'm looking up there. Maybe we've got an anonymous benefactor somewhere.'

And as if by magic, two weeks later, Harry Redknapp hand-delivered an early Christmas gift to Sincil Bank; a neatly packaged 9-0 thrashing of Bournemouth. An unforgettable milestone for the caretaker manager's first game in charge. And a hat-trick for both Gordon Hobson and Murph's scoring machine, Derek Bell. Every team in the lower leagues had its own problems. Murph was struggling with a squad of only 14 professional players, and Redknapp's boys were wearing the wrong boots. From the minute they walked out on to the icy pitch in nylon studs, they could barely stand up.

Asked for his thoughts after the game, Redknapp dead-panned, 'I thought the seventh goal was offside!'

Murph recalls his opponent's reaction; Redknapp escaped into the Lincoln boardroom and sank eight pints. The following week, the Bournemouth Supporters' Association provided the cash to buy a full set of astroturf boots, but some lower-league problems were harder to resolve; Murph still had no money to buy players. Despite the lack of funds, by early January, Lincoln stood six points clear at the top of the table. On the first Saturday of the new year, FA Cup third-round territory, before the demands of TV scheduling spread it over an entire weekend, Lincoln faced a fixtureless few days. They'd suffered a humiliating

3-0 exit from the FA Cup against Fourth Division Hartlepool United.

Simmonite remembers a team meeting in the dressing room on the Friday night, where Murph spoke to the players.

'We've been knocked out of the Cup by Hartlepool, that's not such a bad thing. We're all intact. So, I've cleared it with the chairman, and we're all going to Magaluf next week.'

The players looked at each other, not quite believing what they'd just heard. Murph performed his familiar routine: he raised his arm, shook his wrist and let the bracelet watch he wore two links too big, wriggle down to his elbow. He carried on.

'Not mentioning any names, but I know there's some players here that don't want to go or won't be able to go. Well, I'm telling you now, I've watched Cloughie all these years. And Cloughie takes all his players to Magaluf. It does them the world of good. So, you're all f***ing going.'

He dropped his arm and let the watch snake its way back down to his wrist. Conversation over; they were all heading to the sunshine island of Majorca. The team packed their full kit ready for training, but when they touched down at the airport in the Spanish resort, Murph had another surprise in store.

'Me, Bert, and the rest of the management team are staying in one hotel. You lot are staying in another. We'll see you in five days' time.'

The players didn't need to pack their training kit, the only exercise they got was walking from one bar to the next along the Magaluf Strip. On the Saturday night, Murph phoned home. He was staying at the same hotel where Clough and Taylor had learned they'd won the First Division championship at Derby County in 1972. Murph wanted to find out the result of the Derby vs Nottingham Forest FA Cup third-round tie. It was billed as the Taylor vs Clough grudge match. Clough's former assistant had come out of retirement to take over as Derby manager. A Sunday newspaper had offered to pay Murph to dish the dirt on his former club. He turned the offer down. He preferred to remember the three years he enjoyed at Derby as a coach before his ill-fated spell as manager.

'You don't slag off the good times for the sake of the bad,' he told John Wragg at the *Daily Express*.

'If you do, then life tends to kick you back in the end.'

In the east Midlands derby, the Second Division underdogs beat First Division Forest 2-0. It made Murph even more determined to get his Lincoln side up to the second tier to play a good standard of football in the season ahead. It should have been possible. The Magaluf trip boosted mid-season morale. But when they returned to Sincil Bank, it had a catastrophic effect on results. They lost away to Wigan, and in the next seven games, they won one, drew three, lost three.

The trip cost Murph far more than a poor run of results. It led him to make a decision which he describes as the biggest mistake of his life. It jeopardised the thing he valued most, his professional reputation. Battling injuries in his strike force, Murph needed to consolidate City's position. He asked the board to spend £32,500 to bring in two forwards, Ross Jack from Norwich and John Thomas from Chester. The directors refused. Murph feared promotion would evade him for the second year running, and on a personal level, he would have failed. Faced with the directors' perceived lack of ambition, rumours surfaced that several players were thinking of putting in transfer requests. The *Sports Mail* hinted at an imminent confrontation between the manager and the board. Murph told sportswriter Ray Matts, 'Since I came here four years ago, I've been trying to build a football club, not just a team. Until recently I thought I was getting somewhere, but now I'm not so sure.'

By early February, Cardiff City knocked the Imps off the top of the table. Murph wasn't too worried. It might help the team to relax and discover their lost form. After a 1-0 defeat against Southend, in front of a crowd of only 4,000, they faced their next crucial fixture at home to Plymouth Argyle. The players expected a quiet training session on the Friday, followed by the usual team talk, designed to motivate the squad. Instead, 'Gentleman John' Pickering, Murph's assistant manager, told them, 'We're not training this morning, boys. The boss has called a meeting at the Grand Hotel.'

Colin Murphy plans his attacking moves on the board. (Image courtesy of the Lincolnshire Echo*)*

Murph could have held the meeting with the entire management team, the players and apprentices in the privacy of Sincil Bank, but he held it in the St Mary's Street hotel in central Lincoln — in full view of the paying public. He tipped off Maurice Burton, who travelled to away matches on the club coach. The reporter turned up with a photographer to snap the players on their way out of the hotel. Murph wanted maximum exposure for what had become a very public fight with the board.

Under the banner headline 'City FC staff in protest meeting', Burton reported on a gathering which lasted the best part of an hour. Murph told the players as employees of the club they had the right to know what was happening. He put them in the picture, and the team aired their views. The *Lincolnshire Echo* reporter provided no further details.

So, what exactly did Murph say in the meeting, which he has regretted for the rest of his life?

When I met several former Lincoln players, they happily reminisced about their years at Sincil Bank. Garrulous and enthusiastic to a man, they recounted their favourite Murph stories. In expansive detail, they dissected every touch, every goal, every result from a generation before. Until I asked them about the meeting at the Grand Hotel. A deafening silence.

'I can remember the meeting, but I can't remember the content.'

Full-back Gordon Simmonite. Laid it off.

'Tell me what that meeting was about again. I may well have been there, but I can't remember the detail.'

Defender Phil Neale. Neatly sidestepped.

'We had a meeting, but I can't remember what was said.'

Centre-half Steve Thompson. Parked the bus.

I seemed to have opened a catalogue of can't remembers. Collective amnesia from a group of men who could tell me what they ate for a pre-match meal almost 40 years before, but who couldn't recall what Murph had said at a career-defining meeting in the Grand Hotel. The realisation dawned. A collective silence agreed among themselves. Suddenly, it felt wrong to coax them to break ranks. Through the fragmented memory of his stroke, Murph recalled telling the players never to disclose the content of the meeting. He smiled at the memory of the request and the players' response. Almost four decades later, that group of young men, now long retired from the professional game with grandchildren of their own, had kept their promise. Perhaps more illuminating than what was or wasn't said in the Grand Hotel, is the dynamic force of fraternity and team spirit. The loyalty to a man who always put his players first.

One thing was certain, when Murph called the meeting at the Grand Hotel, he was playing a dangerous game. By openly criticising the board and using a 'them and us' tactic to strengthen the team's resolve, he risked turning the players against the club. Team captain Trevor Peake spoke out to the *Lincolnshire Echo*. The team had only agreed a bonus cut at the start of the season to help the club bring in new players to fight for promotion. He questioned what would happen if they achieved it, 'I can't believe it would be a good Second Division club to play for under this setup.'

Murph hadn't just stirred up the players, he had ignited the fans. Before the Plymouth game, supporters of the 'Blades must go' campaign distributed hundreds of leaflets on the terraces at Sincil Bank. The leaflets urged all City supporters:

TELL THE DIRECTORS TO GO.
AND SHOW YOUR SUPPORT
FOR COLIN AND THE PLAYERS.

They promised to stage a demonstration in front of the directors' box after the final whistle. Chants of 'Blades out' reverberated around the ground, as banners unfurled repeating the same message. Plymouth came from a goal down to beat the Imps 2-1. It was the final catalyst. Four hundred angry supporters stormed in front of the directors' box. A line of police forced them back as they tried to climb into the stand, determined to confront Blades and his fellow members of the board. After an hour of vocal protests, the police announced that Murph would come out to speak to them. The supporters burst into spontaneous applause and thrust placards with 'Blades out, Murphy in' in front of the cameras. Murph picked up the loud hailer and addressed the crowd, 'Leave it to me to deal with. I don't think we're doing much good this way. You can't blame Mr Blades for the performance this afternoon.'

No one moved from the pitch until Murph pleaded, 'For my sake and for the sake of the players, please go home and leave it to me.'

The visibly angry crowd had an invisible army of supporters; a group of Citizens' Band (CB) radio enthusiasts, using their low-power two-way radios to campaign to unseat the board. The CB fad had swept into Britain from the US, popularised by the truckers' movie *Convoy*. With code names borrowed from the hit movie, Rubber Duck and Pig Pen plotted on the airwaves to force the City directors to resign.

After one of the most bitter days in the club's history, Murph's skipper put in a transfer request. Chairman Blades needed a police escort to help him escape from the ground. He returned home to find a message daubed in two-foot letters on an outhouse wall, 'YOUR KILLING LCFC STEP DOWN NOW'.

A weekend of turmoil followed. Blades received obscene phone calls and a death threat at his home. Murph denied suggestions he had orchestrated the demonstration. On Sunday, Blades called the board together. He publicly blamed Murph for inciting the fans and for encouraging the players to talk to the press.

'It is the pressure put on you by managers that is the cynical side of football,' he said to Maurice Burton.

He had some sympathy for Murph but said, 'He thinks he's managing Manchester United.'

With gates which averaged a little over 5,000, Blades accused Murph of having his head in the financial clouds.

On the Sunday night, the 52-year-old chairman and his five-man board of directors called an emergency meeting. They took a unanimous decision behind closed doors. No longer able to tolerate the recriminations and personal abuse, the whole board of directors decided to stand down. Blades accused Murph's meeting at the Grand Hotel of stoking up mob hysteria.

'It was the most diabolical thing a manager could do, and it is absolutely unforgivable,' the chairman said to Burton.

The players were contracted to play football, not to make public statements or bring the club into disrepute. Blades blamed Murph for encouraging the players' dissent. He believed that Murph was wrecking the club for the sake of his own career.

And the manager had to take personal responsibility for the outcome.

'It's a very sad day for football,' Blades said to the *Daily Mail*, 'when hooligans can force a whole board of directors to resign.'

For the first time, Murph had achieved something which Brian Clough hadn't. On a wave of people power, he had unseated the entire board. Murph sat at home and reflected on the mess. Rows, resignations and demonstrations were normally the price you paid for failure.

'I'm a victim of my own success,' he said to John Sadler from *The Sun*, 'and I'm beginning to wonder whether it's worth being successful.'

If you were at the bottom of the league, Murph said, the directors gave you the sack. At the top of the league, they told you to steady on, they couldn't handle it. He would have to wait to see what would happen with the board. If the directors stepped down straight away, it would force the club into liquidation. Someone needed to buy the directors' shares, repay their loans, and take over the running of the club. Until that happened, Murph had no choice but to run the club on a shoestring. He awaited the outcome of a takeover bid, before he could decide about his own future.

Ahead of the next midweek fixture, away to Exeter City, there were no funds available to pay for overnight accommodation. Dubbed the 'rent-a-bed' club by the national press, Lincoln made the 260-mile journey down the M5 and took an afternoon nap in a hotel. After a 3-1 defeat, they drove straight back up north. An elderly supporter had walked into the club office with an envelope stuffed full of £5 notes to pay for the afternoon bed hire. He may have regretted his decision, but his generous £125 donation and request for anonymity earned him a place on the team coach.

Within a week, the financial tide turned. Dennis Houlston, the 44-year-old former Lincoln chairman, made a dramatic swoop to take over the club. He offered to acquire the shares from Blades and his co-directors and set up a new four-man board. More significantly for Murph, he offered his manager a transfer budget for two new signings. The players soon noticed that after a strangely muted few weeks, Murph was back to his shouting best in the dressing room after the game.

The gaffer used to pace around the club with a huge mug of tea in his hand, always whistling. It was the apprentices' job to keep him filled up. Murph wore studs, never moulded rubber boots. The players could hear him coming. Chris Moyses, Youth Opportunities Programme recruit and future Lincoln manager, was walking down the corridor, when Murph yelled out from the changing room, 'Cuppa f***ing tea, Moysie.'

Murph hurled the cup down the corridor for Moyses to catch, just as Chris Thompson, a midfielder on short-term loan from Bolton Wanderers, poked his head out of the boot room. The cup hit Thompson straight above the eye and split his head open.

'F**k me, Chris!' Murph yelled. 'Why didn't you bring it down?'

Murph hadn't given up hope that the team could fight their way back into the race for promotion. Away to Bournemouth on 23 April, he received a stark reminder of how much the Imps' season had declined. The Cherries turned the 9-0 defeat from four months before into a 1-0 victory. Lincoln's 17-year-old apprentice Gary Strodder faced former international George Best, a crowd boosting addition to Dean Court. A 1-0 defeat for the visiting side, and Lincoln had blown their chances of a top-three finish. Murph had simply run out of players.

The 1982/83 season stuttered to a disappointing end. A sixth-placed finish for a team which had built their brand on attacking football. Seventy-seven goals scored, more goals than either Portsmouth or Cardiff who gained promotion. An uncertain future lay ahead. Eight players' contracts were due to expire. Felgate, Peake, Thompson, Hobson, Shipley, Turner, Bell and Hibberd; all free to find another club. Many of the players had narrowly missed out on two promotions. Could Murph tempt the team to keep the faith, or should he rebuild for the future?

It was almost impossible for the manager to plan ahead. He knew his team was good enough to receive offers from other clubs, and the players had strength in numbers. He had developed players to a point where he couldn't always pay them what they were worth. To encourage them to sign new contracts, Houlston invited Murph to extend the two years remaining on his contract to May 1987. The chairman believed he had one of the best managers in the country. Murph had turned down a lucrative job offer from PAOK Thessaloniki, the fourth-ranked club in Greek football. He knew Lincoln had given him a second chance in management, and he still wanted to repay them by taking the club into the Second Division.

At the season's close, Murph lost two key players from his diminishing squad: top goalscorer Derek Bell and skipper Trevor Peake. Murph didn't want to lose his captain of four years, but the offer of £100,000 from Coventry City would catapult the player into the First Division. The gaffer couldn't afford to hold him back. Peake returned to his native Midlands; a career move which would span over 300 games for the Sky Blues.

When we spoke in early 2022, Peake talked about his decision to leave the club.

'I don't think it was the way the club was run. I was still pleased that Colin was the manager, and that I was playing every week. Whilst the board may not have done themselves any favours that year, that wasn't the reason for me putting in the transfer request. I was thinking, I'm 26, 27. If I wanted to play at a higher level, I was keen to know if anyone would take me on!'

Murph was proud to see what his non-league signing achieved after he left Lincoln. Coventry didn't just take Peake on. Four years later, wearing the captain's armband in extra time, he won the 1987 FA Cup Final in a stunning 3-2 victory over Spurs. Not bad for a player Murph had signed from Nuneaton Borough for £15,000.

'It takes four years to build a team,' Murph said to Maurice

Burton at the end of the season, 'and it takes only four months to destroy one.'

He didn't know how prophetic those words might be.

When Peake left for Coventry, Murph not only lost his best player, but he also had to appoint a new captain. Steve Thompson and most of the team saw Tommo as the heir apparent. Tommo and Gordon Simmonite had been close for years, both Sheffield lads who played at Boston United and roomed together on away trips. Murph thought long and hard about Peake's replacement. He was looking for a leader who offered camaraderie, character, fitness – a role model for the team. He called Simmonite into his office and offered him the job.

'Go away and think about it,' Murph said.

Almost a decade later, he used the same words when he invited Simmonite to become godparent to his teenage son, Ben. Simmo said it was an honour to be asked on both occasions.

'He only asked you to be godparent, so he got another chance to sign you!' Ben laughed.

Murph knew Simmonite wasn't the most skilful player in his team, but he could rely on him as captain, week in week out. The popular full-back was delighted to accept the armband.

At the start of the new season, in the early autumn of 1983, Anton Rippon published *Soccer: The Road to Crisis*, a 200-page discussion of the 'plight of Britain's national winter sport'. Rippon spoke to Gilbert Blades in the weeks which followed the chairman's resignation; an episode which the writer describes as 'one of the most controversial episodes in football history'. Blades recalled how Murph repeatedly asked for new players, believing there was money in the pot from the sale of Mick Harford. He said that a youth policy which had produced one player had cost the club £200,000.

Like most managers of his generation, Murph could run a football team, but he had no financial training. Blades said the board had to run the club according to its resources. Murph believed that promotion to the Second Division would generate increased revenue, but his former chairman disagreed.

'Go 15 miles outside of this city and all you'll see are sheep and cows. The support just isn't there,' Blades told Rippon.

Murph hadn't persuaded the board to take a calculated risk to buy in two attacking players so he could sell two more at the end of the season.

The manager and the team had paid the price for the board's lack of confidence.

'It's still a mystery to me why we collapsed,' Peake told me in a phone call, in 2022.

But when I reminded Murph of his decision to take a boozy mid-season break, with his team sitting at the top of the table, he gave a wry smile.

'Dropped a bollock there, didn't I? That bloody holiday cost us promotion!'

Over the close season, Murph received a promotion of sorts. The byline for his weekly newspaper column in the *Lincolnshire Echo* was now accompanied by a curiously unflattering pen and ink sketch. In The Manager's View, Murph's first of the season, he reflected on 'perhaps the best signing I have ever made for City'. Not a player from his impressive back four, but assistant manager John Pickering. The boss credited his number two with producing attacking football from a 14-man squad, using apprentices, non-contract players, and schoolboys. The gaffer looked forward to fighting the new season with the popular man by his side.

'We are not going to win all the battles,' Murph wrote, 'but if we win most of them, we have a good chance of winning the war.'

With funds made available by the new chairman, Murph had signed more foot soldiers for his campaign, including Keith Houghton, the captain of Carlisle United and a latecomer to professional football. Murph wrote about the 29-year-old, 'I am sure he will prove he can run like a new car left in a garage for ten years and not used. In other words, when it comes onto the road, it purrs ... that's Keith Houghton.'

Twenty-three-year-old Scottish forward Ross Jack also signed for Lincoln in the close season. His knockdown fee of £22,000 looked a bargain for a player who was Norwich City's 14-goal top scorer only two seasons before. And John Thomas joined Lincoln at Murph's second attempt. With six goals for Jack in his first eight outings, and 16 goals for Thomas in his debut season, both forwards proved their worth. Murph felt more than ever that he could have won promotion if the board had made the cash available when he asked for it.

Travelling away from Lincoln on a scouting mission, Murph stopped at a phone box and called Maurice Burton to get the results of the Milk Cup draw. Lincoln had struck football gold. A 3-1 extra-time victory against Hull City had earned them a meeting with First Division Tottenham Hotspur in the second round. According to Burton's write-up in the *Lincolnshire Echo*, the manager's comments were unprintable. For a third-tier club it didn't get much more exciting than a draw against Spurs.

On 5 October 1983, Gordon Simmonite led out the team at White Hart Lane in front of a crowd of over 20,000. It wasn't the cup upset the Imps hoped for. An own goal, a concussed captain, and a missed chance in front of goal. Lincoln lost the first leg 3-1. But Steve Thompson picked up the City man of the match award and the adoration of the 2,000-strong travelling support. He showed no respect to England international Graham Roberts, and Murph's young side proved they could play football.

The manager was more than happy with a City performance built on determination and hard graft. Murph couldn't question his players' commitment. In the return leg at Sincil Bank, fans' favourite George Shipley had a plaster cast removed from his broken wrist before the game and put back on again at full time. City needed a 2-0 win at home to take them through to the next round.

A crowd of over 12,000 poured in to Sincil Bank to watch

Thompson, at the heart of City's defence, leave his First Division calling card. Burton's match report suggested that Lincoln's centre-half destroyed Spurs at every turn. New signing John Thomas scored from a header in the 43rd minute; the goal neutralised by an on-target shot from Falco 15 minutes from time. Ross Jack clawed back the advantage with a converted penalty, but it wasn't enough. The glory of a 2-1 victory, marred by a 4-3 aggregate defeat.

Spurs manager Keith Burkenshaw congratulated his opponent for fielding the better side on the night. Murph was disappointed but pragmatic. The White Hart Lane fixture gave Lincoln a £20,000 windfall from their share of the match receipts and £50,000 in total from their Milk Cup campaign. The team had renewed hope and a cash buffer for the season ahead.

Determined to keep strengthening his squad, Murph was tracking a useful goalscorer from the Norwich reserves. The manager spotted an unmissable opportunity in a gangly 21-year-old, by the name of John Fashanu. When Fashanu signed for the Canaries in 1979, half a dozen clubs had turned him down. He lived in the perpetual shadow of his older brother, Justin; the first £1m black footballer, who had signed for Brian Clough at Nottingham Forest. The younger sibling struggled to break through into the Norwich first team. He appeared only seven times in two years, but Murph felt he could do something exciting with the youngster's raw steel and determination. After a single appearance on loan to Crystal Palace, Fashanu realised his time at Norwich was coming to an end. He transferred to Lincoln, two divisions below the Canaries in the Football League. A move which allowed Fashanu and Ross Jack to restore their partnership from the Norwich reserves.

Murph was still enjoying the challenge of hunting for non-league talent he could mould into a player. Cunningham, Peake, and Thompson had taken three years to develop. When he signed Alan Walker from Telford United, Murph knew the powerful defender would need time to settle down. Every opposition team had a big, hard centre-forward. Burnley were no exception. They had Billy Hamilton, the Northern Ireland international, up front. In Walker's debut game against the Clarets, Tommo said he would compete with Hamilton until Walker found his feet.

As they withdrew to the dressing room at half-time, Murph was full of praise for the new boy.

'Well done, Alan, brilliant job.'

Tommo remembers the day well. Murph turned to his number six and said, 'Steven, what's happening?'

Tommo thought, 'Something's not right here, I've got a smashed lip and Walker's getting all the plaudits.'

He tore off his shirt and stormed into the showers, shouting behind him, 'If you don't need me, I'm f***ing off!'

As Tommo turned on three showers and stood under the jet spray, Murph followed him in.

'Steven, Steven, I'm just using some reverse psychology with the lad. Now get yourself back out there.'

Tommo looked at Murph standing fully clothed, getting soaked to the skin. He relented, put his shirt back on, and went back for the second half. They won 3-1.

Less than a month later, in the FA Cup first-round tie against Port Vale, Murph's battling centre-half collapsed to the ground. Bert Loxley ran across the pitch with a yellow sponge and a bladder filled with cold water.

'I've broke me leg,' Tommo said.

'Stand up, lad.'

'I can't stand up!'

'Where are you from?' Bert said.

'Sheffield. Yorkshire.'

'Then you can do it, lad!'

Tommo stood up and fell straight back down again. He was stretchered off the field with a broken leg, leaving behind all the hopes and expectations for the season on the Vale Park pitch. He would be out for the rest of the campaign. In a typical Murph response, the gaffer didn't allow himself to dwell on the negative. He would just have to work harder to see the season through.

Every morning he looked at the fixture list and decided where to go in the evening. He didn't care how far he travelled to watch an opposition team or a player he fancied signing. I asked Judith if it was hard work being a football manager's wife.

'No, not really, he was never there!'

Wherever Murph travelled during the week, he had the same routine on a Sunday morning. He wandered up Blacksmith Lane in Thorpe-on-the-Hill, picked up the *News of the World*, and spent the morning poring over the previous day's results. Murph tested his eight-year-old son Ben on the league table, the fixtures, the goals scored. On a weeknight he would come home with the match programme, sit on Ben's bed and discuss the game. He never discussed football with Judith.

'He was always on the phone to people about who's got a good left foot, this that and the other,' Judith said, 'but he never spoke to me about it. I can remember even when they lost a match. He left the ground, and that was it. He didn't mope about. He probably went over the game with somebody on the phone, but it didn't seem to hang over him.'

And on Monday morning, the whole merry cycle started again.

By November 1983, Murph had completed five years with Lincoln. He was the longest serving manager in the Third Division. Murph needed a cause to keep the adrenalin flowing. Arguing with the directors had kept him sharp. With the board dispute behind him, he needed to channel his constant supply of nervous energy and focus on managing the squad.

Fashanu, Murph's new signing, admits he arrived at Sincil Bank thinking he was a star. The gaffer didn't let him think it for long. Two months after he joined the Imps on loan, the centre-forward signed a contract for £15,000. He played his next game against Bristol Rovers in front of a home crowd of 3,709. On the same day as the Brinks Mat robbers snatched £25m in a Heathrow

Airport gold heist, Fashanu grabbed himself a hat-trick, in a game they won 4-0. The first hat-trick City had seen since thrashing Bournemouth 9-0 at home, almost 12 months before.

Simmonite tells the story of Lincoln's new signing. On the Monday morning after the Saturday game, Murph requested the usual routine for training; in the changing room by ten o'clock, on the pitch for quarter past. With the hint of a 'Look at me boys', Fashanu arrived at the ground at quarter past ten, and wandered on to the pitch 15 minutes later. Murph clocked it but said nothing. Two weeks later, with the next home game against Sheffield United in the second round proper of the FA Cup, Murph instructed the players to be in the changing room for 1.45pm before the team talk at two o'clock. Fashanu ambled in at five past two; brown velvet suit, pink cravat in his top pocket, suede loafers with no socks, and a leather toiletry bag under his arm.

He sauntered to the bench.

'Hello boys. Hello boss. Sorry I'm late.'

Fashanu sat down at number nine where his shirt was hanging up. Murph shot him a glance.

'That's alright, Fash. You sit there at number 12, cos you're f***ing sub!'

Lincoln drew 0-0 in the Sheffield game, but Murph didn't regret his decision. Nobody took liberties with the boss.

Despite the odd dressing down, Fashanu remembers his time at City as where he really learned his trade. Almost 30 years after he left the Imps, he told Danny Kelly from talkSPORT's *My Sporting Life*, 'Murph, he's a legend, wonderful man, been looking for him ever since. You know his ideas on football were just unique.'

Murph knew he had signed a striker who had passion, aggression, and self-belief, but no left foot. Fashanu remembered how the boss came up with a solution. In their Sincil Bank training sessions, he made his striker wear a football boot on his left foot and a sandal on his right; the sandal covered with a full-length white sock. Murph told Fashanu that he couldn't strike the ball with his right foot. The gaffer would know if he did, because he would come off the pitch with a dirty sock. The striker had to learn to use his left foot. If he left the pitch with a virginal white sock, Murph gave him the most valuable reward for any young player – the manager's handshake. The unconventional idea hadn't come from a Lilleshall training manual, but it would later pay dividends for the player and the club.

For the second Christmas in succession, Murph had to play without a full-strength team. In his weekly newspaper column, The Manager's View, he expressed his frustration.

'I happen to believe no one can work miracles and it strikes me that even applies to people like Holmes and Watson, the Marx Brothers, Bilko, Inspector Clouseau, or Winston Churchill. All these had immeasurable qualities, but I don't know whether any of them had the attributes to be able to win promotion for Lincoln City F.C. with all the injuries and suspensions we have had in a squad of 16 players.'

Murph knew the only way to win promotion with a skeleton squad was to go 46 games without injury or suspension,

'And tradition suggests that no one has done that for 50 years.'

He would have to adjust his expectations in line with the club's resources and try to keep his players injury-free. It would be a long haul to drag themselves up from mid-table, but publication of the annual accounts in February brought a welcome reprieve. A prior year loss of £89,000 had turned into a £120,000 pre-tax profit. Cost-cutting and the reduction in player numbers had paid off, but they had come at the price of promotion. Murph questioned whether you should evaluate a successful club by a healthy balance sheet or its results.

'Where do you get the compromise,' he wrote, 'between sound business philosophy and stepping out into the promiscuous unknown?'

Not enough Lincoln supporters were stepping out into the promiscuous unknown. Only 1,575 watched a 4-0 drubbing of

Gillingham at Sincil Bank in early March. The chairman recognised that City's attendance record placed them in the bottom 15 league clubs in the country. It was difficult to justify their rightful place in the Second Division.

If Steve Thompson had been available throughout the season, things might have turned out differently. There may have been no need to sell a player who was still instrumental in Murph's long-term plans. But on deadline day, Glenn Cockerill, renowned for his explosive style of attacking play, was on the move to Sheffield United. It was the second time the manager had sold him for over £100,000. Even allowing for the £40,000 Murph paid to bring him back from Swindon Town, it was an excellent piece of business. Almost £200,000 of profit for a player signed by Graham Taylor from Louth United at the age of 17, for a song. Despite the boost to the club's bank balance, Murph reflected on a dismal season; Peake's departure, Thompson's long-term injury, and a spate of results which decimated the home support.

'I could keep this club in the Third Division till doomsday,' Murph told Maurice Burton.

But it wasn't what the manager wanted. Two near misses for promotion and a 14th-placed finish to the 1983/84 season. He had expected a greater return for finding young talent and developing his own side. The rumour mill suggested he didn't have the stomach to go through it all again. He was linked with a move to managerless Hull City. The north Humberside club had missed out on Third Division promotion by the smallest of margins, one goal short in the last game of the season. If the Tigers wanted to tempt Murph away from Sincil Bank, they faced a £40,000 bill for compensation. Houlston didn't want his manager to go, and Murph had no authority. The transfer didn't happen. But Boothferry Park had landed on Murph's managerial radar. It might just take him another 18 years to get there.

The start of the 1984/85 season had little to commend it. Only Phil Neale had reason to celebrate. Apart from Bert Loxley, Neale was the longest serving member of the Lincoln staff. After ten years of service, Murph recognised the contribution of his stalwart in defence, not by awarding him a testimonial match, but a testimonial season – the first of its kind. The organising committee kicked off with a match against Graham Taylor's Watford. Later, boxing nights and a barn dance at a local farm all contributed to the testimonial pot. In Neale's matchday player profile, he cited Taylor and Murphy as the biggest influences on his career. Two managers who brought him to Lincoln and kept him long enough to help fund a house move to Worcester. Murph was delighted to help secure the future of the captain of Worcestershire County Cricket Club. The gaffer still enjoyed his cricket.

A month after the testimonial game, John Fashanu played a decisive match at Millwall away. Despite a 2-0 defeat for the travelling side, Murph's striker caught manager George Graham's eye. Fashanu had battered the Millwall defence, received racist abuse from the home crowd, and needed a police escort from The Den to the Lincoln coach. Yet, despite the traditional south-east London welcome, three weeks later, after a run of four goals in seven matches, Fashanu signed for Millwall. A £55,000 ticket to the club which christened him 'Fash the Bash'. And a £40,000 profit for City after only 14 months at Sincil Bank. Murph was still pulling rabbits out of hats.

The trade, which Fashanu said he learned with Murph at Lincoln City, would propel the committed centre-forward right the way through the Football League; an FA Cup winner's medal with Wimbledon in 1988 and two England caps the following year. When Fashanu received his first cap, he sent Murph his England shirt. His former manager appreciated the gesture.

'One day I will return it to him,' he said in an interview with *The Independent*, 'but just for the moment I prefer to keep it.'

Murph thought he had found someone to replace his committed striker, another non-league bargain, Devon White. The manager sounded optimistic about his £2,000 signing from Arnold Kingswell.

'White could be another Tony Cunningham. He's raw at the moment, but I believe we have unearthed another jewel.'

Despite the glowing reference, Murph gave White only five outings in as many months. The season was falling apart. With crowds of little over 2,000, Houlston predicted a loss for the year of £100,000. New chairman John Reames feared the football club might have to cease trading. And Murph was fighting to avoid relegation.

Towards the end of April, the World Snooker Championship was taking place at the Crucible Theatre in Sheffield. Steve Davis was looking to make it three titles in a row. And Lincoln were playing Doncaster Rovers at home, desperate for three points from the local derby to take them clear of the drop. Murph described Rovers as the Bank of England of the Third Division; laden with players and with plenty of money, the antithesis of City. In an appalling game, Doncaster had two players sent off. Even against nine men, the Imps went down 2-0. Murph stormed into the changing room after the match, karate kicked the wooden table, smashed the table's legs and sent the contents flying.

'You'll be running that f***ing common tomorrow!' Murph shouted as he stormed out of the room.

The players looked at each other. Nobody moved, until left-back Steve Collins broke the silence.

'Not a bad break for his first visit to the table!'

The lads enjoyed the joke, but it marked a grim end to the season. Only five players had contract extensions which took them beyond July. The Rovers game was a chance for the others to showcase themselves in front of visiting managers in the stands. Murph's former youth team coach, Lennie Lawrence, said to sportswriter David Whaley, 'Over the last few years, they have built up a couple of good sides, but all that has gone now and it's very sad.'

The board had forced Murph to sell players to balance the books; financial stability achieved at the expense of a weakened side. Steve Thompson and George Shipley would join Lennie at

Second Division Charlton Athletic at the end of the season. And Tommo would finally get his captain's armband. But before that, five games remained between the Imps and relegation. With two home draws and an away win, Murph scrambled to salvage the season.

Saturday, 11 May 1985. The final game of the season, and the last appearance in a Lincoln City shirt for several of Murph's players. The Imps faced champions Bradford City at Valley Parade. The ground was packed to near capacity with Bantams fans eager to celebrate their promotion to the Second Division. A league which would bring both increased revenue and more stringent safety regulations. The old wooden Parade Stand had fallen into disrepair. There were holes in the roof covered by tarpaulins. And the outmoded design of the wooden stand, built on the naturally sloping hillside of the ground, would determine the outcome of the tragedy which unfolded that afternoon. A day which would forever scar the lives of over 11,000 fans who attended the game.

At 3.43pm, just before half-time, the West Yorkshire Fire Brigade received a call from Valley Parade. Sixty seconds later, Yorkshire TV spotted a small fire near the front row of the wooden part of Block G. A discarded match dropped under the floor of the stand is believed to have set light to years of abandoned rubbish. The fire spread rapidly through the space beneath the seats. Within minutes, neighbouring timbers were alight. With alarming ferocity, flames ravaged through the wooden seating and up into the bitumen-clad roof. Burning debris fell on the supporters below as smoke poured from the stand. The fans surged forward. Bert Loxley and Murph were in the dugout as panicked supporters clambered over the wall from the terraces. Loxley ran to a young girl and dragged her free.

Murph later recalled the horror of the scene which confronted them.

'I stepped out of the dugout when people started to spill on to the pitch and the flames were just in one corner. Then within seconds, the whole stand was ablaze. I have never seen anything burn like that before.'

Most of the 3,000 fans in the main stand escaped on to the pitch, but some tried to get out through the exits at the back of the stand. The gates were locked to keep spectators without tickets out of the ground. Desperate fans became trapped in a narrow alley between the back of the stand and the wall of the ground. Engulfed by smoke and toxic gases, there was no escape.

The crowd gathered on the pitch, horrified by the harrowing scenes which they watched in front of them. As the fans dispersed from the ground, Murph walked with them into the smoke-filled side streets, searching for his players. He found the team on nearby Cornwall Road; dazed and shocked, still wearing their football boots. Murph joined Bradford's player-coach, Terry Yorath, and returned to the pitch, unaware of the human toll of the tragedy. Clothes, scarves and helmets lay abandoned on the ground, police officers slumped in chairs in the centre circle. They had ripped off their jackets to douse the flames. Murph spoke briefly to a television camera crew, shook his head in disbelief, and walked away from the scene of devastation. He never spoke to his family about what he had seen that afternoon.

The fire claimed 56 lives and led to a collective outpouring of grief across the football family. Within days, the Bradford Disaster Appeal was set up. The scope and imagination of the fundraising heartened the local community; £500,000 raised in the first week and over £4m in total.

And yet on the same Saturday in May, some of the worst violence ever seen at a British football match sullied the sport. At Birmingham City's St Andrew's stadium, at the last home game of the season against Leeds United, a running pitch battle broke out between both sets of supporters, straight after the final whistle. Ninety-six police officers needed medical treatment. Over 80 spectators were injured. And a 15-year-old boy lost his life when a wall collapsed under the pressure of the crowd.

After a devastating weekend of football, the home secretary

Leon Brittan, addressed the House of Commons. He said that football violence at the Birmingham game, orchestrated by both sets of fans, underlined the link between crowd control and crowd safety. Brittan appointed High Court judge Sir Oliver Popplewell to chair an inquiry under the Safety of Sports Grounds Act, 1975. The findings of the Popplewell Inquiry would have a profound impact on football in the 1980s. And a significant influence on Murph's next managerial post.

Lincoln ended the season in a dismal 19th place. To recover from the traumatic events of the Bradford fire, Murph took the squad away to the Balearic Islands for an end-of-season break. Returning on flight KT 101 from Palma de Mallorca, the Lincoln team boarded the plane with a group of players from York City. Ten minutes before the scheduled landing, 15 miles south-west of Leeds Bradford Airport, the aircraft contacted air traffic control. The pilot was told to prepare for landing on runway 14. None of the flight crew had landed at Leeds Bradford airport before, but they didn't anticipate any problems. Only a year before, the runway had been extended to 2,200 metres.

On the approach to the landing strip, which was wet from a recent rain shower, the co-pilot announced, 'One thousand feet per minute descent.'

The third pilot took over the countdown.

'One hundred feet. Fifty feet. Thirty feet.'

On 30 feet, the captain closed the throttle and made a firm touchdown on the concrete. It felt like a good landing, but Murph and his fellow passengers jolted violently forwards. The captain had followed the centre lights, alternate red and white lights from 900 to 300 metres, red lights from there to the end of the landing strip. As soon as he saw the red lights approaching, he applied full braking, but the cockpit voice recorder registered his surprise.

'Gosh, the red lights come quickly, don't they?'

Four seconds after touchdown, 800 metres beyond the landing threshold, he felt no deceleration.

Three hundred and eighty metres from the end of the runway, he shouted out, 'I've got my feet on the brakes as far as I can!'

The co-pilot increased reverse thrust to maximum.

The passengers could see the end of the runway approaching. The captain was running out of time. Frantically, he steered left to swing the plane away from the path of runway 32. The nose wheel of the Lockheed Tristar careered off the end of the runway and continued its momentum across a stretch of rough ground. It screeched to a violent halt, its nose wedged down overhanging a sheer embankment, tail thrust upwards into the air. The plane stopped only metres away from the airport's perimeter fence. Air traffic control alerted the emergency services, which leapt into action. Four fire vehicles sped across the runway, and 12 ambulances arrived in quick succession.

'Don't undo your seatbelts!' the captain ordered.

All 398 passengers ignored his advice. They scrambled for the emergency exits. Murph didn't wait to let women and children go first. He jumped down the nearest escape slide and fled with his fellow passengers across the grass.

'We were just trying to run away as fast as we could,' Steve Thompson remembers. 'We thought the plane was going to blow up.'

Within 90 seconds the flight crew had evacuated the aircraft and the passengers gathered safely on the bank. Once the shock had subsided, the Lincoln team joked about what they should claim on their insurance.

'A Pentax camera and a gold chain,' one player suggested, 'cos they can't prove anything, can they?'

'What are you gonna claim for?' Tommo asked Murph.

'Trauma and loss of hair!'

'They'll get you a f***ing wig then, boss!'

Two years later, the Accidents Investigation Branch of the Department of Transport filed a 40-page report of the incident. It was one of ten landing overrun accidents on wet runways in the UK in the previous ten years.

Murph's wife Judith recalls the plane crash with wry amusement.

'Colin took the ex-chairman with him, without the chairman at the time knowing about it. When the plane ran off the runway, of course it came out that Dennis Houlston was on the trip. And consequently, Colin got the sack!'

Murph recalled the end of his seven-year reign somewhat differently.

'I realised there was no more I could do, and the challenge had gone,' he told the press.

Murph said the long-term contract which tied him to Lincoln had become a millstone around his neck, not a stepping stone to further success. With two years left on his contract, if he chose to leave, his new club would have to pay compensation. If Lincoln made him redundant, they would face a hefty pay-out. He said he struck a gentlemen's agreement with the board. He left Sincil Bank by mutual consent.

In his last interview with David Whaley from the *Lincolnshire Echo*, Murph spoke with obvious regret.

'There is part of me in this club. I have blood in it. I hope I will be able to come back here in the future and still have a lot of friends.'

Forty-one years old and out of work for the first time in seven years, Murph couldn't possibly imagine how soon that return might come.

6

MADMAN OR MESSIAH?

STOCKPORT COUNTY, AL-ITTIHAD, AND BACK
TO STOCKPORT COUNTY

Murph stood outside the ground at Edgeley Park, shaking hands with Stockport County's chairman, Alan Kirk. The well-rounded, white-haired director looked pleased with his new signing. He'd persuaded a Third Division manager, only two months out of a job, to manage a team of Fourth Division strugglers. County ended the previous season in 22nd place. Murph knew he faced an uphill task, but like so many times before, he relished the challenge.

The Popplewell Inquiry would make life difficult for lower-budget clubs in the Football League. Home secretary Leon Brittan, announced that all Third and Fourth Division sides would face the same system of safety certification as those in the higher tiers. Under the government's stringent policy, County needed to complete essential work before they could apply for a safety certificate from the local authority. They couldn't do the work until they had the funds. Murph faced a lower-league catch-22.

The Football League wouldn't let them play home games until the stadium work was complete, but they needed the revenue from home games to pay for the work. County stood on the edge of a precipice. They faced the prospect of being the first

English football club to go to the wall because of the change in legislation.

A welcome handshake from chairman Alan Kirk, at the start of the 1985/86 season, precedes a series of unfortunate events. (Image courtesy of The Stockport County Historical Archive)

When Exeter City refused to switch their early season match from Edgeley to St James Park, it forced Murph to cancel the game. Faced with a fixture crisis and an enquiry by the League Management Committee, he took control of the one thing he could influence: the players' fitness. In his drive for success, extra training sessions in the afternoon and on Sundays became the norm. On the Saturday morning after the cancelled fixture against Exeter, Murph turned his full senior side out in a junior match against Crewe Alexandra reserves, because, 'They were getting paid for doing nothing.'

Murph didn't care about popularity. He wanted maximum fitness. And he needed to see results.

Seventy-five per cent of the £100,000 cost for the ground's development project was recoverable from the Football Grounds Improvement Trust. The body was set up in 1975, funded by the football pools, to provide financial help towards safety work required by the Safety of Sports Grounds Act. But faced with a chronic cashflow problem, County had to complete the work in stages.

Murph started the new season with only 12 full-time professionals, and one of them was under suspension. Murph had a strong sense of déjà vu. He would have to work hard to survive. He started by lobbying his Fourth Division opposition to switch fixtures, so that County could play all their games away from home. In the opening two matches of the season, the team got off to a poor start. But after a 4-1 defeat against Bolton Wanderers in the League Cup, the manager remained bullish.

'It's a tremendous challenge for me to get it right at Stockport. So much needs to be done, but it'll happen.'

In their next league game away to Burnley, County's exciting smash-and-grab tactics took the title favourites by surprise. County snatched their first victory at Turf Moor for almost 80 years. It settled the manager's nerves, but Murph couldn't build a team on fresh air. He needed to spend money. More specifically, he wanted to sign Sheffield United striker Paul Smith, who had netted five goals in seven games while on loan at Edgeley Park.

In the opening weeks of Murph's contract, injuries culled the team down to nine senior players. Faced with a growing crisis, Murph confronted the board. He threatened that if the directors wouldn't adopt a more positive approach, he would quit. In the middle of negotiations, he laid down his trump card, the offer of a two-year tax-free contract in Saudi Arabia.

Alan Kirk promptly resigned as chair. He said it was nothing to do with Murph's revelation; business commitments required him to travel abroad. Kirk, the club's largest creditor, bankrolled the club during his five-year reign, often paying the wage bill from his own pocket. His successor, Dragan Lukic, the owner of the Belgrade Hotel where Murph had weekly lodgings, refused to commit to signing the player his manager wanted. Murph knew County couldn't come close to matching the Saudi offer; a job which offered him financial security for life. The money didn't bother him. If the board proved they had enough ambition to get out of the Fourth Division, he would stay at Edgeley Park. The directors couldn't convince him. Only 70 days after taking over from groundsman turned manager Eric Webster, Murph quit. And County gained a new Football League record as the club with the largest number of managers since World War Two; an unenviable 20.

The Red Sea port city of Jeddah might seem an unlikely location for a Croydon boys' reunion. But Bob Houghton was managing the Saudi Premier League's Al-Ittihad with Colin Toal as his second-in-command. Houghton offered Murph a job as first team coach at the oldest club in Saudi Arabia. Murph sold the idea to Judith. She could move the family to the sunshine and relax around the pool all day. It would give her a break from her teaching career. She took little persuading. Murph flew over to Jeddah before the family went out to join him, enrolled Ben and Lucy in the International School and gave his wife a call.

'It's all sorted. I've got you a job at the school. You start on 4 January.'

Judith laughs at the memory, 'I was really peeved!'

Left at home in Lincoln to pack up their belongings, with an eight- and a ten-year-old in tow, she received another call from Murph.

'Can you bring the Rothmans with you?'

The Rothmans were 14 years of *Rothmans Football Yearbooks*, a cornucopia of match stats, appearances, transfers and goals. The yearbook was the only Christmas present Murph ever appreciated. As soon as he tore the wrapping paper off the 992-page annual doorstop, he would ignore all his other gifts.

'What do I need that for? You can take it back.'

It made Christmas a cheap affair in the Murphy household. The family always got their money back in January.

Judith lugged the complete set of Rothmans on the plane to Jeddah. They came in handy for football quizzes around the pool. It didn't take long for the family to settle down into the Saudi life-style. A complete change from cash-strapped Stockport County, Murph's centre-forward turned up for training in a brand-new Rolls-Royce Corniche. The booming oil industry of the 1970s fed the appetite for football in Saudi Arabia. 1976 saw the launch of the Saudi Professional League, and within five years Al-Ittihad won their first domestic Saudi Premier League championship.

Brought up on artificial surfaces and Brazilian coaches, Murph acknowledged the emerging talent of the Saudi players. Eight or nine thousand fans would watch the average reserve game, and three times that number would turn out to watch the first team play. The Croydon trio joined the Tigers of Asia at the top of their game. They finished the 1985/6 season in second place and reached the final of the prestigious King Cup. The job had much to recommend it.

Murph marvelled at the change of culture. On a visit to the local bank, he saw people coming out with shopping bags full of cash hanging on their arms. He asked his interpreter how they felt safe walking out on to the streets with so much money on show. The interpreter explained that under Sharia law, theft was punishable by amputation of the right hand.

'That Koran is a powerful thing,' Murph later said in an interview with John Wragg from the *Daily Express*. He recalled passport-sized photos of offenders in the Saudi press. With modern footballers as role models, Murph wanted them to follow a code of conduct. When he travelled to countries like Saudi Arabia, people possessed the qualities he was looking for, but they gained them through fear. He questioned which was the better way.

Lying on his sunbed in Jeddah, after a gentle two hours of football training in the afternoon, Murph had plenty of time to keep abreast of what was happening at home. A boardroom coup back at Stockport County sparked his interest. Josh Lewis and his co-director Grahame White ousted Dragan Lukic as chair. And manager Jimmy Melia got the sack after only three months in charge. Chairman Lewis was on the lookout for a tough replacement; someone with a strong enough stomach to ride the Stockport County rollercoaster.

By mid-November, they sat at the bottom of the Fourth Division, six points adrift of the pack. They had lost 11 of their first 15 league games and were odds-on for relegation. In the days that followed Melia's departure, the same name popped up in the corridors of Edgeley Park. The *Manchester Evening News* joined in the speculation with the headline, 'Iron man a target. Murphy's law?'

Josh Lewis contacted Murph to tempt him off his Saudi Arabian sun lounger and back on to the training ground at Edgeley Park. The odds seemed stacked against the new chairman getting his man. Murph received a £40,000-a-year tax-free offer from Al-Ittihad to extend his contract for a further two years. It made commercial sense for Murph to stay in Jeddah. It would secure his financial future. Judith loved the lifestyle. The children were settled in school. But Murph was battling with an unfamiliar feeling. He was on a perpetual holiday. And he was bored.

A niggling frustration that his ability went unrecognised in the Football League fuelled his move to Saudi Arabia. The more time he had to recharge his batteries, the more he missed the day-to-day involvement in an English league club; the aggravation and hassle of being a manager. Through his rose-tinted sunglasses perched on his sun-kissed balding pate, he still saw potential in the Stockport side, 4,000 miles from his Jeddah compound. Unlike most Third and Fourth Division clubs, he believed County possessed the crowd-pulling ability to prosper long term as a Second Division side. They owned the ground to go with it. If only they could survive the drop.

For the first time in the history of the Football League, the bottom club in the Fourth Division faced automatic relegation to the Vauxhall Conference. No wonder Josh Lewis pursued his chosen manager with relentless determination. The new chairman was used to getting what he wanted. After three days of playing telephone ping pong, Murph flew into Manchester airport. Lewis had persuaded him to take on the toughest job in the Football League, at less than half his tax-free Saudi salary – quite some feat of negotiation.

'Madman or Messiah?' the *Manchester Evening News* headline asked.

Only time would tell.

The throng of fans who turned up at a supporters' meeting at The Jacobean Nite Club that evening was in no doubt; one part madman, four parts messiah. The club was packed to the rafters with fans standing on tables and chairs. They stood and cheered as Murph walked into the room, led by Josh Lewis waving V for Victory signs and smoking a fat cigar. The supporters had called a meeting to hold a vote of no confidence in Lukic, but Lewis saved them the bother with his boardroom coup. After a standing ovation which lasted for more than five minutes, Murph spoke to the crowd.

'Two managers have been shown the door since I left this club. I ain't gonna be the third.'

Murph's soft voice was at odds with his no-nonsense message for the players.

'If they don't want to do things my way and want to play the fool, there will be only one winner.'

The warmth of the welcome from the fans astonished Murph.

Over 35 years later, Des Hinks, Stockport County club historian, describes the meeting as 'a moment etched into County folklore'. Murph was visibly moved by the reception. He admitted to Mike Brennan from the *Stockport Express Advertiser*, 'It frightens me. Not because I don't think I can do the job, because I can. But because people have so much faith in me.'

Judith remained unconvinced. She summed up Murph's decision to leave Saudi Arabia in one word, 'Crackers!'

But Murph stayed for just over a year, so his salary was tax-free. Not quite so mad after all. The board shared Murph's confidence and offered him a two-year contract. Lewis spoke of his ambitions to expand County's board from three members to nine and pledged to give his manager fresh money for new players. Murph reflected on how he took Lincoln to the top of the Third Division with crowds of 4,000 and had to sell his best players. If Stockport made it to the top of the Fourth Division, he was confident of getting 7,000 or 8,000 through the gates on a Friday night.

In the 1960s, County moved their home fixtures from Saturdays to Fridays, so they wouldn't have to compete with the more prominent Manchester United and Manchester City. Murph believed County players could further their careers by staying with the club. Stockport enjoyed a catchment area of 150,000 and were better located than two or three First Division clubs. Lewis tempered Murph's natural optimism with one piece of advice, 'Don't underestimate the problem.'

Or as Murph later wrote, rather more elaborately in his matchday programme notes at Lincoln City, 'Only a very, very, very few people were aware of the demeanour of Stockport County Football Club on the 5 November 1986. Reminiscent of the eerie old, haunted house that had been empty for years and was begging for life. No different to the Mauritian dodo.'

Murph's first task was to sign an assistant manager. His former Lincoln captain, Gordon Simmonite, was working at Second Division Grimsby Town. Murph knew they worked well together and offered Simmonite the job. Everyone told the youth team coach he would be mad to join a team at the bottom of the Football League. He didn't listen. Simmo had total belief in the boss's ability and signed his contract there and then. On their first day in the job, he drove Murph to the Stockport ground, parked his car in the car park, and despite a chill in the autumnal air, left his sheepskin coat on the back seat. Returning to the car after training, the side window was smashed, and the coat had gone. The next day, Murph's number two mentioned the theft in passing to his new nightclub-owning chairman.

'Leave it with me, Gordon,' Lewis said.

Two days later, the chairman turned up at the ground and handed Simmonite his coat back. Murph and Simmo exchanged looks. They'd better not mess up; they had a boss with local connections.

Arriving at County midway through the season, Murph realised he needed rigid tactics to keep the team afloat. Simmo remembers his early days as Murph's number two. The boss gave the players strict instructions for the style of play, and a very simple football philosophy. One touch of the ball in their own half, belt it as far as they could, and launch it at the opposition's back four. In the opponents' half, they could have two touches: the first to control it, the second to pull it back down to the area. Murph knew that cultured defender Bill Williams and front runner Vernon Allatt wouldn't want to play that way, but like a strict headmaster he gave them no leeway. He knew the crowds wouldn't like all his decision making, but his greatest priority was to stay in the Football League.

During his first brief spell in charge at County 15 months earlier, Murph suggested they should set up a supporters' club. He reaped the benefit on his return. A casual mention of the state of the referee's changing room at the supporters' club meeting, and within days, a merry band of fans had turned up to redecorate it, free of charge. Murph repaid them with a 2-0 victory against

Cardiff City, County's first home win of the season, and Murph's first league game in charge.

Hartlepool United away. Stockport lost 1-0 to a late penalty against the run of play and faded in the closing stages. Murph responded immediately. He recalled the players for extra training sessions on Monday and Tuesday afternoons, and said to sportswriter Mike Brennan, 'Why shouldn't footballers work every afternoon? People are working morning and afternoon five days a week and then paying three pounds to come and watch us.'

Colin Murphy, sitting next to assistant manager Gordon Simmonite, directs the offensive at Edgeley Park from his sleeping bag. The match on 22 November 1986 brings a crucial 2-0 win against Cardiff City. (Image courtesy of The Stockport County Historical Archive)

The *Daily Express* ran with a story, suggesting that Murph rivalled Brian Clough for his eccentric ways of handling players. It reported that when Murph's full-backs made a habit of passing the ball across their own goal, he made them wear eyepatches in practice matches. The right-back wore one over his left eye, and the left-back vice versa. And when Murph spotted two of his young players with their hands in their pockets during training, he got their pockets sewn up.

Murph enjoyed the media attention. Two weekly newspaper columns raised his local profile, the predictably titled Murphy's Law for the *Express Advertiser* and Back Chat with the *Stockport Messenger*. The *Messenger* promoted the column as the chance to question the new County chief who 'has won a reputation over the years for forthright, hard-hitting opinions'.

Murph wasn't afraid of shaking things up, either in his written responses or on the pitch. His up and at 'em tactics required a great deal more physical stamina than the County players possessed, but they couldn't argue with the success of the no-nonsense style of play. The same direct approach had taken Dave Bassett's Wimbledon from the Fourth to the First Division in five remarkable seasons. Murph desperately wanted to 'do a Wimbledon'. He introduced a gruelling training programme, one of the toughest in the country, and didn't curb his tongue with his team talks. As they walked down the corridor after training one day, Simmo asked Murph, 'What are you gonna to talk about today, Col? Last Friday's game?'

Murph performed his usual ritual. Held up his right arm, shook his wrist and let the links on his watch, roll down to his elbow.

'Dunno, Gordon, I think we should f***ing see!'

Simmo tells the story of how Murph wandered into the changing room where 15 players were sitting after training. He spotted recent signing Levi Edwards; a midfielder with a heart the size of a dustbin lid, willing, enthusiastic, a player who would run all day long.

'Levi, somebody tells me, you come to work on the bus, is that right?' Murph said.

'Yes, boss.'

'Do you sit upstairs or downstairs, Levi?'

'Downstairs, boss.'

'Well, that's what's wrong with your f***ing game, cos if you sat upstairs, you'd have more vision, and you could see where you're passing the ball. Try sitting upstairs.'

'Yes, boss.'

The players fell about laughing. At the next team talk, Simmo asked Murph what he wanted to cover. He got the same response.

'I'll f***ing think of something.'

Murph strolled into the changing room and turned to Edwards, who hadn't yet learned to avoid the boss's eye.

'There's three blackbirds on a telegraph wire above a field. This big, fat foreman comes out with a shotgun, takes his aim and shoots one. How many's left, Levi?'

'Dunno, boss.'

'How many's left?'

'Two, boss.'

'That's what's wrong with your f***ing game, you don't think enough. Because if you were one of those blackbirds, would you still be sat there? No, you'd be flying away, wouldn't you, so there's no blackbirds left.'

As they left the changing room, Simmo laughed.

'Where d'you pull that one from, Col?'

'Dunno. But he's a good lad. Won't do him any harm to shake him up a bit.'

And as a vote of confidence, Murph rewarded Edwards, his non-contract signing from non-league Altrincham, with a contract to the end of the season.

Simmonite remembers a conversation he had with Murph.

'Gordon, we're not in this game to be liked, but if these players don't have some feeling for you, they won't play for you.'

Murph didn't go out of his way to be liked, but he did want to earn the players' respect. He had the full support of his assistant manager. The move from youth league coach at Grimsby Town was a big step up for Murph's number two.

'In them days, we were doing everything, just him and me;

training, coaching, scouting, looking at opponents, looking for new players,' Simmonite said.

He would leave home at seven o'clock in the morning, train the first team with Murph, train the reserves in the afternoon, watch an evening game, and crash into bed at midnight. One miserable December evening, Murph asked him to drive 260 miles from Stockport to watch fellow Fourth Division strugglers Torquay. They arrived at Plainmoor ten minutes late and made their way to the directors' box. Murph shuffled through the seats, sat down and unfolded his sleeping bag from its liner. He stood up, crawled his way into the bag, pulled on his recently acquired deerstalker hat, and wrapped his scarf around his neck.

'You can't watch a game of football when you're f***ing cold.'

They had come to watch a player who was warming up. When the player stepped out of his tracksuit bottoms and started running up and down the pitch, Murph turned to Simmo.

'Come on Gordon, we're off!'

'We can't go, Col, we've just got here.'

'He's got f***ing brown legs. I don't take a player with brown legs. It's the middle of winter and he's been on a sun bed.'

It didn't matter if the lad was good or bad, Murph saw something he didn't like; an example of the long-lasting influence of Jimmy Sirrel.

When I met Gordon Simmonite, I asked him what Colin looked for in a player. Simmonite said,

'He'd got that knack for looking at players and seeing they're going to make it or they're not going to make it. I once asked him, "Col, what do you look at?", and he said, "I don't know". And I thought well you do know, but you'll never tell anyone.'

Undeterred by the wasted journey to Plainmoor, Murph found a pair of players much closer to home. Veteran target man Ernie Moss and 20-year-old midfielder Phil Brown signed from Chesterfield on Christmas Eve. On Boxing Day Murph returned to Sincil Bank for the first time since he left by mutual consent. It felt strange sitting in the visiting team dugout, but there was no time for nostalgia. The Imps, who dominated play, were sixth in the table and went home disappointed with a point. The County fans celebrated with a conga around the terraces, led by Des Hinks dressed as a festive Father Christmas. Vernon Allatt joined in the seasonal spirit with a hat-trick in the next home fixture against Peterborough United. An undefeated December in the league, things were looking up.

Murph went home after the Lincoln match and switched on Teletext. He received the confirmation he was looking for and smiled at the TV. County had dragged themselves off the bottom of the table. Murph opened the fridge door and poured himself a glass of John Smith's ale. He was under no illusions; life in the lower regions of the Football League would always be a constant battle, not least for cash. He had learnt to celebrate the minor triumphs.

Before the January fixture away to Cardiff City, Murph appealed to the supporters' club to finance bed-and-breakfast accommodation for his 'live away' players. He wanted them to be fresh for the long drive to the Welsh capital. The supporters' club readily paid £150 for the hotel bill, so that players who lived in Barnsley, Sheffield and Wolverhampton could be ready for the early start. A good night's sleep helped the Hatters grab an away point. In four games over the holiday period, County took eight points from a possible 12. They looked well set to pull away from the relegation zone, and Murph rewarded his battle-weary players with a week off. He denied that the 'ironman' had gone soft. The demanding training schedule had taken its toll, but the run of improved results showed it was working. Murph took some satisfaction from seeing who benefited the most. Two players impressed him – Vernon Allatt and Levi Edwards. They both knew County might be their last chance of league football and were determined to make the most of the opportunity.

Just as things were looking up, Simmo asked to speak to Murph in his office. He stood in front of the boss.

'I just can't do it, Col. This game's not for me.'

'What d'you mean, you can't do it?'

'I've got an 18-month-old, Col. All the travelling. I can't do it.'

Murph looked at Simmo as though his favourite defender had picked up the ball and booted it into the back of his own net.

'Gordon, what else is there in life, apart from football?'

'I dunno Col, but I'll think of something.'

Simmo applied for a job with the South Yorkshire Police. He received a letter in March telling him he had a start date in October. It would allow him to stay at County until the end of the campaign. The season was playing out against a backdrop of boardroom unrest. In January 1987, former chairman Dragan Lukic demanded the immediate repayment of £70,000 owed to him by the club. By the end of March, current chair Josh Lewis, a man who wore over-sized sunglasses throughout the winter, shocked the supporters by announcing his retirement at the end of the season. He had seen off a winding up order over the club's tax debts, set up a seven-man board and created a new fundraising structure. He told Andy McIntyre from *The Messenger* that once they reached an amicable agreement with the creditors, including the executors of Alan Kirk's estate, 'I believe we will have the foundations to build a Second Division club at Edgeley Park.'

Murph had to dig deep and keep the faith.

After a steady start to the new year, County looked safe from the drop. Murph's players had reached the level of fitness he wanted. Now they were ready to face stage two of Murph's method, a tactical and organisational plan. Before they could do that, disaster struck. Four successive defeats catapulted them back to the bottom of the table. Murph responded by going back to raid the coffers at Chesterfield. He signed goalkeeper Chris Marples. In the goalie's first home game against Cambridge United, County played in the worst gale for a decade. The roof from a nearby timber yard blew on to the Cheadle End terracing before the start of the game, and with the wind against them, County trailed 2-0 at half-time. In a match of blow football, with the icy blast at their backs in the second half, Marples played a blinder and Stockport forced a dramatic 3-2 win.

One local fan of a literary bent penned his praise for Murph's comeback in phrases so flowery, Murph could have written them himself. 'On Murphy' appeared in the letters' page of the local press.

'Edgeley Park is no Camelot, but another Merlin has emerged, and the gallant knights have responded magnificently to his strong words of encouragement,' wrote Stan Broomhead from Offerton who liked Murph, a lot. 'He should be on the short list for the next England managership,' Mr Broomhead suggested.

'Someone who's roughed it and emerged with pride and respect, for conquering a situation where all seemed lost ... He's got no gold rings or bracelets, no Mercedes, but find me another manager who has done more, and achieved more in such a short space of time.'

Stan was wrong about the Mercedes, but Murph appreciated the sentiment. Not all the fans were so supportive of Murph's up and at 'em style. The purists among them criticised his tactic of getting the ball forward quickly and playing in the opposition's half. Murph tongue-whipped his critics and refused to budge.

'What do they want us to do? Go around planting a few daisies? This is the harsh side of the game, and nobody gives you points for playing pretty-pretty stuff.'

Simmonite agreed.

'Until the team is mathematically out of trouble, we will press on banging the ball down.'

As results improved, they could allow the players more freedom. Thirty-seven points from 23 games, compared with six points from 15 before the management duo signed in November. The tactics spoke for themselves.

Towards the end of April, Lincoln arrived at County's ground for a crucial battle at the bottom of the table. When the teams last met on Boxing Day, the Imps were still dreaming of a place in the play-offs and County were struggling in the relegation zone. Four months on, Lincoln had plummeted towards the bottom of the league. Murph didn't underestimate the importance of the fixture. Les Robinson, one of his most influential signings, dominated the midfield. And a late, low cross from Phil Brown allowed Andy Hodkinson to score probably the most valuable goal of any club that season. County bagged a 1-0 win and leapfrogged over Lincoln in the table. The Hatters' euphoria matched the Imps' despair.

A depressed Lincoln supporter wrote to the *Lincolnshire Echo*. He'd hitchhiked to Edgeley Park with his son to watch Murph and Simmonite train their new squad before the game. He wished he hadn't bothered. The County team had accepted their new bosses, who looked happy, as did the fans. The away trip gave the fan a terrible longing for Lincoln's past, the glory days of beating Tottenham at home.

'Please someone somewhere give us a club to be proud of,' he wrote.

The same sentiment echoed around Edgeley Park. The fans took a collective intake of breath. Could Murph really secure their survival and give them back a club they would be proud of? Two weeks later they would find out.

On a bank holiday Monday in Peterborough, County played a scrappy game of football, but earned a hard-fought point. The goalless draw belied its significance. The Stockport fans did the maths. From the depths of certain relegation, Murph had delivered his promise to keep County in the Football League. With two matches to go they were safe at last. They could still influence the fate of teams at both ends of the Fourth Division table. Murph had his eye on Tranmere, Rochdale, Torquay, Burnley and Lincoln, all of whom faced non-league oblivion in the Vauxhall Conference if they finished bottom. He knew which one of those clubs he would hate to push over the edge.

In the last Friday night fixture of the season, Mark Sertori shone in his home debut at Edgeley Park. The Hatters couldn't deny Southend a two-goal victory, but the defeat didn't matter to the County fans. On the final whistle they stormed the pitch in their hundreds, in sheer relief that County were staying up. Murph and Simmonite stood in the directors' box at the top of the main stand, linked their hands in the air like a victorious fight team, and introduced the players to their adoring fans. The squad Murph had assembled bore little resemblance to the one he inherited six months before.

The gaffer praised Simmonite for his influence in changing the club's fortunes. And the County board believed the powerhouse they'd built, fuelled by grit and determination, had a real chance of bidding for promotion in the season ahead. With 18 months of Murph's contract still to run, the directors had no reason to think the manager didn't share their ambition. But they probably didn't have their eyes peeled on Lincoln City away.

By 9 May 1987, Rochdale and Tranmere had climbed to safety. The three remaining teams, Burnley, Torquay and Lincoln faced an agonising fight to secure their future. Lincoln needed a point to survive. On the final Saturday they travelled to Swansea; a last-ditch stand to salvage their Football League status. Travelling on the supporters' bus to Vetch Field, Chris Ashton, Red Imps Association chairman and Mr Lincoln City the Younger, orchestrated the fans in fine voice. Carloads of travelling support flanked the supporters' bus on an anxious five-hour drive. Within 30 minutes of kick-off, Lincoln went 1-0 down. The players' heads dropped, only lifted by the roar of the crowd when fellow strugglers Torquay conceded a second goal at home to Crewe Alexandra. Like Lincoln, Torquay needed a draw.

The Football League introduced the automatic relegation system to add some bite to the season. And a German Shepherd dog called Bryn took the advice to heart. Trailing 2-1 down in the dying minutes of the game, Torquay's right-back, Jim McNichol, ran to make a cross. The police dog, fearing for his handler's safety, swept in and bit the player's leg. With four minutes of time added on, enough to refresh tired legs, 30 seconds before the final whistle, Torquay scored. They had pulled the match back to a 2-2 draw. And Swansea beat Lincoln 2-0. With 48 points apiece, Torquay scrambled clear on goal difference. And Lincoln were going down; bottom of the Fourth Division for only the last 30 seconds of the season.

Thirty-three years later in the national lockdown of 2020, Torquay cemented their saviour's name in club folklore. They launched a signature brew, in a jet-black bottle. And called it Bryn.

Murph and Simmonite struggled to compute Lincoln's ill fortune. On the way home to Lincoln after a usual weekend fixture, Murph would drop Simmo off in Baslow, close to his Peak District home; the hour-long car journey spent deep in conversation. But on the Saturday after the Lincoln result came through, the pair drove home in complete silence. A curious mix of emotions; pride and delight for what they'd achieved at County, but total devastation for Lincoln.

Within 48 hours, small box adverts appeared in the national press, inviting applications for the Lincoln manager's job. Before the last kick of the Swansea game, several candidates had expressed an interest, but the directors couldn't appoint a new manager. The PFA, the players' union, was waiting to confirm the validity of existing contracts for players who would no longer appear in the Football League. Protecting its members from the disappointment of signing for a league club and ending up in the Conference, they underestimated Lincoln City's commitment to saving all its professional staff. Chairman John Reames assured the authorities they had every intention of keeping the players on full-time contracts, despite dropping down to a part-time league. Six players' contracts expired within the month. Without a manager, the directors decided who should stay and who should go; only one player was on their retained list. The incoming boss would have to rebuild for promotion. The board needed to find an individual who was up to the job.

When Lincoln dropped into the Conference, they passed Neil Warnock's Scarborough on the way up. Warnock achieved a double first. His first promotion as manager and Scarborough's first ever taste of the Football League, achieved with a part-time squad. Murph was the second biggest winner of the season. By achieving the seemingly impossible at County, he became the hottest property in the Fourth Division.

Vic Jobson, chairman of Southend and a long-time admirer of the straight-talking Londoner, was tracking Murph's managerial career. Southend had just won promotion to the Third Division, ironically gifted by their closing match victory at Edgeley Park. The Blues' manager, David Webb, had resigned after a disagreement with the chairman, two months before they won promotion. Jobson spoke to the press about Murph.

'It's not our policy to tap up managers of other clubs, but if he wished to apply, he would be welcome.'

Murph was a wanted man, but Southend had appointed Paul Clark as interim player-manager, and Murph realised the Roots Hall job could be more of a general manager's role. With a domineering chairman like Jobson, Murph would struggle to establish an understanding that he was his own boss. The Blues were an attractive proposition, but Murph didn't pursue the opportunity. Five years later, in different circumstances but with the same chairman, he changed his mind.

Murph hadn't severed his ties with the city of Lincoln. He kept his family home at Thorpe-On-The-Hill. The manager's job at Stockport was a weekly commute. One hundred and twenty applicants were reported to have thrown their names into the hat at Sincil Bank. The front runner, Martin O'Neill, in his first managerial post at Grantham Town, believed he had as good as got the job. But when John Reames phoned Murph, he knew why his former chairman was on the line. Reames, a millionaire grain merchant, knew what he wanted; someone who combined confidence with optimism, enthusiasm with determination. Despite parting company with Murph only two years before, Reames said to Tony Hardisty from the *Sunday Express*, 'It was Murphy I wanted to lead us back to respectability. It was no surprise to me that he had done so well at Stockport. He's a damned good manager.'

Murph ran the idea of returning to Lincoln past his good friend, Simmonite.

'You've got to take the job, Col,' Simmonite said.

The boss was worried about leaving his assistant in limbo. It would be several months before Simmonite started his new post with South Yorkshire Police.

'What are you gonna do till October?' Murph said.

'I could go on the dole, Col.'

'You don't have to do that. I'll sort something out.'

Murph wouldn't let his running mate down. He hatched a plan and sold it to Lincoln's four-man board. City couldn't afford to pay Simmonite for the close season, and County had offered him the vacant boss's job. Murph said to his assistant, 'Stall them. Just tell them you haven't decided yet. If you can stay at Stockport throughout the close season so Lincoln don't have to pay your wages, I'll take you as youth team coach. You can work with me till the day before you join the police.'

Murph liked to have his own people around him. And Simmonite appreciated the gaffer's support.

While Murph was negotiating with Lincoln, the Stockport County Supporters' Club wrote a letter, pleading with him to stay at Edgeley Park. They admired the ambition and abrasive style of their charismatic manager. Like Murph, they believed that County, with their enviable facilities and growing population, could one day support a Second Division side. When they were last in the Third Division in the 1960s, they averaged crowds of 12,500, outstripping the support for Manchester City in the league above. But by the mid-1980s, Football League attendance was in decline. Total Football League crowds of 27.6 million in the 1964/65 season had fallen to under 18 million in 1984/85. A combination of economic factors and the availability of competing leisure pursuits had hit the turnstiles.

The Stockport County supporters' club put forward a

compelling argument for their manager to stay, but Murph had already decided. He wanted to manage a football team, not become embroiled in boardroom politics. The bust-up with the directors at Lincoln was still fresh in his mind, and he didn't want history to repeat itself.

Tensions were running high in the Stockport County board after yet another change of chairman. The County directors made no guarantee of money to spend on new players, and the Lincoln City board promised to fund a comeback campaign. Murph needed little persuading. He accepted Reames' offer, and boldly told the local press he was looking forward to Third Division football in three years' time.

Acting-chairman Grahame White released a statement on behalf of the County board. They were bitterly disappointed with their departing manager. Murph had shaken hands with the new chairman before he left to go on holiday and assured the directors, he was planning to stay at Edgeley Park. White claimed that Lincoln had broken the agreement between league clubs not to make an illegal approach. New chairman Dave Hunt later said to the *Stockport Express Advertiser* that when he took over, he gave Murph carte blanche for what sort of contract he wanted.

'If he had come back to me and asked for a ten-year contract, I would have given it to him and that's never been done in football before, to my knowledge.'

County were planning for their long-term future and Murph had let them down. Hunt insisted that £100,000 of the directors' money had rescued the club, not the manager. Disgruntled supporters who bought season tickets in the belief that Murph was in charge could get their money back.

'This club is not about Colin Murphy,' the chairman said. 'It is about Stockport County.'

As a parting gesture the board threatened to file a 'substantial' claim for compensation, reported to be in the region of £30,000. John Reames stepped in with some tough telephone negotiations. Murph was off the hook and on his way back to Sincil Bank. But his decision to leave Stockport confounded convention. Why would a manager in a secure position in the Fourth Division, with active interest from a Third Division club, risk everything for a high-stakes move to the Vauxhall Conference?

'Madman or Messiah?' the Manchester press had asked. Quite possibly both.

7

MISSION ACCOMPLISHED

LINCOLN CITY

Driving in his white Mercedes through the familiar redbrick terraced streets surrounding Sincil Bank, Murph spotted Lincoln City super fan George Ashton. Almost two years to the day since he left the club by mutual consent, Murph was back in Lincoln. He wound the car window down and shouted across the road to the gentleman almost 20 years his senior, 'Don't worry, Georgie boy. I'm back. We're gonna win the league!'

Ashton gave a cautious smile. He wanted to believe the boss, but the club had just suffered two consecutive relegations.

Murph returned to a city still smarting from its spectacular crash landing into the Vauxhall Conference. The Imps started the season as one of the Fourth Division favourites and ended by consigning 95 years of professional league football to the history books. The lure of promotion to the Football League had increased the tempo and competitiveness of the Conference; total attendance had increased by almost 20 per cent in a year.

Over the close season, the leading clubs assembled stronger squads than ever before. Murph knew he had to rebuild a team which could get City promoted at their first attempt. They would be the team to beat; every match against them played like a cup final. He was putting his credibility as a manager on the line. If he failed to bring them promotion, his reputation could be finished.

Despite the devastation of relegation, a new energy pulsed through the club. Managing director Geoff Davey, brimming over with enthusiasm, announced that season ticket sales were up, sponsorship was up, and ground adverts had sold out for the first time. Murph intended to drive the regeneration by demolishing a team which he believed had committed the ultimate sin; they hadn't fought to survive. He needed to 'resurrect some spirt, warmth and feeling in the club, and to regain some respect within the community'. After a wholesale clear-out of his inherited squad, he would look towards the Football League for fresh players, but he wouldn't rush into deciding.

Gamekeeper turned poacher, Murph felt no shame in looking to Stockport County for his first signing. Towering centre-half Trevor Matthewson, the Stockport County Supporters' Club Player of the Season, had turned down a contract renewal. The local press reported that Matthewson felt unsettled at Edgeley Park, playing for a club which lacked ambition. Murph admired his former skipper's solid presence in the County back four. Big club scouts had been tracking the player after some brilliant league performances in his best-ever season, but the 24-year-old defender put his faith in a change of fortune under his old boss. Testament to his relationship with Murph, he was excited by the challenge, unfazed by the drop into non-league football, and confident they could go straight back up. The bookmakers shared his belief. City with their full-time playing staff were the season's favourites, though Murph realised it did them no favours.

'Every team in the Conference wants to prove a point for the quality of non-league football by trying to shoot us down,' he said to sports journalist Bryan Brett.

Murph enjoyed far more media attention than a job in the non-league would usually allow. Every pundit wanted to know why he had taken the biggest gamble of his managerial career. The *Daily Express* ran an article on the toughest job in sport; trying to get Lincoln City out of the Conference at the first attempt. An alliterative copy editor coined a phrase which would define both a manager and a season. The headline 'Murphy's Mission' was soon adopted by the club, and frequently repeated over the next 12 months.

Murph explained the rationale for his return to sportswriter David Spurden.

'It's a challenge and a big, big risk but I know my past has equipped me to succeed in this type of situation.'

Murph reflected on the lessons he learnt at Derby County.

'It matured me overnight. It made me realise what a dog-eat-dog world football is. It also taught me that no matter how hard life may seem at the time, you can get through it. You learn how to survive and there's no bigger word in football management!'

In the middle of June, survival looked precarious. A month away from pre-season training, Murph had only a handful of players guaranteed to start the season. Fuelled by adrenalin, he gave a wry chuckle.

'What a laugh! No pros, no coach, half a stand and only a month away from opening the shop.'

But Murph promised that by the time the season started, he would field a team of full-time professionals and would have signed a new coach. He didn't let on that Simmonite was finalising terms. Murph's number two had total faith that the boss would bounce Lincoln straight back up to the Football League.

'He's a great manager,' he told Julie Sherborn at the *Lincolnshire Echo*. 'I would follow him to the ends of the earth.'

A 40-mile trip from Grimsby to Lincoln was all that was required.

City pledged that despite their non-league status, the new St Andrews Stand, planned in the aftermath of the Bradford City fire, would still be completed. Murph stood in front of the half-built construction, a monument to the spirit of revival at Sincil Bank, shoulders hunched, hands planted in his tracksuit pockets. No hint of a smile. He spoke of putting his neck in the noose, and his managerial reputation on the line, but his parting message sounded more optimistic.

'It's a big gamble but the fans realise I will deliver.'

As if to convince himself, Murph taped a copy of the league table from 9 November 1986 to his poky office wall. The table showed Stockport County at the bottom of the Fourth Division with six points, and Lincoln City fifth from top with 24. Murph laughed out loud.

'I love it. You can either end up in the khazi or at Old Trafford. What a life!'

County fans feared that Murph's departure might consign the club to oblivion. In a supporters' poll, the vast majority wanted Simmonite to take over where Murph had left off. They saw the 30-year-old assistant and keeper of Murph's promotion plans as a natural replacement. But Murph would disappoint them a second time. Not only was he signing Simmo as his assistant at Lincoln City, but he planned for him to return to the Imps' back four. In the deal to move from County, Murph took Phil Brown, Edgeley Park's attacking midfielder with him. Brown had spent less than five months at County, but Murph liked what he saw. His hunch was right. The player went on to score 20 goals in his first season at Sincil Bank.

Neither County nor City confirmed the amount of compensation they paid to release Murph from his contract. When asked if it was the substantial sum they were reported to have asked for, the County secretary dryly observed, 'When you've got nothing, a fiver's substantial!'

Murph wasted no time in shaking up the Lincoln team. He netted £50,000 for captain Gary West en route to Gillingham, taking a £16,000 profit for a player signed by coach turned manager John Pickering three years before. In among the comings and goings, Bert Loxley, who had dedicated 21 years to the club as player, manager and team physiotherapist, was devastated to hear his services were no longer required. Living up to his hardman image, Murph wiped the slate clean. When the Lincoln players reported back for pre-season training, seven new players swelled their ranks.

Laying the foundations for a new start at Sincil Bank.
Assistant manager Gordon Simmonite and manager Colin
Murphy on the construction site at the new St Andrews
Stand. (Image courtesy of Lincoln City Football Club)

Mick Waitt, a 6ft 4in striker, and midfielder David Clarke took a leap of faith and left Third Division Notts County to follow Murph into the non-league. Waitt hoped Murph could reboot his career, as he had done for John Fashanu. None of the new signings needed to drop out of the Football League any more than their manager did. Murph was putting together a team which was prepared to take a gamble, with players who had the confidence and determination to succeed. He recognised the pressures he would face but batted them away.

'It's all part of the game and if you can't cope with them, you might as well go off and run a post office!'

The greatest pressure came from Murph himself. He rarely relaxed. If he had a spare evening, he took a trip up the road to watch Grimsby Town's reserves in search of another signing. Football dominated his life, and his dedication paid off. Before the start of the season, he lifted goalkeeper Nigel Batch, central defender Andy Moore, and future Lincoln City Player of the Season Bob Cumming from Grimsby's first team. With a fee of £34,000, Moore broke the transfer record for a non-league club.

Murph sold the bulk of his inherited team before the start of the season. By September he had bought a new squad, with £40,000 left over. Asa Hartford, the ex-Scottish international who took over the manager's job at Edgeley Park, wasn't surprised when Murph looked to County to raid his old club. Alongside Brown and Matthewson, Murph snapped up winger Dave Mossman and 19-year-old Mark Sertori.

'He has taken four and asked for others, so every time the phone rings I expect it to be Colin,' Hartford said.

Murph was unashamed of raiding his old club. He explained his reasoning to sportswriter Bryan Brett.

'I know at 3pm each Saturday they will go out and give me 90 minutes. I don't ask for more than that and I know we have to have it, as the Conference is a tough league.'

On a flurry of Friday afternoons, Chris Ashton whipped into Murph's tiny office on his way home from school; volunteering at Lincoln City was a huge part of the local teacher's life. His dad, George, had wheeled him in a pram to his first Imps game in 1953. The 35-year-old chair of the Red Imps Association ran up to the telephone office in Grantham Street, transfer instructions in hand. In the pre-internet age, new signings were made by telegram. They had to meet the five o'clock transfer deadline to allow the player to appear the next day. It was no surprise that

Lincoln's spending spree didn't endear them to their non-league opponents. Nor did Murph's high profile in the media. His willingness to speak to the press brought more than his fair share of attention.

He spoke to chief sportswriter Tony Pritchett from the *Sheffield Star* before the start of the season. 'TP' could be waspish in his reporting, but he wrote with genuine warmth about Lincoln's 'deeply respected' manager, who had 'an outstanding reputation in the lower divisions'.

Murph admitted he didn't know how the season would pan out.

'I sense more sympathy than bitterness about our plight. I can take both; I can understand both. It is apathy I can't do with. Maybe I'm at my best when I'm struggling.'

David Pleat told me this was an uncommon trait among football managers, but Colin was a fighter with a great self-belief that his principles would out. When the Conference committee announced the season's fixture list, they put his comment to the test. Murph's men faced a baptism of fire. In their first away game of the season Lincoln played Barry Fry's Barnet, the previous year's Conference runners-up. A fixture handpicked by the committee to guarantee maximum media coverage. Fry was taking no chances. He started pre-season training a week early with one fixture in mind. He predicted that the Imps' superior fitness could pay dividends late in the season, but Murph's newly assembled team couldn't win the Conference. They would have dropped too many points in the early games.

Fry took some satisfaction from the opening Saturday's result at Underhill Stadium. Lincoln lost 4-2. In their second fixture four days later, away to Weymouth, a club blessed with the healthiest bank balance in the league, the Imps' fans had nothing to admire, except the newly completed Wessex Stadium. City lost 3-0.

Murph didn't underestimate the task ahead. He said that in the Conference, they would play teams as strong as any in the

Fourth Division, and a few in the Third. Many of the talented players in the Conference saw it as a lifestyle choice. They could play part time, train twice a week, and still have the security of a job outside football. City's fall from grace would give their opposition the added satisfaction of kicking lumps out of a full-time ex-Football League outfit on a Saturday afternoon. Ever optimistic, Chris Ashton put a positive spin on the non-league challenges ahead. In an interview with Frank Keating for *The Guardian*, he said, 'We've got 21 new clubs to visit, some in places we've never heard of. And our club shop has 21 new crowds to sell our badges to. Tell them that our catering was always considered best in the League.'

Keating duly obliged. He also wrote a pithy summing up of Lincoln City's boss.

'He is an old-school haggler for a bargain and a disciplinarian with a sergeant's haircut.'

Murph had to respond quickly to the two opening defeats. Supported by City's ambitious four-man board and boosted by the £108,000 transfer of goalkeeper Lee Butler to Aston Villa, Murph made an offer of £48,000 to Port Vale. It was enough to tempt Paul Smith, their 23-year-old striker, away from the Third Division. Smith explained to the press why he accepted an offer which would take him straight out of the Football League.

'Colin Murphy,' he said. 'It's as simple as that. He knows how to get the best out of players.'

Smith had played under Murph at Edgeley Park on loan from Sheffield United. When the County board refused to sign him, Murph quit the club. John Rudge, the Port Vale manager, wanted to play Smith wide on the right. Murph wanted to play him up front. It was a straightforward decision for the striker to leave the Valiants. Smith believed City would go from strength to strength. He spoke about the gaffer to Tony Hardisty from the *Sunday Express*.

'He's ruthless enough to rip the team apart and good enough

on the coaching and tactical side to blend new players in smoothly.'

Murph broke the transfer record for a non-league club for the second time that season.

In Manager Murph's Message, the matchday programme notes for the first home game of the season, he set out his intentions.

'If I am able to develop the spirit that the other "bunch of ragbags" that I had here possessed, then one thing is for sure, we are in for an exciting season.'

In Smith's second game, away to Altrincham, Murph returned to the north-west for the first time since he had left Stockport in the lurch. A crowd of almost 800 County fans made the brief journey to the Moss Lane ground to give him a good old-fashioned footballing welcome, an incessant 90-minute barrage of verbal abuse. They booed, heckled and chanted until the final whistle, when a police escort flanked an ashen-faced Murph for the ten-yard walk from the dugout to the dressing room. Undeterred by the abuse, he added salt to County's festering wounds. Within a week, he signed midfielder Clive Evans, the fifth player to join the exodus from Edgeley Park.

When Barry Cheetham, a lifelong County fan, penned *When Friday Night was County Night: Stockport Footballing Memories* over a decade later, he recognised the complex nature of the County fans' relationship with their former manager. The author acknowledged that whenever Murph returned to Edgeley Park, he received a reception 'which might best be described as vitriolic'. Yet he admitted that without Murph's return to the club, County could well have ceased to exist. By way of reconciliation, in Chapter 12 of *When Friday Night was County Night*, Cheetham proposed a 'Be kind to Colin Murphy week'.

Roll forward a further 20 years. Murph was invited to lead Danny Cowley's triumphant Lincoln City team on to the pitch at Wembley stadium, ahead of the 2018 EFL Trophy Final. And the Hatters' fans' feelings had softened yet further with time.

Colin Murphy leads the Lincoln City team out on to the Wembley pitch, 30 years after his promotion-winning season with the club. (Image courtesy of Chris Vaughan for Lincoln City Football Club)

The County supporters' message board pinged with recognition of their former manager.

'Mad as a box of frogs,' one suggested. 'And nicked a few quality players when he left ... but forgiven, he was a miracle worker, and a manager County should never forget. Massive respect for this guy.'

'County saviour,' another added.

'And we repaid him,' recalled a third, 'by singing, we're gonna hang Colin Murphy from the highest tree!'

Des Hinks, County club historian, remembers the complete lyrics of the song with wry amusement:

> *There is a tavern in the town, in the town,*
> *And we're going to burn it down, burn it down.*
> *We're going to hang Colin Murphy from the*
> *highest tree,*
> *So, all the Lincoln fans can see!*

Murph took the criticism in his stride, but two months into the Conference season he was still adapting to the physical style of play. Opponents changed their tactics when they faced City; most teams fielded five in defence. Following a home game against Bath City, Murph wrote in his matchday programme notes, 'When I saw Bath line up and then studied the first five minutes of the game, I was beginning to think they had come to defend Hadrian's Wall, or possibly the Berlin Wall.'

'It's like playing in Europe every week,' Murph sighed when he spoke to the press. He likened it to Juventus arriving to get a 0-0 result to preserve their opportunity for the home leg.

Undeterred by the spoiling tactics, a 3-0 victory against Bath put the Imps firmly among the leaders. City's gates had rocketed since they dropped out of the Football League. Murph played three men up front to break his opponents' back line. McGinley, Brown and Sertori ran the legs off opposition defenders, who couldn't match them for fitness. And Murph employed a special brand of tactics at home.

If you looked through the old iron gates at the South Park end of Sincil Bank, late on a Friday night, you might spot a hosepipe watering the already well-hydrated pitch. Murph had instructed groundsman Richard Alford to improve the playing surface. Improvement meant a sodden and heavy pitch, perfect for tiring out their part-time opponents' legs. It was a trick Murph had picked up from Brian Clough.

When Derby played Benfica in the 1972/73 European Cup, the Baseball Ground sported one of the worst pitches in the country. Sensing that a soft surface might give them an advantage, Clough drenched the pitch with firefighters' hoses overnight. He later confessed there was 'enough water on the ground to have staged an Olympic diving event'. It worked for Clough. Derby slayed the mighty Benfica, 3-0. Murph would have to wait to see if the same tactic paid dividends at Sincil Bank.

In October, as planned, Murph lost Simmonite to a career in the South Yorkshire Police, and Dick Bate arrived as his replacement. The coach educator had survived for only ten games as manager of Southend United. Chairman Vic Jobson hadn't consulted his fellow board members when he made the appointment; an omen which Murph would have cause to remember in four years' time.

By the end of the month, a bumper crowd of 4,624 turned up to Sincil Bank for an explosive top-of-the-table clash against Barnet. Those who made it to the end of Murph's Message learned that Murph the manager had become Murph the soothsayer.

'Experience means decision making, if within all our circumstances we can make considerably more correct decisions than those of the incorrect nature, then most certainly we will learn, the biggest secret is to learn quickly, and this will give us a degree of success which we are all hoping for.'

The fixture showcased its fair share of incorrect decision making; a penalty for the Imps, two sendings off for Barry Fry's men, and a pitch invasion by the police. Seven officers leapt into action to break up a fight in front of the Sincil Bank Terrace between Lincoln skipper Trevor Matthewson and Barnet's Edwin Stein. Fry sprinted across the pitch to get involved and chairman John Reames and director Geoff Davey hot-footed it from the stands. A melee of officials and substitutes piled on to the pitch. Fry and Murph had barracked each other throughout the game, and when a steward escorted Fry off the pitch, Murph rubbed his hands in glee.

'That's you done! That's you up in the stands!' he thought.

Barnet recovered from the fracas to pull a goal back, but Lincoln hung on for a 2-1 win; the 'degree of success' Murph was hoping for. The victors' prize; fourth place in the league, two spots behind their north London rivals. And an end to Barnet's impressive run of 14 consecutive away games without defeat.

Murph hoped new signings Smith and Waitt would become a title-winning partnership. Only minutes into their next home game against Cheltenham, his hopes were dashed. A crunching goalmouth collision with the Cheltenham keeper saw Waitt stretchered off the pitch. Lincoln had lost their top goalscorer to a leg broken in three places. Eight goals in 15 Conference outings; Murph would miss his towering striker. Despite the devastating blow, the Imps put on a convincing display and waltzed home 5-1. Two weeks later, phase one of the new 1,400-seater St Andrews Stand was opened. An £800,000 beacon of hope, jointly funded by the club and Lincoln City Council. Things were looking up.

Simmonite had started with the police training school. He was looking forward to having a two-week break, a rare chance to be at home for the Christmas period with his wife and young daughter. He looked at the Lincoln fixture list and saw they were playing Boston away. He was going to ask Murph to get him a couple of tickets. Before he had time to phone the gaffer, Simmonite received a call.

'It's Colin. What're you doing on Boxing Day?'

'I'm coming down to Boston, Col.'

'How did you know I was gonna ring you?'

'I didn't. I'm coming to the game.'

'Has someone f***ing given you some inside information?'

'About what, Col? I've not spoken to anyone.'

Murph paused for a moment.

'How's your fitness?'

Simmo knew instinctively why Murph was phoning. Boston vs Lincoln, the Lincolnshire derby, was a massive game. Murph wanted his dependable defender back. Murph told Simmo he didn't want the players to know what he was planning. His former assistant joined the team on Christmas Day at a hotel in Boston and signed a contract which Murph faxed to one of his contacts in the FA. To the surprise of his teammates, Simmo turned up to the team talk on Boxing Day afternoon. As the players filed on to the pitch, City fans looked at each other in disbelief. Simmonite was wearing the number seven shirt. Only Murph would re-sign a right-back on Christmas Day!

The gamble paid off. Lincoln won 2-1, and Murph planned

for his defender to stay for the rest of the season. The gaffer was confident Simmonite was one of the fittest players he had worked with. He didn't need to train with the team. He could follow his own fitness regime, but his weekly appearances for Lincoln didn't go unnoticed by Simmonite's police superintendent. The boss wanted to know how much his officer was getting paid.

'If I find you're not playing for nothing, you're out of work,' he said.

Under the terms of his police contract, Simmo couldn't take a second job. He assured his superintendent he was only receiving out-of-pocket expenses. Murph took a pragmatic approach. His returning defender had just moved house; he needed to replace night storage heaters with gas-fired central heating.

'Leave it with me,' Murph said.

Simmonite gave him an invoice for full-house central heating. And Murph got it paid. The end justified the means.

City finished the year in second place, snapping at Barnet's heels. And the manager continued to receive more than his fair share of column inches. The headline 'Murphy's law lifts Lincoln hangover' marked the start of the new year. Murph explained the appeal of the 'illogical challenge' he accepted at Lincoln to Tony Hardisty from the *Sunday Express*. Murph believed he deserved a job in the First or Second Division; his record was good enough. If he could put Lincoln back on the Football League map, maybe it would convince a big club they should offer him a job. If that didn't happen, he would set his sights on taking Lincoln out of the Conference and eventually into the Second Division.

'That's not idle talk,' he said. 'It can be done.'

Five wins in January earned Murph the Vauxhall Conference Manager of the Month award, for the second time that season. He banked the £100 cheque from the *Mail on Sunday* but didn't allow himself to get carried away.

'If we keep doing the correct things competently and enthusiastically then we've got a chance.'

Murph's measured response masked his relentless enthusiasm.

By early February, Lincoln had only suffered one defeat in their previous 15 Conference games. In their steady progression towards the top, only Barnet blocked their way. The north London club stood level on points but had a game in hand. Murph felt satisfied with the team he had put together but getting the right players hadn't been easy. City paid the price for their full-time status. He said in an interview with *Match* magazine, 'Most players in non-league soccer change hands at an average of £15,000, but when we show an interest, the price is doubled straight away.'

Murph didn't underestimate the scrap which lay ahead. Barnet's attacking flair made them a tough team to beat. The Bees had faded in the latter stages of the previous season and lost out to Neil Warnock's Scarborough. Murph knew Fry was determined not to let that happen again.

As Murph contemplated the final push, he took a phone call from Reg Drury, chief football correspondent at the *News of the World*. It had been a big week for two of Murph's former attackers, Mick Harford at Luton and John Fashanu at Wimbledon; both hoping for their first call-up for the England side. Murph was pleased for his former strikers.

'Neither man was easy to handle, but I didn't mind because their natural aggression was an asset on the field,' he said.

Harford won the golden ticket; his first England international, a friendly against Israel in Tel Aviv. Murph was delighted for the man he had inherited at Lincoln and sold to Newcastle for £180,000. He was even more delighted by the number of fans who were turning up at Sincil Bank each week. Home attendances averaged over 3,000, over 50 per cent higher than the previous season.

By the second half of March, tension was rising in the Conference. Barnet battered Wealdstone 6-0 on the same day City limped home from Enfield with a dismal 0-0 draw. Two points dropped for the second week running. Murph knew if both Barnet and City won all their remaining games, the Imps would end the season one point behind and miss out on a return to the Football League. In Murph's Message from the matchday programme against Altrincham, the gaffer left his readers with a linguistic brain teaser.

'I suppose it is fair to say that the ball has been stopped rolling from the general club point of view, and the remaining games will determine its direction, the ball that is, both the rolling one and the football.'

Lincoln responded by despatching an off-form Altrincham 5-0. Doubly satisfying for Murph, Tommy Docherty, his replacement at Derby County, had just left the Manchester club in what would be his last managerial post. Barnet dropped two points against Kidderminster. Five points short of the leaders, but with two games in hand. City had everything to play for.

On the bank holiday Monday, City set a new Conference record in the local derby at home to Boston United. A crowd of 7,542 turned up to watch the Pilgrims gift Lincoln a 5-1 win. With six league games left in their season, City welcomed Conference stragglers Wealdstone to Sincil Bank. Barnet played away to Northwich Victoria. The fixtures wouldn't normally attract much attention, but the matches fell on an unusual weekend. The Football League was hosting its 100-year anniversary tournament at Wembley. No league matches were scheduled. The press, radio and TV had to go somewhere. They chose Drill Field and Sincil Bank.

Murph warned his players.

'This is just the day when you might cock it up, when everyone's coming to watch.'

The Conference appeared to be a two-horse race; all eyes were on who would slip up first. The press didn't see City get a bloody nose (the Imps won 3-0), but they enjoyed a good old-fashioned punch-up. City defender Steve Buckley made an ill-advised tackle on Tony Lynch. Wealdstone's Samson Olaleye leapt to his teammate's defence, butted the former Derby County left-back, and kicked off a mass brawl. All 20 outfield players got involved.

'It's always like that in this league,' Murph laughed. 'When anything happens, everyone's out there, managers, coaches, the lot. I've never seen anything like it!'

Colin Murphy and assistant manager Dick Bate watch it all kick off at the Wealdstone game on 16 April 1988. (PA Images / Alamy Stock Photo)

Murph enjoyed the media attention, but he was more interested in Fry's result against Northwich Victoria. Barnet lost 2-1.

Murph admitted to Tony Hardisty it had been his toughest season in 12 years as a manager, far harder than he expected. Signing 12 players in 12 months would normally be considered an achievement but assembling a new team in six or seven weeks had been the ultimate challenge. The Wealdstone game included only two players who survived the fateful match against Swansea, 11 months earlier. Murph confided to sports journalist Derick Allsop, 'It's the hardest job I've had and if we make it, the most satisfying. But if we don't do it, everyone will say I failed.'

Five matches left to play. Two games in hand. City had closed the gap to one point. After a surprising run of results, Kettering Town stepped back into contention with an outside chance. In

front of an all-ticket crowd, the Poppies beat City 2-0 at Rock-
ingham Road and drew level on points. But it was a last hurrah.
Kettering lost their next two games and dropped out of the race.
Interviewed by sportswriter Alan Biggs, with four games to go,
Murph said, 'People said I was crazy to leave Stockport and come
back here, but we all get motivated by different challenges. It's the
one that others think you can't do, that appeals the most.'

Heading into the final bank holiday weekend, City were sand-
wiched between Barnet, one point above them, and Kettering,
two points below. The Imps needed Barnet to drop points in their
last two matches. Murph told his team to play as if it were the first
game of the season, with no thought of promotion or relegation.
The advice paid off. On 30 April City won 2-1 at home to
Stafford Rangers, and Barnet lost at home to Runcorn. For the
first time all season, the Imps sat unaccompanied at the top of the
Conference table. Lincoln with 79 points; Barnet with 77. The
fans celebrated with a standing ovation and a pitch invasion. City
had played their usual 'route one' style of football, mocked by the
press as 'the Lincoln by-pass' but the fans didn't care. On the bank
holiday Monday, they faced Wycombe Wanderers in their last
game of the season. If they came away with three points, they
would be back in the Fourth Division.

Official gates recorded 9,432 fans pouring into Sincil Bank,
almost five times the home crowd for the first fixture of the
season. In a nod to the amateur league, the programmes sold out
by midday. Chris Ashton recalls the day with obvious delight. In a
match which has gone down in Lincoln City folklore, the crowds
who watched the match far exceeded the official tally. Ashton
reckons at least 12,000 were in attendance.

'Up on the old railway bank which you would never have
known, behind the goal, they was everywhere.'

Twenty-five minutes into the game, an ankle injury for City's
goal machine John McGinley threatened to spoil the party. Super
sub Mark Sertori came on in his place. Sixty seconds later Sertori
leapt at the near post and headed home a corner whipped across

by David Clarke. City just had to hold on. Two minutes after the hour, Phil Brown scored the second; his 20th goal of the season. And Murph celebrated with a triumphant jig around the dugout. As the final whistle blew on a 2-0 victory, City sat two points clear at the top of the table. The Imps' fans poured on to the pitch, cheered, danced, and wiped away their tears.

When the crowds cleared from in front of the new St Andrews Stand, Doreen Ashton, mother of Chris and queen of the Imps' catering corps, was spotted walking across an empty pitch singing, 'You'll never walk alone.' Murph's mission had been well and truly accomplished.

At nine o'clock the next morning, his head thick from celebrations, Murph's phone rang at home. Barry Fry's booming voice greeted him.

'You bastard!'

Barnet had occupied the top slot for six months of the season and missed out on the Football League for the second year running. Nine points from their last nine games cost them the title. But Fry acknowledged what Murph had achieved.

'You know what, Colin, you're a really good team. You deserved it.'

Murph appreciated the recognition. And over 20 years later, speaking to Leigh Curtis from the *Lincolnshire Echo* in 2011, he still remembered Fry's magnanimous response.

'I will never forget that,' Murph said. 'He was first class.'

The Conference committee had hoped City wouldn't head straight back up to the Fourth Division, but they couldn't deny the positive impact of the Imps' presence on the lower league. Of the nine highest attendance figures of the 1987/88 season, City featured in eight: six games at home, and Boston and Kettering away. City doubled the usual crowds at their away games and boosted their own average home crowds by a staggering 86 per cent.

Murph could look back on the season with great satisfaction. He recognised he couldn't have done it without the courageous backing of chairman John Reames. The board hadn't set a budget at the start of the season. They were determined to have the best chance of an immediate return to the Football League. The wage bill for 20 full-time professionals reached £4,000 a week, and Murph made transfers in of almost £200,000. By comparison, Barnet were reported to have spent £60,000 on a quarter of the wage bill.

As Murph cleared out the remnants of his office, before moving to his new quarters in the St Andrews Stand, he reflected on some unlikely happenings of the previous 12 months. He had built a team of 16 full-time professionals almost from scratch and overseen completion of an all-seater stand. His born-again defender Gordon Simmonite had played 13 league games, got full-house central heating, and Murph had got his promotion. It seemed a fair exchange.

In a flurry of post-match interviews, Murph acknowledged the strain of having to win at all costs and knowing that finishing second would be tantamount to failure.

'You couldn't take your average Second Division club, plonk them in the Vauxhall Conference and guarantee success,' he said.

When I first met Chris Ashton in 2015, at his parents' home in Lincoln, close enough to hear the roars from Sincil Bank, we talked about the promotion-winning season.

'That was the greatest achievement in my lifetime to bring us back the first time,' Ashton said, 'and I'll argue with anybody, till the good Lord takes me, on that one!'

Asked by sportswriter Ray Matts why he had taken such a leap of faith and returned to Sincil Bank, Murph smiled.

'Sometimes in this game, you allow your heart to overrule your head.'

Perhaps for that same reason, as the 1987/88 season ended, Murph scotched rumours for the second time of a move to Third Division Hull City. Instead, he signed a new three-year contract at Sincil Bank. He predicted that staying in the Football League could never be as challenging as winning the Conference. The

Mail on Sunday agreed with him and awarded him the Vauxhall Conference Manager of the Year award; a life-size, plinth-mounted, golden boot. To celebrate their triumphant return to the Football League, Lincoln City produced a *Limited Edition Official Souvenir Booklet* for the promotion-winning season. Murph replied to a question about his hopes for the future.

'As long as I act within the courtesies of the framework of the hierarchy within the club, then I am allowed to manage the club in the way that I believe is correct. In return for that confidence, the club, the board and the supporters will get success.'

Put more simply, Murph was hoping for another promotion. Double or quits.

8

THE PHILOSOPHER KING

LINCOLN CITY, LEICESTER CITY, AND LUTON TOWN

'Hartlepool, Crewe, Wrexham. They sound absolutely beautiful music in one's ear.'

Murph's Message, the colourful matchday programme notes of City's ebullient manager, welcomed the return to familiar opposition in the Football League. For the Imps' second consecutive home fixture against Crewe Alexandra, Murph celebrated the arrival of Dario Gradi's team in his now familiar style.

'Tonight's game is against Crewe who we have just played, who we are about to play again and furthermore will again play again. If we all remember that the fires of war should have some good feelings, then we shall not be far short at the finish.'

The return to the Fourth Division had not dulled Murph's linguistic brain teasers. Up went the battle cry. The broadsheets loved the hyperbole. And Murph received the moniker of the 'philosopher king'. Not wanting to miss out on their local bard's offerings, the *Weekend Sports Echo* published Murph's writing each Saturday in My Football World. Four-hundred-word essays on whatever took his fancy, from managerial shake-ups, to rising transfer fees or English football's European ban.

Murph started the new season with a plan to return to what he called 'the good old days'. He wanted to make the club's players and staff 'Lincoln people'. Like Graham Taylor before him, Murph believed that living close to the club fostered a strong community spirit. He might not achieve his plan in one season, but he aimed to bring his squad back into the city. Murph also started the season without a coaching team. His number two, Dick Bate, had joined Howard Wilkinson as coach at Leeds United. Murph was on his own, 'following the reserve team, carrying the sponge and all the rest'. He was an old school manager used to doing everything, but he needed an assistant.

Colin Murphy, hammer in hand, opens the bidding for Tony James at the start of the 1988/89 season. (Image courtesy of the Lincolnshire Echo)

He could hardly contain his delight when he signed former Charlton Athletic coach Eddie May fresh from a coaching job in Iceland. It was his third time of asking. And Murph invited the man who made his team tick, midfielder Bob Cumming, to step up to the mark as player-coach. Cumming turned the gaffer down. He could see the hours Murph worked as a manager and the toll it could take on family life. He wasn't prepared to make the sacrifice.

Murph had more success in encouraging Mick Waitt, still recuperating from his broken leg, to get involved on the coaching side. Waitt took charge of City's reserves, but after only six weeks in the assistant manager's role, Eddie May broke up the management team. His family didn't want to move from Romford to Lincoln, and he couldn't satisfy the conditions of the job. The much sought-after coach had become the first casualty of Murph's new 'live locally' campaign. May reluctantly handed in his notice.

Although Murph was disappointed, it allowed him to resume one of his favourite partnerships. In the convoluted workings of football management, Murph brought back his former number two at City, the man who replaced him in 1985, for a brief and unsuccessful stint as manager. Murph couldn't wait to get back to work with 'Gentleman John' Pickering, described by Trevor Peake as the 'best coach in England' and by Murph as a man with an 'unquestionable football knowledge and pedigree'. As Waitt developed his coaching methods, he regarded Murph and Pickering as the two major influences on his career. A trajectory, which would lead him 12 years later, to become head coach of the New Zealand national team.

Pickering was coaching at Second Division Newcastle, when a scouting mission in early October took him to City's home game against Scunthorpe United. Although the Imps returned with three points, Pickering saw that the City squad didn't have the strength of the team he and Murph had moulded in the early 1980s. He wanted to be a part of the Imps' revival, to get them at least back to the Third Division where they had left off three years before. Another ex-Imp shared Pickering's ambition. Gordon Hobson returned to Sincil Bank for a club record fee of £60,000. The 30-year-old striker arrived from First Division Southampton, sidelined in the reserves after an ankle injury, which allowed a young Alan Shearer and Matt Le Tissier to break their way into the Saints' side.

Murph recruited Hobson to help develop his youthful players. Shane Nicholson and Mark Sertori would benefit from the experience of Murph's inside-forward, just as Fashanu, Harford, Cockerill and Cunningham had done in the generation before. The shorter pacy player was the perfect partner to towering centre-forwards. Hobson made an immediate impact on his return to Sincil Bank. He scored four goals in as many league games.

Under the headline 'Lincoln thriving on Murphy's law of gobbledegook', Stephen Bierley from *The Guardian* reported on the match against Scarborough. City and Scarborough were two teams which had passed each other on the Football League bypass, into and out of the Fourth Division. An entertaining game of football and a 2-2 draw led Bierley to conclude, 'Ruskin wrote of Lincoln's cathedral that it was "worth any two other cathedrals we have". At Sincil Bank Murphy shares a similar reputation. His programme messages may sometimes be obscure, but his deeds are obvious to all.'

As if jinxed by the positive endorsement, a losing streak of three games followed shortly on from a winning run of four. Unremarkable statistics, but two of football's favourite pundits took great delight in Murph's response. Ian St John and Jimmy Greaves, one a Scottish international, the other a Tottenham and England legend, are forever etched in any football lover's heart as the buy one, get one free, *Saint and Greavsie*. They were the cheeky chappie double act, whose irreverent Saturday lunchtime stroll around the Football League on ITV lasted for seven glorious years. Only axed in 1992, when the newly founded Premier League signed a rights deal with Sky Sports, and £304m of Rupert Murdoch cash sounded the death knell for having a laugh.

Murph was a *Saint and Greavsie* kind of guy, a likeable Londoner with a twinkle in his eye, always armed with a crowd-pleasing quote. The showman in him delighted in inviting the ITV film crew into his office at Sincil Bank. With his polo shirt collar turned up, leaning back in his chair, he read from his latest matchday programme notes.

'Music soothes the savage breast. The cobra has been tamed. Losing. A losing sequence, namely three games, always appears to put doubts in people's minds, irrespective of the club's predicament and the doubting Thomases doubt no more and the judges become experts. The cobra has an excellent habit of wriggling free and indeed Gordon Hobson wriggled three at Burnley with the assistance of his colleagues and what an excellent way to bounce back.'

Part way through the season on a losing run, Murph's intuition told him he'd better watch out. He delighted in telling his interviewer,

'When we won that next game, that's when I thought the cobra's been tamed. And that little rat of a front player I've got Hobson, he's gone and wriggled away and done the game for us at Burnley and got the hat-trick. So, I thought then, she's been tamed. We're all right, we're still in work.'

Being in work remained a powerful incentive for Murph, still haunted by his public and humiliating sacking at Derby County over a decade before.

Murph can't recall when he started writing, but players regularly saw him on the Lincoln City training ground, *Rothmans Football Yearbook* under one arm, *Collins Concise Dictionary* under the other. Just as likely to be scrabbling to pick the right word as pick the right player.

'In this job, you need to have lots of virtues,' he told the ITV crew. 'Now one of them is a driver. I drive 25 to 30,000 miles a year, at least that's what I tell the taxman. And when you're driving and driving, you think of all sorts of weird and wonderful things. And maybe that's when these ideas come to you.'

Asked by the ITV crew whether his team talks were as baffling as his programme notes, Murph was quick to respond.

'I really think it don't matter how you talk to a team. The only thing that matters is what they do between three o'clock and 20 to five. You really can do what you like with them during the week, and you really can say what you like to them in the team talk, and if that makes 'em run round like deranged ferrets for an hour and a half, you've done your job, ain't you, cos they win.'

And so 'deranged ferret' entered the lexicon of football punditry. And the name of Lincoln City's new fanzine was born.

Colin Murphy, the self-styled bard of Lincoln City, with his tools of the trade.
(Image courtesy of the Lincolnshire Echo*)*

In the run up to Christmas, City found themselves tucked in the table behind the leading pack. Two months later, Murph's Message from the Tranmere Rovers game suggested if the team didn't at least make the play-offs, it would be their own fault.

'We shall want our arses kicking if we do not run the situation very close or as close as can be considered close,' Murph wrote.

Four consecutive league defeats followed his rallying cry, and the Imps plummeted to 11th place. Heading into the final six weeks of the season, City faced Stockport County at home. Murph reflected on his departure from Edgeley Park, and how a great deal was said when he left.

'I am the only person who has said "nowt" and I consider it to be in the interests of Stockport County that I say "nowt". It is important to remember that the "Club" or "Clubs" are bigger than all of us and they must perpetuate, whereas one day I suppose we are going leave the earth, later rather than sooner I hope!'

Murph ignored the barrage of hate chants from the travelling County fans, still angered by his departure two years before. He was less forgiving of County's persistent use of the offside trap which dragged out a 0-0 draw. In the space of three weeks Lincoln had dropped from seven points off the top of the table, to seven points off a play-off spot, but Murph refused to admit defeat.

'Only an uneducated elephant would say it's all over,' he said to Neil Custis from the *Lincolnshire Echo*. 'As General Custer said, "You keep going." But they all got shot!'

With six games remaining, Murph's Message at home to Colchester United remained upbeat. He reminded his readers that 'one's greatest glory is not in never failing, but in rising every time we fall'.

Despite his optimism, the season limped to a disappointing end; poor away form in the second half of the season, combined with a treatment room full of injured players. When the fans' Player of the Season, Tony James, hobbled on to the pitch on crutches to receive his award, it summed up a disappointing campaign. The manager tried to salvage the depressed mood with an uplifting message for the final home fixture against Leyton Orient. *The Times* Daily Diary page picked up on Murph's programme notes for the Orient game, calling it 'a vignette of football noir'. Its author rejoiced that the beautiful game now also had beautiful literature. In Murph's valedictory article, he reflected on the past two seasons.

'At the time of this communiqué from my bunker, the battle-field for the next war is undecided as the campaign is planned. But for sure amidst the gathering of ammunition we are well set to win more battles than the past two campaigns, which can only therefore lead to success. What a horrific, horrendous, halluci-nating two years! Two years we can safely say, I would think that not any Football Club will ever again have to endure. Thanks for coming, thanks for "reading". Just short of 4,000 of you every week for the past two years. Incredible. Unbelievable ... I am sure you will come again in these numbers, again, if we are to give you the good commencement. Commencement? Bombing commences next August, full battle dress required. Angels one five, over and out.'

Tenth place in the league, and second place in the Fourth Division Programme of the Year awards; The Wirral Programme Club preferred Wrexham's matchday offerings. Undeterred by the snub, Murph's Message was destined to continue.

For its inaugural issue in August 1989, the editorial team of the *Deranged Ferret* fanzine couldn't quite believe their luck. They wrote to the club asking if they could interview 'somebody' and struck editorial gold; an hour in the office with the bard of Sincil Bank. Murph answered whatever questions editor Roger Bates threw at him. When Bates asked if he enjoyed the publicity from Murph's Message, the gaffer explained it wasn't his intention to self-promote. He had always been interested in the illogical and the eccentric and wrote things as they came into his head. But he realised, 'If you're not careful, it gets out of hand and people expect you to continue.'

He questioned his own motives.

'Am I doing it because I want to do it, or am I doing it because they want me to do it?'

It started in the first place to be a 'very, very genuine feeling, expression and consequence'. If it had extended beyond that, it was not his intention.

Whatever his motivation, and whether he was playing up to the image, Murph prided himself on his use of language and long words. When he penned his programme notes, he could extend a sentence longer than a goal kick. Chris Ashton, stalwart of the Lincoln City Supporters' Club, coined the phrase 'doing a Murph' for writing an impenetrably long sentence. Murph's record stood at 99 words.

Putting his literary pursuits to one side, Murph took the squad to Aldershot army camp for pre-season training. He wanted to build a sense of camaraderie for the start of a new campaign. While he was there, he spotted a 25-year-old corporal from the

Royal Artillery PT Corps, a player with no Football League experience. Never one to miss an opportunity, Murph signed the centre-forward for £200. Matt Carmichael repaid the investment with two goals in his first two league outings. And to shore up the defence, Steve Thompson returned to the team on a free transfer from Sheffield United, replacing the departing Trevor Matthewson as captain.

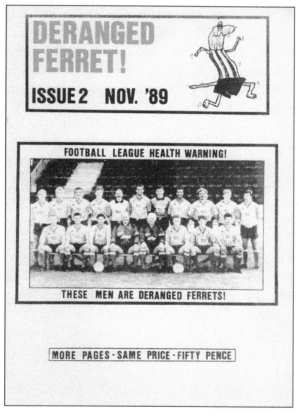

(Image courtesy of Roger Bates)

Tommo knew John Pickering was planning a move to Middlesbrough, but Murph's assistant would stay at City for another six months.

'I went back while John was still there,' Tommo remembers. 'I was virtually knackered; I had a cyst on my knee and was struggling to play. I assumed I was going to join the coaching staff.'

Murph told Tommo he would sign him; he could play a few games and he would take him on as his number two at the end of the season.

'Oh, and by the way, the chairman wants you to have your hair cut.'

The player sported the same long curly hair and moustache as he did when Murph first signed him a decade before. Tommo spoke to John Reames. The chairman wasn't bothered if the player had hair down his back. Tommo got the message. It was Murph's way of saying, if you're coming into management, you've got to toe the line.

After a year of consolidation in the Fourth Division, Murph was determined to get the club back to the Third.

'It is impossible for us not to do better than we did last season,' Murph said to Neil Custis from the *Lincolnshire Echo*.

The manager predicted they needed an extra seven or eight points to get them into the play-offs. Or as he wrote in the opening Murph's Message of the season, 'Our conkers are in order, a little bruised, but much more well mature, some have dropped and some are still gaining their varcity but they are more resilient with the vinegar and oven having taken respect. In this respect, I once remember owning a 46er and if this is to be the case, this season will complete on the sunny side of the strata. Best wishes, good voice, ear plugs inserted, stand by for take-off.'

The season was launched with a shrewd transfer deal. Murph had bought defender Tony James from Northern Premier League Gainsborough Trinity for £6,000 and 11 months later sold him to David Pleat at Leicester City for £150,000. Quite a return on the fans' 1988/89 Player of the Season, who made only 25 full appearances for the club.

'Selling is not the problem. Replacing is the problem,' Murph wrote in A View from the Dugout, his new weekly column for the *Lincolnshire Echo.*

The gaffer was delighted that with dogged determination, big frontman Mick Waitt had made his way back from injury after almost two years, ready to team up with Gordon Hobson.

Four games into the new season and City were the only club in the Football League with a 100 per cent record; seven goals for, and one against. At the top of the Fourth Division table, two points clear of Southend, Murph gave a cautious response in his matchday offering against York City.

'Have you ever smelt the scent of the Queen? A sniff you might say of the promotion air. I have always considered that there is an extremely thin line between confidence, complacency and failure. It is probably more difficult to stay at the top than get to the top ... Well, at the moment we have a 4er or a 12er dependent upon your interpretation. The poor conker must be begging for a stretcher. However, there must be no respite, we must strive and sweat every inch to retain the position they have so proudly, justly and spiritually accured.'

He was pleased to take a more straightforward, congratulatory phone call from his old friend Lennie Lawrence, seven years into the job as manager of Charlton Athletic. Lennie reminded Murph that the last time City were promoted to the Third Division, they had been scrapping it out with Southend at the top of the table, and City finished second to the Blues. Murph welcomed the positive omen. Less welcome was a 2-0 away defeat at Roots Hall, which knocked the Imps off the top spot and allowed Southend to take their place.

To consolidate City's position, the board approved the signing of established winger Alan Roberts from Sheffield United for a record-matching fee of £60,000. Determined to develop a side which was capable of 'beating people by attacking means', Murph described the acquisition in A View from the Dugout.

'We have gained a right sided conker which has baked in the oven for seven years. On the subject of conkers, I'd like to inform you all that I'm still in the world championships. Roberts in. Any more to come? Wait and see.'

Murph's purchase of Roberts didn't pay off. A serious knee injury prevented the right-winger from playing more than ten games for the club. Before Robert's debut game against Halifax Town, City were sitting in second place. In his matchday programme notes, Murph wrote, 'The course is plotted so we know what we have to do to remain on course. Without a shadow of a doubt, we need to be vitreous silica.'

With the same resilience as refractory glass, City withstood the high temperature of the Halifax game, and won 2-1. Murph's Message assured the fans, 'If we continue to perform certain acts correctly, then the correctness will manifest itself with correctability and we'll know then that correctitude will result.'

Murph's elaborate musings didn't escape the attention of Chrissie Maher, director and founder of the Plain English Campaign. Set up to 'oppose gobbledygook, jargon and legalese', the independent group was celebrating its tenth anniversary. Murph's Message stood out as a prime candidate for their Golden Bull Award; a trophy which celebrates 'the worst examples of written tripe'.

'We've had some superb entries this year,' Maher said, but none better than Murph's programme notes. In fact, she admitted in an interview with *Today* newspaper, 'It's the best we have had in the whole ten years of the campaign.'

Prompted by sitting third in the league, Murph scented promotion and his matchday article for the Grimsby fixture reminded the home fans of the perils of complacency.

'We cannot fall into the trap of committing practical haplography. It is also a dangerous feeling to consider that where we are in the league is of acceptable standard, because standard is relevant to the standards we have set, which thereby may well indicate that we have not aspired to the standard, which we set ourselves.'

Practical haplography had everyone reaching for their dictionary. Even the broadsheets took up the linguistic challenge. A column entitled Murphy's lore, on the Comment page of *The Guardian*, reminded its readers what practical haplography meant, 'the practice of saying or writing once, what ought to be stated twice'. They imagined the literary analysis which took place across the terraces at Sincil Bank. Far removed from its sports pages, *The Guardian* published two columns of fanciful linguistic gymnastics and a truncated match report of the local derby. Lincoln trailed 1-0 at home to Grimsby. Graham Bressington crossed to Paul Smith. Smith scored. The final whistle blew. And the unidentified *Guardian* feature writer concluded, 'The pair had only done once what they should have done twice: an omission which can only be described as a practical haplography. Thus did the fate which the seer of Sincil foresaw, come precisely to pass. Funny game, football.'

Six years later, Murph found himself in good company. The NHS won the Golden Bull Award for its 229-word definition of a bed.

Undeterred by the criticism of his matchday missives, the gaffer maintained his usual standard in their next home game against Stockport County. 'Irrational immunities' rubbed shoulders with 'fantoccinical' and Murph's Message offered a welcome literary distraction to a lacklustre, goalless draw.

'How joyful for them not to have acrimoniated in the non-league,' Murph wrote of his former employer, top of the table after 13 games. 'How delightful for them to be making a success of defeating extinction. To be savoured. Let us hope we are all able to be pulmonic.'

The *Daily Express* took up the story and Christopher Hilton reported that City's commercial manager, Wayne Jenner, bet his friends £1 they couldn't read Murph's programme notes without backtracking. He hadn't been forced to pay out.

Not to be outdone, *The Banker*, the magazine for City supporters, devoted a full-page spread to the all-new superhero from Banker Products – Murphman™. A deluxe model with a genuine Cockney accent, the ability to walk on water, and a vocabulary decoder 'to work out what he's talking about!'. All for the bargain price of £9.99!

Murph's fame extended far beyond the Lincolnshire Fens. From the *Chicago Tribune* to Maine's *Bangor Daily News*, the press celebrated the gaffer for the way he kicked English.

His notoriety didn't stem his flow of matchday offerings. Murph explained his thinking to *Today*. He drove thousands of miles a year on scouting missions and always tuned in to Radio 4. He couldn't help but pick up a few words along the way. He had never read a novel in his life, but he loved digging into newspapers. While many people read their newspaper in the smallest room in the house, that was where Murph kept his *Collins Concise Dictionary*.

'Let's face it, you spend a fair amount of time in the loo, so I like to make the most of it.'

If he drove along the motorway and heard an analogy on his favourite radio station, he took note.

'I've got no delusions of grandeur or anything.'

These thoughts filtered into his programme notes. Murph enjoyed the craft of writing. He viewed it as an extension of his personality and told the *Daily Express*,

'We've all got different ways of expressing ourselves. In certain professions, some people think it's a crime to be well read.'

Paul Weaver of *Today* concluded, 'While some managers are obsessed by the long ball, Murphy's interest is clearly focused on the long hyperbole. He is the Stanley Unwin of the written word.'

On the football pitch, Murph spoke more directly than he wrote.

'If people don't like it, I might just stop it one day and say "Bollocks!".'

The international press couldn't protect Murph from a season in decline. After a flying start in the opening fixtures, the Imps began to fade. By late December they had dropped to seventh place. Murph's Message for the Boxing Day match was reduced to a list of Murphy's Fundamental Laws. Rule number one. When nothing can go wrong, it will. With the loss of Gordon Hobson to injury from August to November, Murph had no 20-goal-a-season striker to fill his place. A 4-3 victory against Cambridge United on Boxing Day couldn't have come at a better time.

'Well, what a corker!' Murph wrote. 'A corking game, some corking incidents, corking goals, and the cork was well and truly corked in the last corking minutes.'

The gaffer was relieved. Man of the match Hobson was back from injury. Murph suggested, 'We are now in an excellent position to prepare for the remainder of the season's traumas in a chivalrous manner.'

He spoke too soon. They lost the next home game, 3-1. But a change of fortune in late January brought an unbeaten run of six games; three wins, three draws and only two goals conceded.

'Sixteen games to go, one third of the season remaining, we must not flutter,' Murph wrote as they sat fifth in the league.

They swept David Webb's Southend United team aside in a 2-0 home victory. With the Blues' vice-chair John Adams watching from the directors' box, Murph had as good as hand-delivered his CV to the south-east Essex club.

Seventh in the table by the start of April, their lowest position of the season, with nine games remaining, City should have been heading for a place in the play-offs. Until they drew at home to Torquay and were no longer in the frame for an automatic promotion spot.

'There can be no greater dignity than holding your hands up in the air and saying, well, we cocked the job up,' Murph wrote. 'No excuses, no deceiving, just straightforwardness with a hole not big enough to crawl into.'

A dismal three wins in the last 14 games, City limped home to a tenth-placed finish for the second consecutive season. The Imps scored only 48 goals in 46 games, the same number as relegated Colchester United. There were few highlights to savour from the 1989/90 season, apart from Murph's record-equalling signing of Grant Brown for £60,000 from Leicester City. The impressive centre-back and *Deranged Ferret* Player of the Year would continue to bolster City's defence for an extraordinary 12 seasons.

Despite the recent glory of a return to the Football League, when the fans had hailed Murph as the Imps' messiah, the gaffer's time with the club juddered to an unsatisfying end. In his final Murph's Message of the season, the manager thanked the fans for their support. He accepted the criticism he had received and appreciated the sincerity and spirit with which it was offered.

'Because as I have often said in the past, one must care, and the manifestation of the cares will be expressed with conviction, and that is the way it should be.'

The fans bemoaned an opportunity lost. They talked of a season which recorded too many players on loan, too many panicked signings, too much defensive play, and the 'unforgivable omission' of keeping Phil Brown from the starting line-up.

Murph's Message read like a well-crafted letter of resignation. And sure enough, on 20 May 1990, for the second time in five years, Lincoln City announced their manager would leave the Bank by mutual consent.

Murph didn't tell Steve Thompson about his decision. The player heard it second hand at the Collingham Cricket Club. He spoke to Murph on the phone in the pavilion.

'What the f*** are you doing? Where does that leave me?' Tommo said.

'Steven, I had to go. I've been there too long. They've offered me a good severance pay. You've got a year left as a player.'

Tommo knew he didn't have a year left. His knee was giving way. It felt as though Murph had left him in the cart. But with the gaffer's full support, Tommo applied for the vacant manager's job. He lost out to the former FA Cup-winning Leeds United and England striker Allan Clarke.

As soon as the replacement manager took over, he packed his rival off to the FA rehabilitation centre at Lilleshall.

'I must have been there three months,' Tommo recalls. 'I was like Lord Lucan. Everyone goes "Where's Tommo gone?"'

(Image courtesy of Roger Bates)

The player received a recall when Clarke had won only one of his first eight league games. It wasn't enough to stop the rot. Three defeats later, Lincoln sat bottom of the Fourth Division, and Tommo was offered the manager's job. He is quick to acknowledge Murph's influence on his first managerial post.

'The coaching was based on John Pickering. The managing was based on set plays, 11 v 11,' Tommo said. 'Colin's management of players was a massive influence, because I had no coaching qualifications at that time. I used to phone Colin up and ask him what he thought. He was like a guiding light.'

In May 1990, Murph looked back on almost a decade as manager of Lincoln City. Ten years which brought promotion and relegation, elation and heartache in almost equal measure. He had believed he could take Lincoln into the Second Division, but in the end he had to settle for knowing he had fallen short, but done his best. He picked up the consolation prize; the knowledge there would always be a warm welcome for the outspoken southerner in his adopted home in the east Midlands.

Deranged Ferret, still going strong in its fifth edition, ruminated over Murph's departure at the start of the new season. Contributor A.B. felt sure the lack of success and Murph's predilection for a 'route one' style of direct football had hastened the manager's departure, but there was something more to the story. A.B. suggested Murph had become 'a victim of his own cult status'. The eccentricities, the programme notes, the media attention. The board couldn't allow the man to become bigger than the club. Murph had to go.

He didn't hang around for another opportunity to manage in the Third or Fourth Division. Within two weeks, Murph took a call from David Pleat, who invited the out-of-work manager to join him as coach at Leicester City.

'I would always try to take someone I knew,' Pleat told me. 'So, I took Gordon Lee, who had been my coach years before at Shrewsbury. He was a very good man, a man of high principles. And of course, I knew Colin. I went from Tottenham at a difficult time in my life. I had been terribly unfairly treated by the press. When Leicester came up, I knew I needed staff there who would be loyal to me; good, hard workers. I had Gordon and Colin and I couldn't have had two better people. Not just five-a-side people. They were what I call proper coaches. Colin was more of an assistant. Gordon was my right-hand man. They were the type of people who weren't worried about titles.'

The Foxes had swung with pendulum-like regularity between

the First and Second Divisions for the previous ten years, but this season marked an unholy scrap for survival at the bottom of the second tier. Following a poor start to the 1990/91 campaign with seven defeats in a row, a relegation clash with Blackburn Rovers cost the manager his job. After four years in charge, it was the start of a new era. Terry Shipman resigned as chair, and first team coach Gordon Lee took over as caretaker manager. Murph stayed until the end of the season, but he didn't wait to see Brian Little arrive to turn the club around. He left Leicester to rejoin David Pleat as assistant manager at Luton Town.

In the merry-go-round of football management, Pleat returned to the club he had left five years before. Murph recognised the buzz of being invited back, but the Hatters had only narrowly avoided relegation from the top flight when the First Division expanded from 20 to 22 clubs. Murph told sports reporter Simon Oxley why he accepted the job.

'I have always felt the First Division is a rich prize not to be sniffed at, and hence I am here.'

I asked Pleat how Murph's role differed from the coaching job at Leicester.

'He sat alongside me, although I never felt he was that comfortable in that role. He might have thought he could have done better,' Pleat said. 'I was a very imaginative coach. People said I didn't pay enough attention to the defensive aspects of the game, but I wanted to entertain. Colin was better at defensive work than attacking work on the coaching field. Some of his coaching sessions might have been long, thorough and somewhat predictable, but repetition is important and can never be underestimated. The complete opposite of the Ron Atkinsons of this world, who were just, "Go out and enjoy yourselves." Players will accept anything provided you're a winning team.'

In the 1991/92 season, Luton were not a winning team. The management duo fielded a group of young players and couldn't save the Hatters from the drop. Relegated from the First Division on the last day of the season, they missed out on the launch of the

Premier League by just two points. In the usual rounds of managerial speculation, the press linked Pleat with the vacant job at Southend. But the Blues' chair, Vic Jobson, knew who he wanted – the manager's number two. At the second time of asking, Murph was on his way to Roots Hall, home to Southend, described by talkSPORT host Danny Kelly as the last football club before you fall into the North Sea.

Total immersion swimming. The gaffer was in for a rough ride.

9

STAN THE MAN

SOUTHEND UNITED AND SHELBOURNE

Murph stood on the Roots Hall pitch in front of the old North Stand, clasping a Southend United scarf in both hands above his head. Wearing a grin as broad as the Thames Estuary, he looked every inch a lifelong Blues fan. But it would take more than a well-curated photoshoot to convince the Southend supporters that David Pleat's number two was the right man for the job.

The chairman was at loggerheads with the fans who blamed him for the departure of their promotion-winning hero, David Webb. The Southend manager had turned a miracle in south-east Essex, lifting the club from the Fourth to the Second Division in successive campaigns. For the 1992/93 season, following the Premier League split from the Football League, the divisions were re-numbered upwards. David Webb's Second Division outfit became Murph's First Division side.

Webb had resigned over a contract dispute made worse by Jobson's interference in his role as manager. After Webb walked out of the club for the first time in March 1987 over 'a matter of principle' the chairman approached Murph to take the job. The Stockport County manager turned him down, opting for the greater challenge of taking Lincoln back to the Football League.

Five years later, property developer Jobson was delighted to get his man. His fellow directors didn't share the chairman's enthusiasm. The 70 per cent majority shareholder appointed Murph without consulting the three-man committee, set up to discuss Webb's replacement. The local Southend paper, the *Evening Echo*, reported that one director only heard Murph had got the job when he read about it in the paper. There were echoes of Dick Bate's appointment, five years earlier; a manager unilaterally chosen by Jobson, before the chairman sacked him ten weeks later.

Murph had every reason to feel nervous. On his arrival at Roots Hall, his appearance caused a stir. A group of Southend supporters spotted him at the club and speculated why he was there. Jobson issued an immediate denial to the *Evening Echo* that he was about to appoint a new manager. He said he would take time at the start of the close season to consider all options. Twenty-four hours later, Jobson informed the national press of Murph's appointment. It did nothing to improve the chairman's already sour relationship with the fans. Many of them relied on the local newspaper for news of the club.

Murph started his new job with a kitbag full of problems: supporter protests, boardroom turmoil, and player unrest. He said he accepted the job because he believed in the team's strength. The Blues were well organised and competitive, and they played the game how he liked to play it, getting the ball into the opposing half and playing a bit of football. He didn't mention his over-riding reason. Southend would give him another chance to manage in the Football League. He had never aspired to be a number two.

In Murph's first week in charge, Howard Southwood, sports editor at the *Evening Echo*, asked him a loaded question.

'How does it feel following on from the most successful manager in the history of Southend United Football Club?'

Murph didn't flinch.

'I followed current England manager Graham Taylor at

Lincoln, and Brian Clough and Dave Mackay at Derby, and I felt I did pretty well.'

Murph brushed aside comparisons with the man he had replaced. He faced a greater challenge; convincing disenchanted Blues fans he was more than the chairman's puppet. Murph reported to a chairman who had a complex relationship with the fans. Jobson courted controversy but had also saved the club from extinction. In 1984, when he joined the board of directors, the club lay bottom of the Fourth Division, and hadn't paid the players' wages for three weeks. The club was forced to borrow money from the PFA to settle the debt.

Two years before Murph's arrival, Southend started looking for alternative sites for a new stadium. The chairman estimated that turning Roots Hall into a 10,000 all-seater stadium to comply with the Taylor Report, Lord Justice Taylor's recommendations for ground safety following the Hillsborough disaster of 1989, would cost more than £2m. Players would have to be sold to finance the work. Jobson proposed developing a council-owned sports ground in Southend. The supporters agreed, but the council didn't. Jobson proposed moving the club 30 miles west of Southend to a 100-acre site in Basildon. The fans tore into him. The move would rip the heart out of the club. Three months before Murph accepted the job, a new anti-Jobson, pro-Webb pressure group emerged, and United for Southend staged their first sit-in at Roots Hall. Not for the first time, Murph had accepted a poisoned chalice.

The Blues ended the previous season in 12th place, though midway through the campaign they were on course to go straight up into the newly formed Premier League. On New Year's Day they sat top of the table, but anti-Jobson protests and calls for the directors to resign punctuated a disappointing second half of the season. The players knew the manager was leaving and performances slumped. When Murph joined the club, he insisted that the wrangling with the board was merely a sideshow; the focus of any football club had to be the team. His first job would be to persuade eight out-of-contract players that their futures lay at Roots Hall.

An elaborate game of deal or no deal. For the first three players through his office; no deal. Former Player of the Year Peter Butler, goalscoring winger Andy Ansah and future England international Chris Powell, were all queueing up to leave. Many of the players believed they owed their success to David Webb, who signed them after they had been released by other clubs. Ansah suggested to the local press that if the club still had ambition, his contract didn't reflect it. Southend weren't trying too hard to persuade him to stay.

Murph was negotiating players' contracts when a chasm was opening up between the Premier League and the Football League, the haves and have-nots of English football. Sky Sports was celebrating a major sporting coup; a £304m deal for the exclusive rights to televise live Premier League games over the next five years. No wonder Murph's First Division hopefuls had their hearts set on leaving Roots Hall for a top-flight club.

Dean Austin, Southend's fresh-faced full-back, delivered Murph his first body blow. The 22-year-old jumped ship when Premier League Tottenham Hotspur offered him a lucrative contract. Jobson slated Spurs for 'stealing' Austin for a tribunal-fixed fee of £375,000, despite having signed him from non-league for only £12,000 two years before. Jobson complained that Southend couldn't hope to compete with the big boys on the Premier League stage unless they could build an all-purpose stadium to generate future funds. Goalkeeper Paul Sansome softened the blow for the new manager and committed himself to Southend for another three years. But United for Southend, who wanted a wholesale change of personnel in control of the club, urged their fellow supporters to boycott season ticket sales.

Jobson used an interview with the *Evening Echo* to communicate with the fans. He didn't care what United for Southend had to say; he didn't recognise them as a legitimate body. He cared they had already cost the club an estimated £100,000 in additional police presence and lost ticket sales. And Murph cared that if he didn't sort out the five remaining contract rebels before the start of the season, he risked getting caught with his trousers down. He tried to placate the fans by meeting with the club's executive vice-presidents and convince them there could be life after Webb. But it was a bad-tempered affair, which gave him a bitter taste of the challenges ahead.

Against a backdrop of internal backbiting, Murph made his first signing, a major sporting coup. He used the gentle art of persuasion to tempt his old pal, Bob Houghton, back to England as his number two. Houghton had spent 18 years coaching and managing in Sweden, the US and Saudi Arabia, and guided Malmö FF to the European Cup Final against Nottingham Forest in 1979. For a couple of years, he had been thinking of returning to England, but Houghton told the club's *Blues News* that only a handful of managers could have tempted him back. Murph was one of them. Jobson boasted to Howard Southwood that he had found his dream team.

'I am sure our pair can achieve similar success to the Clough/Taylor partnership, without the aggravation,' he said.

He wasn't the only chairman who would compare a Murph partnership to the famous management duo, but Jobson's prophetic words might come to haunt him.

Murph and Houghton took charge of a club which was strapped for cash. Southend spent over £800,000 the year before on ground improvements to satisfy the Taylor Report. They faced further expenditure to update a decaying ground. The money couldn't come from ticket sales alone; they would need to trim their 26-player squad. Murph and Houghton relished the challenge, but they faced early disappointment with their chosen team selection. A thigh injury would put Brett Angell, Southend's top scorer from the previous two seasons, out of action for at least four months. Not for the first time, Murph put a positive spin on losing his star player. It would be up to the rest of the team to go out and grab their opportunity.

Southend were the only team in the league which hadn't bought in the pre-season. Murph tried to reassure the fans it was his decision not to spend; a lack of funds hadn't constrained him. He would dip into the market when the time and the player were right. Murph later admitted in an interview with Colin Bateman from the *Daily Express* that his first two months at the club were anything but easy. The challenges had nothing to do with football. The fans had turned on both the manager and the team. He had to prove himself to the players, and it affected what they achieved on the field.

Four games into the season, four straight defeats, and Murph already had four players on the long-term injury list. When Southend crashed out 7-1 on aggregate to Derby County in the League Cup, Murph knew he needed to shore up his battered and bruised defence. He also needed an on-loan striker. In days gone by, it would have been easy to arrange. A couple of phone calls to a fellow manager and the deal would be done. Murph now faced a situation where the manager said 'Yes', only for the manager's chairman, to say 'No'. Murph felt frustrated by how the job was changing; chairmen wanted to make decisions about players, and managers were losing control.

Quizzed at the annual shareholders' meeting in September, about whether he had advertised the manager's job back in May, the chairman admitted that only one interview took place. The *Evening Echo* reported on the meeting.

'We had 40 people put in for the job,' Jobson said. 'Some were from Warley Mental Home, some from St Albans Football Club and even a cricket manager applied, but if you are involved in the football world for some time, you know who you want for the position and who you think can do it.'

As the meeting progressed, Jobson added, 'People have said Colin Murphy is a nut case. Anyone who takes on the job he has got, must be a nut case. Anyone who gets involved in the administration of a football club must need his head examined because we rarely get any thanks.'

Murph wasn't looking for thanks, he was looking for results. But at the 11th league game of the season, a 1-0 defeat at home to Grimsby, he got neither. He endured 20 minutes of constant chanting. The fans were already baying for him to get the sack. Chants of 'Murphy out' echoed around the ground long after the final whistle. Murph understood the fans' disappointment that Webb had left, but he underestimated their depth of feeling.

Colin Murphy under pressure at Southend United. (Image courtesy of Southend United History)

Newly appointed Southend skipper and former contract rebel, Dave Martin, leapt to Murph's defence. The 29-year-old midfielder pleaded with the fans to get behind the team; the boys couldn't battle against the opposition and their own supporters. Andy Ansah's signature on a new two-year contract gave Murph a welcome reprieve. Based on Southend's defensive record, they should have been sitting in the top half of the table, but with only nine goals scored in 11 games they were third from bottom.

In late October, the club looked forward to hosting the first ever live TV game at Roots Hall. United for Southend relished it too. The game against Cambridge United, shown on Anglia TV, would allow them to escalate their campaign to get Jobson out, and distribute hundreds of leaflets inside the ground. Their pamphlet blamed the chairman for three things; the resignation of 'the only director with any money', Hi-Tec sportswear boss Frank Van Wezel; the departure of their all-time favourite manager, David Webb; and the appointment of Murph, whose team selection they claimed to be 'as mystifying as his legendary programme notes'.

In Murph's matchday notes for the Cambridge fixture, he introduced fans to 'The Winning Way' a poem which David Campese, the Australian rugby union winger, used as a talisman to his success.

'It is perhaps worth, at this time in our development, when things look less than rosey to consider the poem here,' Murph wrote.

He reminded his readers that winners take chances, and they don't give up.

'Winners are flexible,' he quoted from the poem. 'We are flexible, let us hope that together with patience we shall also find flexibility in the hearts of our own supporters as today we take on Cambridge.'

But the Blues' fans weren't interested in poetry, they wanted results. They questioned why club favourites Keith Jones and Pat Scully couldn't make it into Murph's first team, and suspected Jobson was pulling the strings. The chairman didn't respond. He had kept a low profile since the start of the season and granted only sporadic interviews to the press.

Murph, by comparison, had nowhere to hide. They didn't win the Cambridge match. It ended in a 1-1 draw. And in the next away game against Luton Town, Southend fans booed him on to the pitch and jeered him off it at half-time. Murph soaked up the criticism.

'As management, we only have to sit on the bench and take it,' he said to the *Echo Sport*, 'but the one thing about criticism, it never hurts unless you know people are right.'

He was more concerned about the negative impact on the players. He didn't question the team's commitment; they scrapped it out to turn a 2-0 defeat at half-time into a 90-minute draw, but he worried that the atmosphere was dragging the players down. Houghton called for calm on the terraces, and the Southend United Official Supporters' Club called for a meeting between the directors and the fans to heal the growing rift. The club turned the request down.

In tragic unison, the relationship between manager and chairman was falling apart. Murph wanted to sign Steve Jones, a striker from non-league Billericay. With 26 goals in 21 games, it convinced the gaffer the star striker could play in a higher division. Jobson disagreed and publicly blocked the £30,000 transfer. He said Jones didn't have First Division qualities. West Ham manager Billy Bonds disagreed and jumped in to sign Jones for his newly relegated First Division side.

Murph kept a dignified silence, though speculation was widespread whether he could carry on working with a chairman who questioned his professional judgement. Sports reporter Dick Marshall wondered whether the Southend fans who were singing 'David Webb's yellow army' would cut their new boss some slack when they realised it was pointless criticising the manager for not making new signings. Murph could no longer do his job. When Jobson referred to Murph and Houghton in the press as 'very good coaches', it suggested to the fans that the chairman was managing the side.

The *Evening Echo* reported that Jobson had compared the rebel supporters who were calling for his resignation to the Hitler Youth. He claimed their intimidating tactics were preventing decent fans from attending games. The controversial outburst enraged United for Southend. Angry fans filled the *Echo Sport* letters page with nine variations of anti-Jobson and anti-Murph rhetoric. The copy editor had a field day.

'Jobson ego trip must be halted.'

'Who is boss? Is it Vic or Murphy?'

'Time for the crew to leave sinking ship.'

After three days of negative articles, Jobson retaliated by serving the *Evening Echo* with a writ, claiming damages for libel. Its editor, sports editor and the paper's owners, Westminster Press, were all named in proceedings, including a claim for an injunction to prevent the paper from publishing any defamatory articles. Faced with the ongoing crisis, an unusually taciturn Murph limited his comments to what was happening on the pitch. He suggested others were better placed to comment on what was happening off it.

When Southend next played away to Swindon Town, despite going 3-0 down in less than 30 minutes, the match brought some unexpected highlights. Murph made a brave gamble to give two 18-year-olds from the reserves their first team debut. Steve Brown and Scott Ashenden provided crosses which clawed two goals back. The scoreline ended 3-2. The late comeback provided some encouragement, but it didn't prevent the Southend fans from unfurling a 15ft, professionally printed banner with the simple message, 'JOBSON + MURPHY MUST GO'.

The fans saw chairman and manager as a job lot. Murph's more immediate headache was a mounting injury crisis and a call by United for Southend for supporters to boycott the next home game. Those who answered the call to stay away from a relegation battle against Notts County forever regretted their decision. In an eventful week, leading marksman Ian Benjamin left Southend in a shock move to Luton Town. Playing on a week-to-week contract, he could no longer put up with the protracted negotiations. He said he didn't blame Murph for the delaying tactics. The gaffer had been honest and straight in his dealings with the player. The problem lay elsewhere in the club.

Only 3,219 fans braved the elements to watch the debut performance of Benji's towering 6ft 4in replacement: Southend's lowest league gate for almost two years. The stay away fans missed a corker. Murph had brought his new striker from Premier League Crystal Palace's reserves on a one-month loan deal with a view to signing a permanent contract. It was a good deal for both player and manager. Murph would get a striker with strength and pace, and the 21-year-old would get the chance of regular first team football. The 400 fans who protested in the car park, before and after the game, missed a brace of goals for their new signing, a 3-1 victory against County, and Southend's first win in ten league games. Southend fans would forever remember the name of their latest acquisition; future England international Stanley Victor Collymore a.k.a. 'Our Stanley'.

David Pleat remembers the Collymore signing.

'I went to watch Crystal Palace one night. Collymore was playing, and Colin was at the game. Collymore was playing outside-left, out of position, looked a bit lazy, did nothing for me. I've got a feeling that was the game Colin decided to sign him for Southend. I said to him, I'm surprised at you signing that boy. "The sun doesn't shine all the time," Colin said. "I'll see if I can make the sun shine with him at Southend".'

It was the second time Murph had struck a bargain from Palace's reserves. John Fashanu was on loan with the Eagles when Murph signed him at Lincoln City. It was a much-needed positive omen for the struggling boss.

In the curious revolving doors of professional football, Collymore returned to Southend with great fanfare almost 30 years after he joined the club. In late 2021 he offered his services as a senior football strategist, to shore up Southend's recovery after dropping into non-league for the first time in over 100 years. In conversation with Ian Ladyman from the *Daily Mail*, Collymore remembered his early days at the club, 'At Crystal Palace, I was never gonna get in the team ... Then Colin Murphy, the Southend manager, brought me down here. He actually wanted me.'

Collymore recalled how he felt as he was driving into Roots Hall, 'This is it. Your debut. No more bull**** and hiding. You are playing Notts County tomorrow and it's on you.'

If local fans wanted to read the match report for the next Collymore game after County, they were disappointed, but the manager was relieved. Southend lost 1-0 at home to Sunderland. Page 46 of the *Echo Sport* included two matchday photographs, a 'What the fans have to say' article and a large white space extending across three column widths. It contained a small box by way of explanation.

'This space had been reserved for Howard Southwood's report of Saturday's game at Roots Hall. Southwood was banned from the ground.'

The local newspaper endured an uneasy relationship with the Southend chair. Jobson complained that sensationalist 'lock up your homes' advice before certain home games would cost Southend dear, if local families stayed away. The ongoing spat between the chairman and the newspaper was escalating, and it did nothing to ease the pressure on the manager. Two weeks before Christmas, plagued with player injuries, Murph counted only three league wins and 18 goals from the first 20 games. Trailing 2-0 away to West Ham, it was difficult to ignore the vocal Blues' away support, chanting 'David Webb's yellow army' throughout the second half.

While Murph watched the game, knowing that he might be hanging on to his job by his boot laces, the seat next to him in the dugout lay conspicuously empty. The following morning, he confirmed the rumour. Bob Houghton, his impressive number two, had left the club. A knock-back for Murph, Houghton was returning to work in Saudi Arabia. Murph played down his disappointment and explained his philosophy; if you find anything in life that's any good, it will always be difficult to keep hold of. He didn't regret taking the risk.

Murph felt the same about Collymore. He sensed that the 21-year-old would be hard to keep. Murph had first spotted the talented striker playing non-league football for Stafford Rangers. When Collymore moved to Crystal Palace, Murph tracked his progress. Bobbing up and down on the team sheet as a first-team substitute and playing for the reserves, Collymore's career failed to gain momentum. But only a month after he exploded on to the

Roots Hall scene, with four goals in five matches, Murph predicted he'd found a player who would earn the club £1m and would one day play for England. The gaffer was wrong on one of those counts. Collymore would sell for a lot more than £1m.

Murph compared the player's touch and technique to Mick Harford at Chelsea; his aggression to John Fashanu at Wimbledon. Murph had predicted in his Lincoln days that Harford and Fashanu would play for England. He'd got it right both times.

If Collymore 'uses that which is between his ears, he could one day be worth a lot of money', Murph said to Southwood, 'people here won't see a more exciting player.'

Even the not very catchily named Southend United Supporters' Club Football Club made a reluctant nod to Murph's new signing. In *The Fanatic*, their Southend Sunday League official programme, hand-typed, photocopied and largely dedicated to criticising Jobson and Murph, the Blues' beleaguered manager received a begrudging reprieve. In an article entitled 'On the up?' cautiously optimistic and hence relegated to page six, a contributor who signed himself,

Russ

P.S. Jobson out

wrote, 'I'll give Colin Murphy some credit if it was he who realised that, with the backdrop of poor league performances, dreadful results, much terrace disquiet, the sale of Benji and a three figure gate looming, something clearly had to be done.'

The author acknowledged that Collymore's performance at Swindon Town, on a miserably wet afternoon, had lifted the endless gloom for 90 minutes.

The official Sunday League programme is stored in the archives of the British Library at King's Cross, where on request, it can be delivered to the Rare Books and Music Reading Room. In exchange for depositing your reader pass as collateral, you will receive a 24-page A5 pamphlet. A slim yellow bookmark inside the front cover carries the dire warning, 'Special material. Not to be left unattended at any time.' No photography is allowed, and you must sit at a desk reserved for the use of restricted or special material. I asked the librarian why a football programme would be special material.

'I can only assume there is something terrible in it!' he said.

Despite languishing second from bottom of the First Division table, Murph looked forward to facing Millwall, fourth from top, in the third round of the FA Cup. A home tie in front of their biggest crowd of the season. A Collymore low drive, which hit the back of the net in the opening minutes, justified Murph's enthusiasm. The 1-0 victory, Southend's first FA Cup win in ten years against a Football League side, gave Murph a stay of execution. Yet victory came at a high price. As the final whistle blew, Millwall fans erupted on the terraces, ripped out advertising hoardings, brandished screwdrivers and tore up seats to use as weapons against the police. Reinforcements dressed in riot gear provided backup, but seven police officers were injured, and 20 people arrested. In a press conference with the *Evening Echo*, Southend's vice-chair, John Adams, responded to the violent outburst.

'What went on at Roots Hall was not the unacceptable face of British football, but the unacceptable face of Britain as a whole. It's a tragedy for Millwall F.C. who have tried so hard to try and bury their image from the past that it should be wrecked in this way.'

Jobson didn't comment further on the *Evening Echo's* 'lock up your homes' advice.

Murph had more than enough footballing problems to deal with. Repeated injuries in his strike force led to so many pairings up front, it was hard for the players to develop an understanding. In among the interminable gloom arrived a slither of hope. While they were staying at a hotel in Huddersfield on the eve of the fourth round of the FA Cup, Collymore's roommate threw him the paper.

'Have a look, they're saying you should be in the England team!'

Collymore laughed. Not at the thought of a First Division

player being selected for a World Cup qualifier, but at the recognition of how far he had come. He didn't allow the attention to distract him. He ravaged the Terriers with two more goals at Leeds Road and catapulted Southend into the fifth round of the FA Cup, for the first time in 17 years, and only the fourth time in their history. No wonder the Blues' fans loved Stan the man. Murph didn't dismiss the 'Collymore for England' stories. He had already spoken to his striker; a story which the gaffer recounted to Trevor Haylett from *The Independent*.

'It was a mucky morning, and the tide was going out on the Thames estuary when I pulled Stanley up in training and reminded him of one or two things and what he was capable of. You say a lot of things to players at five to three to wind them up and make them perform for you. Telling them they will play for England one day is different, because you're putting your credibility and a personal relationship on the line.'

At the end of the Huddersfield game, the Blues' fans swamped Collymore and threw him high into the air. They had found a new hero who frightened defences with his power and pace. Murph faced a different barrage of questions, not about whether Southend could survive relegation, but whether Collymore would be good enough to play in the Premier League. And if he did, what his price tag might be. Murph hesitated in his response, but Jobson leapt in.

'He's not for sale!'

As Collymore grabbed the headlines, Premier League teams ignored the chairman's warning and queued up to watch him play. Scouts from Everton and Nottingham Forest watched him despatch his tenth goal in 15 games, against Bristol City. Collymore was uncommonly modest; John Cornwell and Keith Jones were creating chances for him, and the boys at the back were soaking up the pressure to allow him to hit sides on the break. Collymore was enjoying his football again. It hadn't been a straightforward journey. Dumped by Wolves as a teenager, he played for Stafford Rangers in the Vauxhall Conference before spending almost two miserable years at Crystal Palace. Premier League Wimbledon had come in for him, but he had a gut feeling he would be no better off. With the Dons as groundshare tenants of Crystal Palace, if he moved to Wimbledon, he would still have stayed at Selhurst Park. Collymore explained his decision to Trevor Haylett.

'Colin Murphy impressed me as an honest manager with a good knowledge of the game and I liked the plans he had for me. I just needed to feel wanted, and this was a chance to make a name for myself. Now I have regular first team football, I'm thriving on it. All round I'm a much better player.'

Murph didn't play Collymore on the right or left wing where Palace had used him, but in the central position which the striker preferred. Collymore felt he had the right platform to show what he could do.

Fans got behind the team, vocal in their support, none more famous than the Basildon queen of rhythm and blues, Alison Moyet; regularly spotted in full voice on the terraces of the North Bank. In an extraordinary resurgence of support, almost 5,000 Southend fans travelled up the M1 to watch the Blues play Sheffield Wednesday in the fifth round proper of the FA Cup. Murph phoned his old pal Simmonite and invited him to the team's hotel in Sheffield.

'Come for a pre-match meal, Gordon, join me at the game if you want.'

'I'm off sick at the minute, Col. With the TV cameras at Hillsborough, I can't very well be sat in your dugout, can I?'

'Why don't you wear a f***ing balaclava?'

Simmonite declined the balaclava and sat at the back of the stand. He watched Southend crash out of the competition, 2-0 to Trevor Francis' Premier League side. The eventual FA Cup finalists outplayed the Blues, yet when the *The Roots Hall Roar* fanzine later published 24 years of seasonal memories, Southend fan Andrew Leeder remembered it as his game of the season.

'From the depths of the Murphy era came a ray of hope, not from the pitch but from the stands.'

The legion of fans who made the 500-mile round trip proved that despite the despair, good times were just around the corner. By contrast, only 3,896 fans turned up for the relegation clash against Bristol City, three days before. Murph, still the bard of the matchday programme, described his team as 'a bit like an old lighter with a dodgy flint'.

Vice-chair and proud Yorkshireman John Adams pleaded for rebel fans to accept a call for peace, to return to the home games and help fight relegation from the terraces. Adams became the front man when Jobson withdrew from the press. Murph tried not to get involved with public relations. He had to concentrate on First Division survival. He pinned his hopes on the new striking trio of Collymore, Brett Angell, back from a nine-month injury, and pacy winger Andy Ansah. For the first time since he took over as manager, Murph relished the luxury of being able to handpick a team, instead of selecting the only 13 players who were injury-free. But with the transfer deadline less than a month away, Aston Villa, Nottingham Forest, Leeds United and Queens Park Rangers were all reported to be circling Roots Hall's new star striker. Murph might not have too long to field his holy trinity, but at least he had time to breathe. He wouldn't have to decide about Collymore until a concrete offer landed on the table.

'We are not necessarily suggesting the boy is for sale,' he said to Howard Southwood. 'In fact, you might argue he is not up for grabs until we extricate ourselves from the predicament we are in.'

Anchored towards the bottom of the First Division, Murph could still savour the moment. He was sitting on a player, a bargain buy at £150,000, whose goalscoring record could conceivably notch up 30 goals a season.

'It wouldn't be stupid to rate anyone who can do that in this division as being worth two million pounds,' Murph said to the *Blues News*.

He allowed himself a wry smile. The value of his prolific striker had increased 13-fold in just four months! After all the traumas surrounding the club, questions over how much Collymore might be worth and where he might go offered a pleasant distraction. The player seemed content to leave Murph to sort it out; he was confident the boss would look after his interests. The transfer dealing clock ticked down to 25 March, and the first verbal offer came in. Thirteen goals in 23 games commanded a price tag of £1.5m. The bidders, Nottingham Forest, teetered on the brink of Premier League relegation and manager Brian Clough needed to boost his strike force. Southend turned down the offer. Days of wrangling followed.

In a paso doble of negotiations, Forest came back with an offer of £1.75m plus £250,000 after 20 games. Collymore was keen to accept the offer; attracted by playing alongside top goalscorer Clough Junior, in front of a crowd three times the size of Southend. Clough Senior was a legendary manager and Collymore would be half an hour from his home in the West Midlands, a dream deal for the ambitious lad from Cannock, Staffordshire.

Murph couldn't allow the bidding to distract him. Just when he needed to make the last push of the season to avoid relegation, his team was falling apart, victim to a freakish spate of illness and injury. A gashed knee, calf strain, pulled hamstring, flu virus and chicken pox all added to his catalogue of woes. Murph's midfield hardmen, captain Dave Martin and John Cornwell, both received match suspensions as they crept over the 21-point disciplinary barrier. Press speculation over Collymore's future threatened to affect his game. Southend's goalkeeper Paul Sansome picked up a red card against Notts County, and the team crashed to a 4-0 defeat. The local papers offered every permutation of Murphy 'feeling Blue'.

To Jobson and Adams' surprise, Clough didn't turn up to watch the Notts County game. Collymore still believed he was heading to Forest for the agreed deal, but hours before the transfer deadline, the Reds withdrew their offer. They countered with a £250,000 loan deal until the end of the season. Jobson rejected it;

he wouldn't be backed into a corner. He believed Forest had drawn out negotiations to keep other clubs away. Clough's side had snatched a crucial win against Southampton, and the manager's interest in Collymore appeared to have waned. Clough said he would decide at the end of the season, when he was sitting with his colleagues in the sun. He paid the price for his indecision. Forest were relegated from the Premier League at his final home game at the City Ground; an emotional end to Clough's 18-year reign at the club.

With the Collymore deal off the table, after a desperate 2-1 defeat against Tranmere Rovers, Jobson called Murph to his office. If he checked his calendar, April Fools' Day, Murph might have predicted what was about to unfold. Six hours of gruelling conversation with the chairman, and Murph's managerial fate was sealed. In a statement issued from Roots Hall, the directors and the manager 'mutually concluded' that in the best interests of the club, Murph would step down as manager with immediate effect. Jobson was sorry to let his chosen man go.

'I know Colin Murphy has made probably the biggest financial contribution to this club of anyone past, present and probably future,' he said to the waiting press.

Murph's signing of Collymore was a stroke of genius, the bargain of the season. Collymore scored 18 goals in 33 games. But Murph knew he had paid the price for failing to calm terrace unrest and for a debilitating jinx of injuries, which conspired against him. For much of the season, the queue for the treatment room had curled round the building like a hot dog stall on matchdays. Murph had worked particularly hard at Southend and saw very little goodwill in return. Rightly or wrongly, football is a results business, and fans invest significant time and money in following their team. Trying but failing is insufficient reward for many supporters.

The board wasted no time in appointing Murph's successor; a well-known character in the lower divisions, who endured a tempestuous relationship with ticket tout turned chairman, Stan

Flashman. Across two stints at Barnet, Murph's replacement had guided the Bees out of non-league football after three second-placed finishes. In a spectacular display of football shenanigans, he had an actioned-packed week before he joined Southend. Sacked for the seventh time by the chairman on the Tuesday, re-instated by the Barnet board after the chairman resigned on the Wednesday, he met Jobson at a reserve game on the Thursday and accepted the manager's job. Enter the Roots Hall record books, Mr Motivator and a good pal of Murph's from the lower leagues, the irrepressible Barry Fry. Murph felt no animosity towards his old pal for accepting the job. Only minutes after the club announced the appointment, the two men were spotted deep in conversation. Fry, a natural extrovert, burst on to the Roots Hall scene with his trademark humour.

'What's my biggest ambition in football?' he said to the press. 'To get Southend into the Premier League – where they don't belong!'

It didn't take long for the Blues' fans to fall in love with their new boss. The showman had arrived, and results followed. After only two wins in their previous ten league games, Southend stunned Sunderland with a 4-2 comeback in his first game in charge. In his programme notes for the next home match against West Ham, Fry bounded on to the scene with a Barry Fry Writes column.

'Remember the old song "From a Jack to a King". Well, here I am "From Bee to a Blue" and right out of the Blue, so to speak,' he wrote. 'Now, the opportunity has occurred, and I've grasped the nettle or the reins whichever way you want to look, for Colin Murphy who I know is a good and true man.'

After a 1-0 victory against West Ham in front of a sell-out crowd, Fry spoke to the club's newspaper, *Blues News*.

'I told Vic that I would have walked to Southend, that's how keen I was to take the job. It's a lovely little club and I've always fancied it. I think Southend could be a sleeping giant.'

Fry promised not to resort to the long-ball game in his rescue mission, but to give the fans an entertaining game of football with plenty of goals. He kept his promise; five wins in the last nine games secured Southend an 18th-placed finish. Fry delighted the fans by naming Keith Jones as captain; a player sidelined for much of the season by Murph, believed by many supporters to be Southend's most influential player. Fry didn't criticise Murph's efforts during his year in charge, and told the *Echo Sport*, 'David Webb was an excellent manager, and popular with the fans. I don't think anyone would have had a cat in hell's chance of following him successfully.'

Howard Southwood mirrored Fry's support. Writing about Collymore's goal tally and his current market value, the sports editor reflected on Murph's contribution to the season. He suggested in the *Evening Echo* that if Southend survived the drop, the fans might, 'Spare a thought for the quiet, almost introverted, man who may well have played a more significant part in that survival than perhaps many people will give him credit for.'

Murph's severance deal with the chairman apportioned some credit. It included a clause entitling the manager to five per cent of any profit made on the subsequent sale of Southend's star striker. It was a shrewd move on his part, although enforcing the clause would prove to be a greater challenge when Vic Jobson refused to pay up.

As soon as Murph was released as manager at Southend, the press linked him with the vacant job at Lincoln City. Strongly tipped to take over from Steve Thompson, axed after a poor run of results in a promotion-chasing season, Murph wasn't tempted to return to Sincil Bank for a third time. With Fry established as manager, the chairman wanted to keep Murph at Roots Hall and offered him a new role as director of football.

The appointment reflected the tidal change in job titles and footballing responsibilities in the early 1990s. Technical directors, coaching directors, and directors of football were vying for position, their respective responsibilities frequently ill-defined. An alternative model of football management was emerging, which reflected a continental influence. The team manager trained and selected the team, the director of football looked after scouting, contracts, transfer fees, wages and almost everything else.

Colin Murphy in the hot seat at Southend United. (Image courtesy of Southend United History)

The distinction meant little to the fans. They were more interested in results. And in what would happen to Collymore, their top-scoring striker. In the close season, they found out. He transferred to newly relegated Nottingham Forest, signed by Frank Clark who had replaced Brian Clough.

Clark recognised Collymore's future potential. A down payment of £2m accompanied Forest's agreement to a long list of potentially lucrative demands:

1. An extra £250,000 if Collymore scored 25 goals the following season (he hit the 25-goal target across all competitions).

2. £250,000 if Forest gained promotion during the next four seasons (he helped them straight back to the Premier League, as First Division runners-up).

3. £250,000 if Collymore played for England (he received three caps).

4. Fifteen per cent of any future fee the striker might earn for Forest (in June 1995, he moved to Liverpool for an English record fee of £8.5m).

Fry was quick to acknowledge Murph's contribution to the deal.

'It was Colin Murphy who brought him here for £150,000, and I didn't do anything to make Stanley better than he already is.'

The sale made Collymore the most expensive player in the First Division. Cash in the bank allowed Jobson to loosen the purse strings and let Fry buy a host of players, almost an entirely fresh team. Even the cynics from Southend United Supporters' Club Football Club hero-worshipped the new boss. *The Fanatic* programme of early October praised the gaffer for his colourful interviews and programme notes.

'Long may it continue,' they wrote. 'The only time the likes of Dick Bate and Colin Murphy raised a titter was when they revealed their next team line-ups.'

By the end of November, the Blues had leapt to joint top of the First Division. There was much to celebrate, but still *The Roots Hall Roar* wrote in unflattering terms about the man it called 'Mad Murph'.

The editor's notes from issue 17 talked of 'a man whose tactics were straight out of the Charles Hughes school of 'direct football' a man with a personality from the Nigel Mansell school of charm.'

They devoted half a page to the Colin Murphy Appreciation Society First Annual Meeting; a mock-up photograph of a lone man in a raincoat, sitting in an empty stand! The fans questioned how Jobson found the money to pay for a director of football when Fry said he had to trim the squad to cut back on the wage bill. The new manager at Roots Hall could do no wrong. Until he denied he was interested in a move to Birmingham City, and less than two weeks later, handed in his resignation.

The venom directed at Murph throughout his time as

manager was nothing compared to what Fry endured when he left Southend. Attracted by the big budget of a struggling First Division side, the Southend fans labelled him 'Judas Fry'.

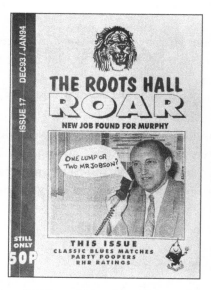

The Roots Hall Roar celebrates Murph's appointment by Vic Jobson, as Southend United's new director of football.

Jobson didn't waste any time in finding a replacement. He looked to Peter Taylor, ex-England international and a former junior Blues player, to take over from his exuberant manager. Taylor remembers the first time he sat in a room with Murph. Taylor was working part-time as player-manager at non-league Hendon. His chairman wanted a fee to release him, which Jobson refused to pay. Murph intervened.

'You can forget about my bit on the Collymore deal, chairman, if it helps you pay for Peter to come as manager.'

Taylor was astonished at the generosity of a man he had only just met. It was an influential meeting, which marked the start of a professional ten-year relationship; a stint in the Premier League and two back-to-back promotions. Only none of their success would come at Southend.

Twenty-eight years later, Taylor recognises there was a fair chance Murph knew he wouldn't get paid for the Collymore clause in his contract.

'That was the reputation of Vic unfortunately, and John Adams, and certain owners of football clubs at that time. Hopefully now, the League Managers' Association has cleaned a lot of it up.'

Taylor was right. Four years after Murph left Southend as director of football, he appointed counsel to appear at the High Court in London on his behalf. Murph's counsel argued that under a contract which determined the terms of his release as manager, his client was entitled to five per cent of 'any profit' made on the Collymore sale. This included sums based on Collymore's future performance and onward sale, not just on his original transfer fee to Nothingham Forest. The *Evening Echo* reported that Southend had counterclaimed that Murph should pay £16,000 for breach of contract, after failing to give notice of his eventual departure from the club. Jobson hadn't expected Murph would have the stomach to take the fight to the High Court. The chairman had a history of litigation. If Murph lost the case, he knew the costs would cripple him, but as a matter of principle he refused to be cheated out of what he believed he was due. In Mr Justice Eady's summing up, he rejected Southend's claim that Murph wasn't entitled to the money 'under the true meaning of his contract' and found in Murph's favour. The former manager wasn't in court to hear the verdict, but he walked away with £77,996 plus costs. It was a useful contribution to his pension pot, but more importantly for Murph, he knew that justice had been done.

Taylor remembers the time he worked with Murph at Southend. It was a difficult job following on from Barry Fry.

'Barry, to be fair, was in a different class. He's a great, enthusiastic manager. He spent a lot of money and I had to do the opposite. So having somebody around like Colin with his experience, very level-headed, I'm sure helped my style of managing. It was a tough start at Southend, but Colin calmed me down.'

Taylor took over the reins with Southend in third place and ended the season in 15th. It was a challenging introduction to managing in the Football League.

Eight months after Fry left the club, issue 18 of *The Roots Hall Roar* published the 1993/94 Readers' Poll Results. D**khead of the Year was won by Barry Fry. The author noted it was the first time in living memory that Jobson hadn't appeared in the top three. The editorial pointed out that, 'any attempt to sue would be a waste of time as we're skint.' It was signed "D. Duck (no relation)".

In the Readers' Poll category for 'Craziest comment/decision by Vic' the top spot went to 'Re-employing Colin Murphy'. Murph came in two places above 'Suggesting a ground share with West Ham'.

Murph couldn't have been less popular with the fans, but Taylor still remembers how his director of football was always popular with the board.

'They appreciated Colin because he was always thinking long term. He had very good standards. If I was the owner of a football club, he'd be one of my first signings, because I'd know the place would run properly.'

Eighteen months after Murph left the Southend manager's job to become director of football, *The Roots Hall Roar* issue 19 ('still no relation', 'even more skint') re-emerged from a two-month slumber to publish a Southend United Mr Men XI. From Mr Clumsy (in goal) to Messrs Lazy and Grumpy (up front), the team selection extended to a trio of the fans' least favourites. On the unfancied subs' bench, from left to right, sat:

Mr Greedy (Barry Fry)
Mr Mean (Vic Jobson)
Mr Nonsense (Colin Murphy)

No wonder Murph reflects on his time at Southend as 'the unhappiest period of my life'. After two and a half years of total misery, he was glad to get away.

In the late 1990s, the Wolverhampton Business School published an academic paper, *Director of football, cosmetic labelling or a sea-change? The football manager's formal job role.* It quoted Harry Redknapp's comments about new roles in a changing era of football.

'Players don't want to retire and be managers anymore,' he said. 'They want to be directors of football. No real pressure!'

But Murph was old school, pre-1990s. As director of football, he missed the pressure.

Offered a hands-on opportunity with Shelbourne, an Irish club in Dublin, Murph didn't hesitate to pack his bags. He needed to get away from the toxic territory of the Thames Estuary. A warmer welcome awaited him on the mouth of the River Liffey, in the manager's job at Tolka Park.

The *Irish Sun* suggested that an away game at rural Monaghan United may have clouded Murph's early impressions of Irish football. A reporter asked him what he made of the League of Ireland in Gortakeegan, where cows grazed on the hill behind the goal.

'Well, it's a bit different,' Murph said.

The league was different too. Only 12 teams competed in the Premier Division, with each club playing each other three times.

In his six months in charge at Shelbourne, Murph guided the club to a third-placed finish, only two points behind champions Dundalk. Shels qualified for the UEFA Cup preliminary round and reached the Football Association of Ireland (FAI) Cup Final, for only the second time in 20 years. A crowd of 15,000 watched the match at Lansdowne Road, but there was no happy ending for Murph's men.

'We didn't play,' captain Mick Neville told the *Irish Times*. 'We never got the ball down, we never got going at all. Total frustration at the end of the day.'

The press criticised Murph's defensive style of play. He used two stoppers in central midfield, and Shels lost out 2-1 to first-time winners of the FAI Cup, Derry City.

The gaffer was disappointed, but not devastated by the result. He had spent long enough out of the English Football League, and he was itching to return. He received an offer to go back to the club he had left 17 years before: struggling Second Division side Notts County. Murph couldn't resist the challenge.

In the Top Trumps of football management, he swapped Vic Jobson for Derek Pavis; one domineering chairman for another. Murph faced another high-stakes game of winner takes all.

Would he have the grit to handle Pavis?

10

THE WEMBLEY BLUES

NOTTS COUNTY

'I've found the next Clough and Taylor!'

Derek Pavis boasted to the local press. The perma-tanned Notts County chairman had reached the end of a turbulent season at Meadow Lane. It was June 1995, and the Magpies had moved from the relative high of winning the Anglo-Italian Cup at Wembley to the devastating low of relegation to the Second Division. The club needed shaking up with new management and Pavis claimed to have found the perfect pair: Murph and his former no-nonsense centre-half, Steve Thompson.

Tommo, who replaced Peter Taylor at Southend, had saved the First Division club from almost certain relegation. In his four months in charge, he achieved the highest win percentage of any Blues manager, including local hero David Webb. It was clear why Pavis picked his new management team, both grafters and fighters with experience in the lower divisions. Two of the most successful managers in County's history, Jimmy Sirrel and Neil Warnock, had learned their trade in the lower leagues. But what did Murph and Tommo see in a club, fresh from relegation, in the third tier of English football? A club which had fielded three different managers and a caretaker trio in less than nine months.

They both say it was an exciting opportunity. Murph saw it as a great chance to get a big club going again. They knew each other well from their Lincoln City days and believed in the club's potential. Meadow Lane boasted an impressive 20,000 all-seater stadium.

In the 1992 close season, three stands of the former stadium were demolished, and the Main Stand re-built and re-named as the Derek Pavis Stand. The chairman was the bedrock of Notts County, driven by ambition and not averse to self-promotion. If Murph and Tommo held any reservations about accepting the job, the offer of a three-year contract secured the deal. It was a generous offer from a lower-league club. One year of contract for each of the mistakes Pavis admitted he'd made in recent months; sacking Mick Walker (after 591 days), appointing Russell Slade (for 121 days) and putting Howard Kendall in charge for 79. As Pavis said when he appointed his new management pair, 'If I don't get it right this time, they'll run me out of town.'

Thompson recognised his job share with Murph was unusual. Only two clubs in the Football League shared management responsibility: Mick Gooding and Jimmy Quinn at Reading, and Alan Curbishley and Steve Gritt at Charlton Athletic, both joint player-managers in the First Division. Pavis said he was following the continental idea of having a team manager (Tommo) to deal with coaching, training and everything that went on in the dressing room, and a general manager (Murph) to deal with contracts and administrative affairs. Pavis wanted Murph for his experience, knowledge, and contacts, and Tommo to instil a sense of discipline and organise the team.

'He can be a tough nut when necessary and we haven't had one of those for a long time,' the chairman said to the *Evening Post.*

The distinction between team manager and general manager seemed to be lost on the press. They ensured Murph grabbed 90 per cent of the headlines and took 100 per cent of the flak in the months ahead.

Colin Slater, BBC Radio Nottingham Notts County commentator for almost 50 years, wrote about the Murph and Tommo partnership in his autobiographical history, *Tied Up With Notts*. The voice of Notts County marvelled at how two such different characters – Tommo, 'a no-nonsense type of person, who ... portrays himself as the archetypal Yorkshireman' and the seemingly 'more reserved and quietly spoken' Murph – could work side by side 'in apparent harmony and with evident mutual respect'. Yet despite their distinct personalities, it was a relationship which worked.

The three-year contract would give the club stability and allow the management duo enough time to put the Magpies back on track. Notts County, the world's oldest professional football club, had endured probably the most traumatic season in its 133-year history. Pavis said he would give his managers free rein, apart from in the transfer market. He had learned his lesson from giving Kendall the freedom to sign players; £500,000 in less than three months. It hadn't saved County from the drop.

For the first time since Pavis took over as chair eight years before, the club was running an overdraft. With a squad of 31 players, he needed to introduce a new regime; the club couldn't buy without selling. It didn't faze Murph. He knew how to run a club on very little cash. Sixteen names on the transfer list gave Murph and Tommo plenty of players to choose from.

Tommo's arrival at Meadow Lane wasn't without controversy. Southend's vice-chair, John Adams, claimed that Tommo had shaken hands on a new two-year deal with Vic Jobson, just before the caretaker manager left the club. Southend approached the Football League to seek compensation. Pavis rejected the claim; Thompson wasn't under contract at Southend. It didn't stop Adams from accusing Murph of enticing his former captain away from Roots Hall. Murph denied any wrongdoing and faced a Football League tribunal. The Football Commission cleared County of malpractice, but Jobson had no intention of giving up the fight. Murph knew from bitter experience that the chairman wasn't afraid of a protracted legal wrangling. The grievance would rumble on.

The muted response to Murph and Tommo's arrival disappointed County's ambitious chair. Notts County fanzine *No More Pie in the Sky* reported that the appointment had been met with a strange sort of silence. Pavis was more encouraged by Tommy Lawton, the greatest player in County's history, who shared his excitement for the new management team. Lawton, an ex-England international, wrote in his weekly column for the *Evening Post* that success would depend on Murph and Tommo having time to turn things around and being allowed to manage without interference. It was common knowledge that the chairman was more hands on than any of his previous managers would have liked.

Pavis promised he wouldn't meddle with the day-to-day management of the club, but admitted he found it frustrating he couldn't control the players in the same way he directed the Pavis Group of companies when he was in charge. He vowed he would leave the managers to exert their own influence. Only time would tell if this teeth-whitened leopard could change his spots.

Murph and Tommo set straight to work on building the squad's fitness and discipline. They organised punishing pre-season training at an army bootcamp to root out the cause of the club's fall from grace. Pavis blamed the 'non-triers' in the team for their relegation nightmare, but Murph believed there was enough talent in the squad to win promotion straight back to the First Division. In an interview with David Stapleton from the *Evening Post*, he said he demanded total commitment from the players.

'They should be thinking about getting Notts County up at every available opportunity, when they're driving their cars, walking down the street, even lying on their beds at night.'

Murph said it was a wonderful feeling to be top of the league on Christmas Day, and he aimed to establish a brand of fast, flowing football to achieve just that. He dreamed of the 1961

Double-winning Spurs team which he admired in his youth; a move away from the long-ball game which County played under Neil Warnock during his four years in charge.

In the last week of the close season, Murph and Tommo took the Notts County's reserves to Lincoln United to play in the Lincoln Challenge Cup. Their opponents played in the Northern Premier League Division One, five levels below County in the football pyramid. It was a chance to give the County boys a pre-season run-off. Murph wasn't banking on getting his goalkeeper, Mike Pollitt, sent off in the 83rd minute. Faced with a three-match suspension and only two goalies in his squad, Murph remonstrated with the referee.

'You can't send him off, it's a pre-season friendly!'

At 90 minutes, with the score at 0-0, Keith Roe, the Lincoln United chairman, told Murph the match would go to extra time and a penalty shoot-out.

'No, it f***ing won't!' Murph said.

He turned to Tommo.

'Steven, tell the boys we're getting on the bus.'

As Roe continued the argument, Murph walked back to the team coach. They drove straight out of the Ashby Avenue ground. Match abandoned. The season hadn't started when the *Evening Post* reported that Murph was about to receive a letter filing for compensation. He didn't regret his hot-headed decision. He had a new boss who matched his forthright approach.

Tommo recalls an early incident at Meadow Lane. On the first day of training, a County player came to see the management team; he wanted to speak to the chairman. His teeth were kicked out at the end of the season, and he wanted Pavis to pay for the dental work. Murph and Tommo offered to go with him.

'Does your hair grow while you're playing for me?' Pavis asked.

'Yes, chairman'.

'Do I pay for your haircuts?'

'No, chairman'.

'Well, I'm not paying for your teeth either, so f*** off!'

As they walked out of the chairman's office, Murph glanced at his team manager.

'Steven, I think this one's going to be entertaining!'

It didn't take long for the pair to feel the weight of their over-bearing boss on their backs. Murph and Tommo liked to arrive at Meadow Lane for an 8am start, organise training and look to wrap things up by late afternoon. Invariably, as they were ready to leave, Pavis would turn up in the office he had given to Murph, water the rubber plant, and keep the two men talking until six or seven o'clock. And if the chairman wasn't there in person, they saw his flattering likeness in the picture he left on the office wall.

'Look at them eyes, they're moving!' Murph laughed as he and Tommo looked at the outsize image of their employer with his coiffed silver hair.

But the management duo knew Pavis held the purse strings, and they had to keep him onside. They wanted to recruit a natural leader and a defensive rock and signed 30-year-old Gary Strodder for a £140,000 tribunal-fixed fee from West Bromwich Albion. Murph recruited Strodder as an apprentice at Lincoln; he knew he would defend with his life and inspire the team around him. Pavis sanctioned a further signing. Goalkeeper Darren Ward joined from Mansfield Town. The chairman was so keen to get the player he wanted, he dipped into his own pocket to come up with the £150,000 fee.

With Strodder as captain, Murph and Tommo got off to a dream start; four wins and a draw in the first five league and cup games. The second-round draw of the League Cup allowed Murph to realise one of his great managerial ambitions; to pit himself against his good friend, Howard Wilkinson, manager of Premier League Leeds United. Wilkinson had learned his Football League trade at County over a decade before. The press tried to bill it as a grudge match. The Leeds United manager laughed it off, although he said to the *Football Post*, 'Ask me if I still have a soft spot for Notts County, and I'll give you an answer after we've played them!'

The spirit in the County team was riding high when the Magpies played the first leg at Elland Road, a stadium rebuilt and ready to host Euro 96. The Magpies held the Whites to a 0-0 draw, and Murph revealed that Player of the Season Shaun Murphy had refused to leave the pitch despite suffering concussion. After colliding with Welsh international Gary Speed, Murphy stumbled around seeing double, but with three defenders out of the game through injury, he took a couple of aspirins at half-time to get himself back on the pitch. Murph praised his namesake's commitment and the attitude which rubbed off on the rest of the team. And Wilkinson lauded Notts for their performance.

'They were as organised, committed, determined and surprising as you would expect from a Colin Murphy team,' he told David Stapleton.

The second leg at Meadow Lane didn't quite go according to plan. Two goals from big frontman Devon White weren't enough to counter Leeds' attacking play. And Speed's 25-yard drive in the 90th minute broke County's heart. Although Leeds won 3-2 on aggregate, White came away as the overall winner. He took his tally to 13 goals from 14 matches, the best scoring statistics in the Football League. Carried away with enthusiasm, Murph predicted his forward had doubled in value.

'People tell me he can't play, but that's the story of my life. They used to tell me Mick Harford, Tony Cunningham, John Fashanu and Stan Collymore couldn't play,' Murph said to the *Evening Post*. 'I knew they could, with a bit of work and guidance.'

Murph said White lacked a deft touch, but he more than made up for it with his physical presence. With new signing and future Welsh international Darren Ward in goal, and White up front, Murph felt County should have a fighting chance of promotion. The players sensed the start of a new era at the club. Paul Devlin asked to come off the transfer list. Forward Vinny

Arkins, Murph's top-scoring striker signed from Shelbourne, and Ian Baraclough followed Ward from Mansfield. Tommo had signed Baraclough in his three-year stint as manager at Lincoln. He was Murph's type of player; a battling defender who relished a chance to surge down the line. And Murph saw 34-year-old former player-manager Steve Nicol as a vital part in their push for promotion. The ex-Scottish international exerted an outstanding influence on both the midfield and the younger players. Murph said the Liverpool medal winner trained every day as if it were a cup final.

By November, the Magpies were showing the strength of their passing game. Four weeks after extolling White's virtues, the management shocked the Meadow Lane faithful by leaving him out of the team. They switched Devlin into the middle with Arkins as a link player to give themselves more pace and mobility up front. Twelve goals from three games and none of them from White got the fans talking. They knew the team could play the long ball up front to their 6ft 3in striker, but a 4-3 away win over close rivals Burnley proved they could play controlled and flowing football too.

In the three games before Murph and Tommo dropped White, his confidence looked to have dipped. But he was still the fans' favourite, and they would need him back when the going got tougher and the pitches got heavier as the season progressed.

In a shock move while White was out of the team, Nicol left County for a return to the Premier League with Sheffield Wednesday. Despite the disappointment at the loss of their midfield general, a run of 16 league games with only two defeats earned Tommo the Second Division Manager of the Month award. The Magpies sat second in the league, three points behind Swindon. County had been playing leapfrog at the top of the table with Dario Gradi's Crewe Alexandra for the previous three weeks. Their seasonal fixture would fill one of the old Derby colleagues with festive cheer. Murph admired Gradi's approach with his young team.

'They play the way the game was designed to be played,' Murph said.

And when Crewe came to Meadow Lane, they did just that; played the game from the back and their short passing tactics paid off. Macauley scored, while 18-year-old Danny Murphy, a future multiple cup winner with Liverpool, impressed in midfield. Murph was disappointed but sanguine about the 1-0 defeat. He said to David Stapleton of the *Evening Post*,

'We've played against not the best players in the league, but the best team. We've been working with our boys for five months. They've been working with that team for five years. Sometimes that comes home to roost.'

Stapleton reported that when Gradi first went into management, FA Cup-winning manager Lawrie McMenemy told him he didn't have to play kick and rush like the other teams in the lower divisions, so long as he knew how to cope with their style of play. The Crewe manager was trying to play in the Second Division like Manchester United or Nottingham Forest were playing in the Premier League, stroking the ball through to midfield. It was gratifying for Murph's former assistant that his playing style was paying off. For the opposition, it raised an important question. What was the best style of play to win promotion from the Second Division, in a league better known for its physical strength?

Tommo pointed out that most promotion challenges are built from the back. Notts weren't a traditional kick-and-rush team; they could get the ball down and play in more advanced areas of the pitch. Baraclough was coming to grips with Murph and Tommo's 'Be adventurous' advice and getting forward to support *No More Pie in the Sky*'s Player of the Season, Andy Legg. But both Murph and Tommo knew they needed to bolster the team, conscious of the maxim, 'Buy while you're strong'. They still had six players to offload from their transfer list. But it didn't stop them going on a £250,000 spending spree in the January sales, just in time for the FA Cup third-round draw, a fixture which brought a touch of Brazilian glamour to Meadow Lane.

Bryan Robson had pulled off the signing of the season when he brought Juninho from São Paulo to newly promoted champions Middlesbrough. For the Meadow Lane showdown, manager Robson, two weeks short of his 39th birthday, selected himself to play in midfield. It was a tactical decision to slow the pace down and hold the ball up to pass to 'The Little Fella', the former Brazilian Young Player of the Year. The Magpies harried Middlesbrough for long periods of the game. Shaun Murphy and Gary Strodder landed crunching tackles on the Boro's £4.75m signing, but County couldn't hold on to the 0-0 half-time score. They suffered a battling 2-1 exit. Murph put a positive spin on the defeat. The FA Cup drew attention away from the primary aim of the season.

'We lost, and that's always disappointing. But I have to say the ideal would have been a draw so we could go up there, get a replay, pick up the money, get beaten and get on with the main job in hand.'

Most fans would agree with him. The priority was winning promotion at the first attempt. Murph recognised County still had some catching up to do with the front runners; the best team (Crewe), the strongest group (Swindon) and the best all-rounders (Blackpool), as he called them.

Despite defeat in the FA Cup, Murph wasn't shy about what he and Tommo had achieved in their first six months in charge.

'We've had to clean the place up, sign players, and make a transfer profit to go up in one swoop. If it's about medals, I should get the George Cross!' he said to David Stapleton, 'but if we fail in the aim, and I'm convinced we'll get into the play-offs, I think we'll murder it next season.'

Murph continued a relentless search for new players and joked that he knew all the grounds with the best meat pies, the service stations and the lay-by vans. He had eaten at them all. It was never a nine-to-five job, and it could be lonely, but it suited him. He didn't play golf, he didn't follow the horses, he wasn't a gambler. Football was his life and he never switched off. The reward came when he spotted new talent and sold someone at a healthy profit.

While the management duo found the players, they needed Pavis to sanction the deals. When Murph spotted a player he liked, he would take Tommo with him to the chairman's office. The conversations followed a familiar pattern.

'Chairman, we've got another player.'

'Another one, Colin?'

'Yes, chairman, I'm putting a jigsaw together.'

'How many pieces has this bloody jigsaw got, Colin, 16 or 64?'

In the early days, the relationship worked well. Murph and Tommo got their players and kept Pavis, known to be a frustrated manager, at arm's length.

In his drive to build a new team, Murph signed forward Tony Battersby from Sheffield United. He was the type of player Murph liked to buy, strong and quick, a relative unknown.

'When you sell them for a load of money, you can't gloat, of course. All you can do is celebrate behind your own four walls and have a few drinks,' Murph said to the *Football Post*.

Murph didn't get to celebrate this signing, Battersby returned only eight goals in 39 games, but with Arkins up front, and Devlin switched to the centre, he had the resources to sell the man who had lost his place in the starting line-up for the past two months. The player just happened to be the crowd's favourite, Devon White. News that their popular goals man was up for sale shocked County fans. They could relate to him as one of their own, a genuine Magpies supporter, born within a mile of the Meadow Lane ground.

By January, Murph and Tommo had built a side which featured seven players they had signed in a month: goalkeeper Ward, defenders Wilder and Strodder, Baraclough and Rogers in midfield, and Arkins and Battersby up front. Eight players, if you counted Ian Richardson on loan from Birmingham City. It delighted Murph to finally get his man. He had made an unsuccessful bid for the left-footed midfielder three years before, when Richardson was turning out for non-league Dagenham and Redbridge, and Murph was at Southend. The management team couldn't question the chairman's commitment; he had paid out £900,000 since the start of the season. And they couldn't question the players' dedication. Graeme Hogg, the ex-Manchester United centre-back, declared himself fit to play against Wrexham despite sporting a pair of cracked ribs.

Although Notts were sitting comfortably in fourth position, the fans didn't withhold their criticism. Season ticket holders phoned the *Evening Post* sports desk, concerned about the future of the Magpies if White were to leave the club. Tommo stressed they were going to carry on doing what they thought was right, not what would make them popular.

In the previous season, Birmingham won the Second Division championship with 89 points, when there was only one automatic promotion place up for grabs. The reduction of the Premier League from 22 to 20 clubs had a knock-on effect on promotions and relegations across the lower leagues. In the 1995/96 season there were two automatic promotion slots out of the Second Division. By the halfway mark, Notts reached Murph's 43-point target. If they could match that in the second half, they should at least be on course for a place in the play-offs.

Murph recognised the points had come at the expense of flair and creativity, but with so many new players, they needed time to settle down. Tommo was less apologetic if entertainment was lacking. While he was brought up on smooth operators such as Tony Currie and Glenn Hoddle, County were playing in the Second Division, and they had to play a physical game to get out of the league.

'The higher up the ladder you get, the more football you can play,' Tommo said to the *Football Post*.

The management duo admitted that County looked more comfortable away from home. At Meadow Lane, the boo boys harangued them for not playing enough football. Murph pledged to take the criticism on board but needed more time to find a winning blend with a sea of new players. Fans recognised he put out a fit and efficient team, but they wanted to be entertained. In the *Football Post*, still the weekly mouthpiece for disgruntled local fans, the letters page suggested that since the departure of Steve Nicol, the team had reverted to long-ball football and the midfield was regularly overrun.

White's departure to Watford for £100,000 devastated the fans. He had scored 24 goals in 42 appearances since his return to Nottingham 14 months before. They were disappointed to see him swap a bit part in a Second Division promotion drive for a regular place in a First Division relegation battle. Murph made no apologies.

'When managers change, it's inevitable that players change. Selling players is never a problem. It's who you replace them with that counts.'

Murph hadn't doubled his money on White, as he predicted. He'd made a loss of £10,000. And he took an enormous gamble in offloading his most prolific goalscorer.

When the general manager got off the team bus for the next away game at Edgeley Park, he met a chorus of boos from the Notts County supporters. The atmosphere didn't improve when Stockport scored their second goal in the closing minutes. A group of irate fans surrounded the general manager in the dugout. The police ejected them from the ground, but Murph realised once again he was facing an uphill struggle to improve his relationship with the fans.

Ten days later, it was Tommo who broke the silence on why they let White go. Pavis pushed his team manager to centre stage in front of the press, irritated by his general manager's inability or unwillingness to placate the supporters. Tommo said White had led them to play in a direct way, and they were trying to adopt a more fluent approach, controlling games from midfield. Bemused by the managers' decision, the goal-getting giant left his heart in

Nottingham when he motored up and down the M1 to Glenn Roeder's Watford, a club destined for relegation.

Murph and Tommo wanted to return to the Notts County glory days. In an era when Jimmy Sirrel was manager, and Mick Walker his youth team coach, Youth Training Scheme (YTS) trainees had rolled off the Meadow Lane production line of young players. If the management duo could keep the club's sense of ambition, they could resurrect a youth policy and hold on to the strongest players. Murph and Tommo said it was a travesty that the squad they inherited with 31 professionals prevented many of the younger players from getting a game in the reserves. They only had to look at Dario Gradi's setup at Crewe, the envy of many Premier League clubs, to realise what they could do with home-grown talent.

If Murph incurred the wrath of the Meadow Lane fans when he offloaded White, it was nothing compared to their reaction a month later when he sold Paul Devlin and Andy Legg to Barry Fry's First Division Birmingham. Murph was quick to point out that Pavis backed his decision, part of the long-term restructuring of the club. It was a canny move from the general manager to deflect criticism upwards.

As Devlin and Legg moved out of Meadow Lane, two Garys came in their place; Gary Jones from First Division Southend and Gary Martindale from Second Division Peterborough United. Martindale was a penalty box predator, described by Murph with evident delight as the 'poor man's Ian Rush'. And Jones who scored 11 goals in 13 games had kept Tommo's Southend side in the First Division. Murph defended his signing of four strikers since the start of the season. He spoke of the contrasting qualities of Arkin, Jones, Martindale and Battersby to the *Evening Post*.

'We've a very clever striker, a hard-working striker, a goalscoring striker and an all-round striker. It's a plentiful situation up front.'

Plentiful or not, the quality of the strike force wasn't filling the Meadow Lane seats. A 2-2 home draw against York City played out in front of a crowd of 3,462, the worst gate in the Second Division for ten years. As they sat in a state-of-the-art stadium, many Notts fans would have preferred to be on the terraces. They looked with envy at Blackpool, Bradford, and York, where they could still stand up to watch their football. Meadow Lane was one of the first clubs to act on the Taylor Report. Although Pavis sympathised with the fans, there was no going back. If County won promotion to the First Division, none of the grounds would cater for standing. He insisted the Magpies were ahead of the curve.

Murph and Tommo's more immediate problem was hauling County back into the promotion race. Success was hanging in the balance. They took a tumble away to Archie Gemmill's relegation-worried Rotherham side, and lost to top-of-the-table, Swindon. Only a 4-2 win at home to Bristol Rovers salvaged the results. Gemmill played under Murph at Derby County, and Bristol Rovers manager John Ward played for him at Lincoln. Ward spoke to the *Football Post* of his respect for his former boss's enthusiasm and knowledge of the game.

'If I was a chairman, I'd put my faith in him. For Colin's sake, I hope they win promotion, so long as it's not at our expense!'

The home support against Bristol Rovers gave Murph a temporary stay of execution. Promotion still seemed within reach. The fans clapped the team off the pitch with a fresh sense of optimism and gave the famous Notts County anthem its first outing in several months. To the tune of 'On top of Old Smokey' they roared the song which has only three lines:

> *I had a wheelbarrow. The wheel fell off.*
> *I had a wheelbarrow. The wheel fell off.*
> *County, County, County!*

Murph could savour the moment, but it was better that he didn't think of the original lyrics of the traditional folksong.

'On top of Old Smokey, all covered with snow, I lost my true lover, for courtin' too slow.'

Six games to go until the end of the season; only time would tell if Murph and Tommo were courting too slow. Tommo believed the management pair were on target; the purchase of ten new players and two more on-loan additions was paying off. Burnley who suffered relegation alongside County had only two loan signings to their name. The Clarets were fifth from bottom, while the Magpies were fourth from top.

A new deal struck with Sky Sports guaranteed First Division clubs an automatic payment of £650,000. Pavis was desperate for promotion. He wanted to recoup some of the £1.4m he had spent on replacement players. He only needed to look at the Birmingham success story to see what was possible. Second Division champions the previous season, the Blues had doubled their season ticket sales within a year.

Faced with the last league game of the season away to Chesterfield, County still had a remote chance of bagging automatic promotion, and the Spireites were still in contention for the play-offs. In the time-honoured end-of-season scramble, Oxford United smashed Peterborough to grab second place, and Blackpool won at York to finish third. Chesterfield converted a penalty to drop County into fourth. The play-off semi-finals beckoned, with Murph pitted against fifth-placed former Derby running mate, Dario Gradi.

In the run-up to the first leg, Gradi enjoyed the underdog's relative lack of pressure. During his 13 years in charge at Gresty Road, he had never spent more than £80,000 on a player and faced a constant battle to balance the books. Although the pair disagreed with how the game should be played in the lower divisions, Gradi had a great respect for Murph's judgement, not least in his ability to spot a player. He expected the County team would be like every Murph team, industrious and well organised. They would try to wear Crewe down. Gradi didn't expect that Crewe would be 2-0 up at Gresty Road within 20 minutes. After a rollicking from Murph and Tommo in the dressing room at half-time, County clawed it back when Martindale came off the subs' bench to score an injury-time equaliser. The 950 away fans turned up the volume. They knew County were only 90 minutes away from their fifth trip to Wembley in six years.

Pavis urged all local football supporters to get behind the team. It didn't matter if they were County, Forest or Mansfield fans, their vocal support could make all the difference. Notts County averaged home gates of only 5,000 for the season, but 9,640 fans took up the chairman's call to attend the second leg of the play-off semi-final. Crewe changed their side and their tactics, hit the ball long and tried to match County for power and strength. But a screaming volley from Martindale marked his 26th goal of the season and showed why he picked up the Second Division golden boot before the game. Murph took great satisfaction that Crewe barely created a clear-cut chance. A 1-0 victory proved enough to beat his erstwhile number two.

Pavis enjoyed stepping into the spotlight. He had poured £3m of his own money into the club and felt vindicated by his choice of managers. A former board member at the City Ground, the chairman had watched Forest move from the bottom of the old Second Division to two European Cup Final wins (now the UEFA Champions League). He dreamt of similar glory at Meadow Lane.

Champagne flowed in the dressing room after the Crewe semi-final match, but Pavis noted how Murph was happy to sit with a mug of builder's tea. The general manager accepted the plaudits for reaching the play-off final at the first attempt, but he insisted that trimming the wages bill had been a bigger achievement. He joined the club when too many players were on lucrative long-term contracts. By selling them on, he imposed a new pay structure and stripped £250,000 a year from the wages bill.

With Crewe out of the promotion race, County looked forward to another trip to north-west London. As ticket sales opened for the Wembley showdown, Bradford City fans rushed to their phones. They had never played under the Twin Towers before. Notts County were old hands; they had won two consecutive play-off finals under Neil Warnock. Murph thought that Tommo as team manager should lead the boys out onto the pitch. But Tommo deferred to the 'senior man' and insisted that Murph should do the honours. Like a father beaming with parental pride, Pavis explained to the press that the 'You first!' discussion was typical of the respect which existed between the pair.

It was Murph's second time at Wembley as a team official. He was sitting on the bench as reserve team coach when First Division champions Derby County beat FA Cup winners West Ham in the 1975 Charity Shield. Twenty-one years later, he could only hope for the same result. The general manager rubbished the theory that the team should go to Wembley to enjoy the day; winning was the only thing that mattered. He warned that other players and teams made it to Wembley and forgot how to play. It mustn't happen to County.

Throughout the season, the odds were stacked against Murph and Tommo's men; the play-off final would be no different. Bradford clinched their place in the final with nine wins in their last 11 league games. They took almost 30,000 fans to Wembley, three times the number of County's supporters. The Magpies fielded a young side. Only Gary Strodder and Tony Agana had considerable league experience. Eighteen-year-old Shaun Derry pulled on the number two shirt, promoted through the ranks of Murph's injured players. Only a month earlier, he was still a YTS trainee.

On Wembley's manicured turf, experience showed. Notts didn't pass the ball out to their on-loan winger, Steve Finnan, and the team didn't settle down. Eight minutes in, and they were a goal adrift. Murph couldn't criticise the desire and discipline of his players, but they were an inexperienced side. Seemingly jinxed by Murph's warning, they had forgotten how to play. A second Bradford goal after half-time killed the game. As the final whistle blew, the players trudged off the pitch. They returned in tears to the County dressing room.

Sitting next to Murph on the team bus back to Nottingham, Tommo cursed their bad luck.

'Steven, what are you so upset about?' Murph said.

'Col, we could have been playing in the First Division next season.'

'Yeah but think of all those unhappy Sunday mornings when we'd got beat. We're better off where we are!'

'F***ing hell, Col, I'm not so sure about that!'

The close season was a quiet time for the management pair; a midfield playmaker to feed the front men proved elusive. Pavis slammed the greed of a new breed of footballer and said he wouldn't break his wage structure for anyone. And Murph and Tommo vowed to play a more entertaining game, while still pushing for promotion. But County's captain, Strodder, warned against getting carried away with passing the ball. In the Second Division he said you had to be direct; get the ball up to the strikers, play it out wide and get the crosses in. Promotion wouldn't be easy. The Second Division looked strong. Newly relegated Watford, Millwall and Luton Town would all be determined challengers.

Murph feared the long-term fallout from a play-off defeat. He said that beaten clubs tended to move into a downward spiral and end up sacking their managers within the year. He didn't intend to be one of them. But six league and cup games into the 1996/97 season, and only one win, Murph blamed the 'Wembley blues'.

'But people should beware. Whatever I've done over 20 years in management, if I've been in a hole, I've crawled out of it,' he said to Stapleton from the *Evening Post*.

Murph wasn't crawling out fast enough for the travelling fans. A 1-0 away defeat to Wycombe Wanderers, and only six goals in ten league games. Chants rang and banners unfurled around Adams Park. It was the same message Murph received at Southend three years before. Only the chairman's name had changed. This time the banners read, 'PAVIS AND MURPHY OUT'.

Complaints from the fans filled the weekly letters page of the *Football Post*. They didn't hold back from telling Murph what they thought of him. It was the worst County side they had seen in 51 years. Murph had driven a wedge between the club and its followers. Murph, Pavis and Thompson should give the fans an early Christmas present and leave the club.

Pavis was quick to respond to the criticism. He published a full-page diatribe in the next matchday programme against Bristol Rovers, couched as an interview.

'What especially niggles the chairman,' the anonymous author wrote, 'is that the antagonists seem to totally miss the point that without his financial backing at this time, we would almost certainly go out of business.'

The headline and the body of the text left no room for misinterpretation.

'Chairman says he's ready to go.'

The club owed Pavis £2.3m. He had guaranteed a further £1m of overdraft. Debts were growing at a rate of £7,000 a week. Pavis named a price of £3m to sell the club. There were no takers, but he stoked an army of critics. The article spawned a run on the contents of Nottingham's airing cupboards. Protest banners which started out as pillowcases, extended to king-size sheets. To ease the pressure of running the club, Pavis appointed Geoff Davey as managing director. Davey joined County from Lincoln; he knew both Murph and Tommo well.

Pavis looked with envy at what was happening at Nottingham Forest. They sat third from bottom in the Premier League, but a takeover was still in the balance with 14 bids to buy the club. Frank Clark, the troubled Geordie manager, said he had so many problems he didn't know where to start. Murph kept smiling and put up an optimistic front. If he gave in to the stresses of the job, he knew the battle would be lost. His number one reason to be cheerful; Pavis had backed his judgement in the transfer market, dipped into his own back pocket again and found £300,000 to sign Steve Finnan from Birmingham. Designed to lift the supporters and the club, Finnan was the wideman the fans wanted; already tried and tested after a three-month loan deal in the run-up to the play-off final. Murph liked what he saw in the quiet Irishman, and later Fulham and Liverpool liked it too. Almost a decade later, Finnan helped bring the UEFA Champions League trophy back to Anfield. It was Liverpool's fifth European Cup title.

But the high-profile signing didn't stop Murph from coming under fire. After County's fourth home defeat of the season, 2-1 against Shrewsbury Town, a band of 30 fans occupied the back of the Jimmy Sirrel Stand. They refused to leave the ground. Murph claimed he didn't feel under pressure; that only came from poor performances and lack of opportunities. He argued that neither of those situations applied. He watched what he described as 'a riveting second-half performance' against Shrewsbury. Despite the positive spin, Lady Luck seemed to have deserted him. The Magpies faced their second match since Finnan joined without their star signing. While County were playing at Kenilworth Road, Finnan was in Dublin representing the Republic of Ireland U21s.

Murph railed against the rules which allowed Premier League clubs to take the weekend off for international matches, while they forced lower-league clubs to honour their domestic fixtures. He said if managers had the skill to develop their own players or were talented in the transfer market, the rules penalised their success. It was a transitory irritation; the bigger problem was a 2-0 loss away to Luton Town. It left County floundering in the league, one notch above the relegation zone. The press speculated if County didn't crush non-league minnows Newcastle Town in their opening FA Cup game, Murph would be out of a job. Despite the pressure, the general manager showed no signs of feeling the strain. Interviewed by Ian Ladyman at the *Evening Post*, Murph said the pressure didn't differ from playing Crewe in the play-offs or Bradford in the final.

'You have to be of good temperament and the most important

factor, you have to believe you will win the next match. You have to deal with pressure with the minimum of fuss.'

Murph sounded convincing when he said that Newcastle would be just another game, but the statistics suggested otherwise. Nineteen managers in English league football had already left their jobs since the start of the season. Notts County had the worst record in front of goal in the Football League. Murph was hanging on to the job by his fingernails, but he had two trump cards up his sleeve. The Finnan signing was a vote of confidence, and if Pavis sacked his management duo, he would have to make a very public admission that he had got it wrong. For the fourth time in two years.

Murph still had the support of the board and local journalists, but the *Football Post* continued to fill its weekly letters pages with complaints from the fans. Some claimed to have stopped venturing to away games, berated by their fellow supporters for showing positive appreciation for the team. More crucially, the players were breaking ranks. Defender Shaun Murphy, Player of the Season for the last two years, made it clear he was keen to leave the club. Martindale said the continual changes to the forward line had knocked his confidence in front of goal. Murph had failed to decide on his favoured pairing up front. He paid the price with an unsettled strike force.

It risked overshadowing his achievement of tackling the financial problems of the club. The £250,000 cut in the annual wage bill and £1.5m generated from player transfers were keeping the Magpies afloat. Murph knew he had made progress in his 18 months as general manager, but the 'Murphy Out' campaign was gathering pace. He didn't know if he would get time to follow his ideas through. His relationship with his chairman was straining at the edges; a barrage of phone calls was grinding Murph down. Day and night the phone rang at home. Murph's wife Judith remembers picking up the phone at one o'clock in the morning.

'Colin, it's the chairman,' she said, handing Murph the receiver.

'Tell him I'm repairing the roof!' Murph replied.

It was not unknown for managers to be harangued at home by chairmen in that era, but times have changed and in the modern game, a bombardment of late-night calls would be viewed as 'unnecessary interference'.

Pavis was a man under pressure. To compound the club's problems, Notts County faced a fresh compensation bid from Southend. The Football League Commission had thrown out Southend's claims that County poached Tommo 18 months before, but Vic Jobson was adamant that his caretaker manager had shaken hands on a deal, days before he left Roots Hall. Although the Football League's regulations didn't allow for an appeal where there was no financial penalty, Southend's QC argued that the club incurred a penalty by paying the costs of the case. The High Court ruled Southend had the right to a second hearing. The Blues may have regretted their victory when they came up against County's defence.

Murph liked James Hunt QC as soon as he met him — an outstanding barrister with a lifelong love of literature. Hunt met with Murph and Tommo to go through the details of the case. The general manager questioned the barrister's thinking.

'Mr Hunt, can I bring you to a point of law?'

'Mr Murphy, do I tell you how to pick a football team?'

'No.'

'Then don't tell me about a bloody point of law!' Hunt boomed.

The general manager kept quiet. The barrister did his job. And County won the case.

Ten days before Christmas, Murph was grateful that Brian Clough turned up in the County directors' box for a home match against Rotherham. It was Clough's first appearance for three years at Meadow Lane; designed to quash rumours of his ill health. It was also a welcome distraction from a lacklustre 0-0 draw against a team which was lying bottom of the Second Division. Murph reflected after the match how County played a very direct, positive game in the previous season. The fans didn't like it, but it won matches. This season they were playing a less direct game, which had maybe reduced the positivity of their play. If he had a certain type of striker in the box, he might have scored a goal out of 'error, chaos or bravery' but he had footballers in the box and the only thing they were going to score was a good footballing goal. Put more simply, 'We didn't score and therein lies the problem.'

They were still the lowest scoring team in the Football League; wherein lay the problem. Cold comfort that three days later, Frank Clark, Murph's counterpart at Nottingham Forest, was forced to resign. Murph recognised the irony. Clark's biggest success was signing Stan Collymore from Southend, and his biggest mistake, letting him go to Liverpool for £8.5m without a replacement striker in the wings.

On a blustery Friday night in the week before Christmas, Notts County played away to Dario Gradi's Crewe Alexandra, seven months after the play-off semi-finals. Revenge is a dish best served cold. County were outclassed; Robbie Savage and Danny Murphy bossed the midfield and Crewe crushed County in a 3-0 defeat. At the end of the match, Murph and Tommo took a dejected walk across the Gresty Road pitch. They glanced up at the stand where the away fans lay in wait. A makeshift banner caught their eye, a king-size white sheet with uneven black lettering and a simple message.

'TROWSERS F.C. MURPHY + PAVIS MUST GO.'

A goodwill greeting from the Nottinghamshire Sunday Football League team.

Murph turned to Tommo and said, 'Well, old friend, it looks like we're on our way out.'

'It doesn't say Thompson. It just says Murphy. I reckon I'm still all right!' Tommo laughed.

Pavis wasn't at the game to watch County's collapse, but Murph was under no illusions. County had scored only two goals in six league games. They were one place off the bottom of the table. Murph phoned Tommo over the weekend.

'Steven, get a big bag and bring it in Monday.'

'What's the bag for?'

'We're getting the f***ing sack! We'll go in Monday, take the bikes, the balls, the whole bleeding lot.'

On Monday morning, 23 December, Murph and Tommo drove to Meadow Lane. They met Pavis in Murph's office. Tommo remembers the conversation well. The chairman stood behind the large marble table and cleared his throat.

'I'm sorry Colin, this is the thing I didn't want to do. I've got a tear in my eye.'

'What've you been doing?' Murph said, 'Cutting an onion?'

'Colin, you know what I mean. I'm going to have to let you go.'

Murph didn't move.

'Chairman, could you just give me and Steven a minute together to gather our thoughts?'

Pavis nodded. He walked out of the room. And Murph turned to the chairman's favourite rubber plant and peed in the pot.

'F***ing hell, Steven, that should kill it!'

The chairman returned, and Murph asked about the financial situation. Eighteen months earlier, he and Tommo had signed generous three-year contracts; 12 months' money if they got the sack in the first year, nine months' if they were released in the second, and six months' in the third. Pavis confirmed he would honour his agreement. Murph and Tommo would receive nine months' money in three months' time. Of all the sackings at Notts County in the previous ten years, Pavis said this was the most difficult.

He couldn't fault the financial impact of his management team. Pavis still had a great deal of respect for his general manager, but sitting second from bottom in the Second Division, he couldn't wait any longer. Murph's relationship with the fans compounded the poor results. When he sold the crowd's favourites, White, Devlin and Legg, he hadn't tried to explain himself. The fans hadn't taken to him or his peculiar turn of phrase. They said they couldn't understand what Murph said. Living outside the city, in the family home in Lincoln, he was viewed as an outsider.

Sacked two days before Christmas, it was unusual for Murph to have any time at home over the festive season. If he looked at the TV listings for Christmas Day, he might have guessed who would replace him. It wasn't the fans' favourite, Neil Warnock, nor the bookies' favourite, Burnley number two John Ward. No, at 12.40pm on BBC2, Murph could watch Woody Allen in *Play it Again, Sam*. Former Blackpool boss Sam Allardyce, out of work since losing to Bradford in the play-off semi-finals, was about to make his big-screen appearance at Meadow Lane.

Allardyce embodied the precarious nature of football management. After Blackpool finished third in the Second Division, their highest league position in 19 seasons, chairman Owen Oyston sacked him from his prison cell. Pavis showed less generosity to his incoming manager than he did to his outgoing team. He offered an 18-month deal with a year's extension if Allardyce kept the club in the Second Division. He didn't. They finished 24th at the end of the season. But Allardyce bounced back in spectacular fashion; Third Division champions with six games left to play, the following year.

The local press raked over Murph and Tommo's demise. The sacking was inevitable, but journalists wrote less with a sense of condemnation than regret. A young Ian Ladyman, future football editor of the *Daily Mail*, said it was a shame Murph hadn't connected with the fans.

'For the Colin Murphy the fans didn't see was one with a wicked sense of humour, an infectious laugh and an admirable sense of optimism.'

Murph was well mannered, entertaining and good company,

the sportswriter wrote, but nobody outside the club saw much of that.

Sacked from Notts County, it forced a parting of the ways for the management team. Tommo joined the coaching staff at his hometown club Sheffield United, but Murph ventured further afield. He moved from Meadow Lane to the Red River Delta of Vietnam. From denigration to adulation, Murph was in for quite a surprise.

11

GOOD MORNING, VIETNAM
VIETNAM NATIONAL TEAM

Murph stepped off the shuttle bus into the oppressive heat of Noi Bai airport and caught his breath. He stopped for a second to take in the scene. Six short-sleeved officials formed an orderly queue on the tarmac in front of him. The official reception committee of the Vietnam Football Federation (VFF) and the government Sports Department had come to meet him. Murph patted down his checked blazer and striped silk tie, slipped one hand into his pocket, and cleared his throat. An eager representative stepped forward, thrust an enormous bunch of pink peach blossoms into his outstretched hand and bowed gently.

'Mr Colin, welcome to Hanoi.'

Mr Colin grinned broadly. He had travelled 6,000 miles east of Meadow Lane to take up the post of national coach of the Socialist Republic of Vietnam, and he jolly well intended to enjoy it. As the TV cameras rolled to celebrate his arrival, Murph spoke to the English-language daily newspaper, the *Viet Nam News*. The long-term future of Vietnamese football excited him. They were a fast-developing national side. He couldn't wait to take over, he told the reporter. The charm offensive had begun. After two periods of disappointment at Southend and Notts County, Murph needed to make this job work.

Sports brokerage firm Strata approached Murph in the spring of 1997. He was armed with a glowing reference from Manchester United manager Alex Ferguson, another early advocate of coaching, whom Murph had met through the FA. Murph jumped at the chance of a move abroad. The export market for British football managers was well established.

Roy Hodgson guided the Switzerland national team to both the last 16 of the 1994 World Cup and Euro 96 qualification. Terry Venables was managing an Australian side which would narrowly miss out on World Cup qualification. And Terry Yorath, Murph's old adversary at Bradford City, had vastly improved the stock of the Lebanon team. Encouraged by the success of his fellow Brits abroad, Murph felt excited by the job opportunity. He left behind a country on a tidal wave of change. Tony Blair had won a landslide victory for a Labour government after 18 years in opposition. And closer to Vietnam, on the Southeast Asia continent, the sovereignty of Hong Kong had just reverted from British to Chinese rule.

Murph faced his own set of challenges. The Vietnamese national team had fielded three different coaches in as many months. The National Football Championships (NFC), the top level of domestic football, lay in complete disarray; plagued with violent incidents on the pitch and match fixing off it. Outgoing prime minister Vo Van Kiet tried to stem the tide of corruption. He called for top officials to be suspended and ordered them to take part in self-criticism and self-punishment sessions. Although self-flagellation satisfied Communist ideology, match fixing proved more lucrative. Some attempts were as amateur as the league itself; back passes into open goals, which infuriated the fans of the domestic game and left teammates in tears.

Despite local corruption charges which brought football into disrepute, Murph could not have arrived in Vietnam at a better time. An English football frenzy was kicking off in Asia, fuelled by increased exposure to mass media channels. No longer confined to traditional regional support in Hong Kong and Singapore, vast numbers of new fans were emerging throughout Vietnam and Thailand; all desperate to pin their colours to the red, white or blue mast of an English Premier League team.

They loved Arsenal's Dennis Bergkamp for his flair and creativity. They had admired Manchester United's Eric Cantona for his passion and unpredictability. And they would embrace Murph for his promise to boost team morale and his British passport. England held most-favoured nation status in Vietnam, as the founding fathers of the country's favourite sport and home of the Premier League.

The football frenzy was no overnight phenomenon; its hungry belly had been rumbling for some time, nourished first by the 1982 World Cup finals in Spain when the state-controlled Vietnam News Agency produced a small football news sheet for the first time. The local population, starved of western influence and culture, loved it. The government didn't and promptly banned its publication. But the groundswell proved relentless, and by the time England hosted Euro 96, it was unstoppable.

The Vietnamese nation had fallen in love with football from live coverage of international matches, a by-product of the decade old Doi Moi (renovation) policy of economic reform. This market-driven capitalist system favoured not just the brave, but the resourceful. Enterprising noodle stall holders rigged up televisions in the densely populated side streets of the Old Quarter of Hanoi, beneficiaries of the recent phenomenon of reliable electricity. And three generations of locals gorged on their favourite diet of piping hot pho bo and European football. Every game screened live. Every goal celebrated.

The swathe of English clubs, which went public on the London Stock Exchange in the 1990s, realised they were no longer simply football clubs, but global brands. For the likes of Manchester and Leeds United, merchandising revenue was becoming big business, and Vietnam offered a captive and growing market. They didn't just want the mug, the poster and the T-shirt. They wanted the foreign football coach too. Murph knew he was no Alex Ferguson or Arsène Wenger, but he would become a big drawcard in Hanoi. And he would enjoy the ride.

The VFF had suffered two acrimonious divorces from foreign coaches: Edson Tavares from Brazil and Karl-Heinz Weigang from Germany. Both men left the job following disputes with the governing body. The VFF wanted someone with a fighting spirit who would settle the national squad. Fifty-three years old with 21 years of management experience, Murph fitted the bill. Bored with bombing up and down the country for lower league games, or 'selling on the Collymores and Fashanus with little fanfare', he was ready to embrace a complete change.

'As I was not going to be appointed Manchester United manager, I didn't really see the point in doing the same old thing,' he later said to Ian Chadband from the *Sunday Times*.

And to the VFF's delight, Murph accepted a short-term contract.

The resignation of interim coach Tran Duy Long made Murph's path to the top job easier. Tran sent a letter to the Sports Department after two months in the role, cataloguing his own shortcomings and asking to be released. The department happily obliged. In early June, lowly Turkmenistan, 20 places below them in the FIFA world rankings, punished Vietnam 4-0 in Ho Chi Minh City's home stadium. And only days after Tran's resignation, in their final Group Eight World Cup qualifier match in Beijing, China battered them by the same scoreline.

When Murph took over the squad, Vietnam had finished bottom of their Asian World Cup qualifying group with an unfortunate goal tally; two goals for, and 21 against. They had a humiliating zero points. After six consecutive defeats, the team lacked any kind of competitive spirit. Morale was at an all-time low. During the 1960s and 1970s, South Vietnam's football team was an unstoppable force in the region, and one of the best sides in Asia. Even the US bombing of Hanoi in 1966 hadn't disrupted the running of the Premier Football Championship in North Vietnam.

Murph was determined to reignite the passion of the national team, no longer separated into North and South Vietnam, but unified as one nation at the end of the Vietnam War. Rubbing his hands together, he told the *Viet Nam News*, 'I'm looking forward to the job ahead. As long as I can work peacefully. By that I mean not be interrupted.'

The VFF couldn't promise no interruptions. They liked committees and set one up to assist their new manager. Not keen on the idea of running a team by consensus, Murph said, 'Players are not stupid. They can see the coaches who just pay lip service to the committees, and they can see the coaches who are prepared to stand up like a man and fight their corner.'

His first chance to fight the players' corner would be at the 19th Southeast Asian (SEA) Games, a biennial multi-sports competition established for the Southeast Asia continent.

'Like the European Championships for us, or the African Cup for Ghana. It's the biggest competition after the World Cup – and it begins in October!' he said.

Murph's experience of scouting players the length and breadth of England prepared him well for his new role. Instead of bombing up and down the M1 in his white Mercedes, he flew in the relative comfort of Vietnam Air, 1,000 miles from the capital city of Hanoi, in the north, to the commercial centre, Ho Chi Minh City in the south. The city of Saigon was renamed Ho Chi Minh City after the fall of South Vietnam in 1975, and the dual names for the city are still used interchangeably today.

In his hunt for fresh blood, Murph watched every NFC team play. Twenty-five players took to the pitch in Vietnam's first friendly against Hanoi Army Club U19s. A 0-0 draw failed to impress the domestic press, but Murph made no apologies. As well as training the national squad, the VFF had employed him to set up a junior system for young players, aged 10 to 16.

He described the challenge to Ian Chadband, 'Like doing Glenn Hoddle's and Howard Wilkinson's job simultaneously.'

Hoddle, the England manager, and Wilkinson, the recently

appointed technical director of the FA, might not have accepted the job offer.

Unfazed by the 1,000-mile commute, within four weeks of starting his scouting mission, Murph had hunted down eight new players to join the 25-man squad. A three-month run up to the SEA Games gave him little time to prepare, but he knew he wouldn't fail from lack of effort.

The Games attracted over 4,300 athletes from ten countries. This time they would be more than their usual sporting showcase; they would be a test of friendship in the region. The financial crisis, which started in Thailand in July, would grip much of Southeast Asia. As the Thai baht collapsed, currency contagion spread across Indonesia, Singapore, Malaysia and the Philippines. All the Games' participants were suffering from a loss of economic confidence. The competition needed to reinvigorate the sense of community in the region, and Murph needed to regain football credibility for his new paymaster. There was a tremendous amount at stake.

The draw for the SEA Games did him no favours. Vietnam faced Group B contenders Indonesia, Malaysia, Laos and the Philippines, far tougher opponents than the teams which defending champions Thailand played in Group A. Murph realised he faced greater problems than the group selection. Although over 20 years had passed since the end of the Vietnam War, the country was still suffering from a lost generation. Over two million Vietnamese citizens are estimated to have been killed during 30 years of post-World War Two conflict, first shaking off the French colonial administration, then in the prolonged bloody battle against the United States.

Murph's assistant coach served in the war against the Americans. Murph asked him what he did.

'I killed people.'

'You shot people? With a gun?'

'Yes,' his coach said quietly. 'I was a very good shot.'

Murph didn't underestimate the long-term impact of the

Vietnam War. The team of footballers Murph inherited were financially poorer and physically weaker than their Thai and Indonesian counterparts, but he admired their level of skill.

'There's no shadow of doubt in my mind that technically they are English Division One,' he said. 'They hit these balls around and they pass these balls around with alarming accuracy; short balls, long balls, one touch, two touch.'

Two years before Murph's arrival in Hanoi, Vietnam enjoyed its greatest moment of sporting glory for decades. Against all odds, the national team fought its way through to the football final of the 18th SEA Games in Chang Mai. The match ended with a humiliating 4-0 defeat against host nation Thailand. Thousands of Vietnamese football fans took to the streets of Ho Chi Minh City, hurling stones and Molotov cocktails at the police. Two years later, the nation still felt the pain of the defeat. In a country with a population of over 79 million, Murph estimated that two-thirds of them were fanatical about football. In an interview with sports journalist Vicky Wayman from the BBC, he talked about the nation's passion for the game.

'They love it. They live it. They can't get enough of it. Their passion is huge. It's really exciting to be working in a football arena where everyone cares.'

These were Murph's type of people. They played football in the streets, in the town square and on every available stretch of wasteland; bare foot and bare chested, in 100ºF of heat and almost unbearable humidity.

Murph had learnt to work in the intense heat in Saudi Arabia, and became accustomed to the climate in Hanoi, a city with only two distinct seasons, rainy and dry.

'But the one thing I really miss,' he said to Wayman, 'is the cricket. That's summer to me.'

In the middle of the English cricket season, Central TV despatched a film crew to Vietnam, to make a four-part documentary of the man who had managed clubs on both sides of the River Trent. Reporter Dennis Coath stood in Ho Chi Minh

Square between the Communist Party headquarters and the Presidential Palace, and spoke about 'Murph's mission'. He bubbled over with enthusiasm.

'If Vietnam win the Southeast Asia Championships, it'll be President Colin Murphy in there!'

'It's a tall order,' Murph said. 'If we succeed, the satisfaction would be tremendous. If I fail, I'll probably end up at the bottom of the Red River with all the alligators!'

Murph had two months in which to prepare his players; to monitor their fitness, training, discipline and diet. He also wanted to toughen them up. As he watched his star striker Le Huynh Duc, known as Vietnam's Maradona, play in training, he joked with his assistant coach, 'Every session we must say to number three of the Army, 100,000 dong, every time you kick him!'

Murph pumped his fist and clapped his hands as he spoke. He knew the players needed to be battle hardened, but he also admired their resilience.

'They've all got blooming strong legs. Now if you ride a bike from five to 16 years of age, it must affect your muscle development. That's an exact science. Maybe that's why they clip the ball around so correctly.'

As the SEA Games approached, few gave Vietnam any chance of bringing back a medal, but Murph encouraged the team to ignore their critics.

'The minute you get on that plane, you have to believe you can win,' he said.

His unbridled enthusiasm uplifted not just the players, but the entire country. Murph appreciated the power of football in the national psyche.

'It's part of their lives. They get up at half past five in the morning, and play football before they go to work, or before they go to school. To an extent, it's frightening for a coach if you were to consider the consequences of failure,' he said to Dennis Coath, blinking nervously as he spoke.

The reporter suggested the national coach had no cause for

concern. The Vietnamese nation greeted Murph as a messiah; his popularity had knocked record rice crops off the front pages of the national press. Murph's beaming face appeared everywhere, from the *Viet Nam News* to the central newspaper of the Communist Party of Vietnam. The government set up six national programmes to receive priority treatment, and sports development was one of them.

Both the prime minister and his deputy, come sports minister, made an official visit to Murph at the team's Soviet-built Olympic training facility. Vietnam's economy boasted the highest growth rate in Southeast Asia, and they wanted the standard of sport and sporting facilities to match the country's economic progress. The newly appointed prime minister recognised the growing importance of sport in Vietnam by granting the Sports Department ministerial status.

The decaying training facility with its reed-like grass fell far short of European standards, but speaking through an interpreter, the prime minister and his deputy expressed the hope that in ten or 20 years' time, Vietnam could qualify for the World Cup. Murph didn't disagree with them. Coath mused whether the Vietnamese could fully understand the man who had won a Golden Bull award for his legendary programme notes.

'Well, sign language is a wonderful, wonderful facility, Dennis, and if that don't work, it's smoke signals!' Murph said.

As he set off for the launch of the SEA Games in Jakarta, Murph's comment wasn't too far wide of the mark. Forest fires were raging through the Indonesian archipelago, and gauze masks and inhalers were last minute additions to the national team's kit.

At their opening match in the Gelora Senayan Main Stadium in Jakarta, the Vietnam players marvelled at the 110,000-capacity venue, almost five times the size of the national Hang Day Stadium in Hanoi. The Vietnamese dominated play in their opening battle against Group B favourites Malaysia, but went down 1-0 to an early opportunistic goal.

'We won in a losing match,' the *Lao Dong* newspaper

reported, and the voice of Vietnamese workers questioned the quality of the referee.

After his first competitive international, Murph praised the consistency of the team's football. He knew it took at least six months to put together a stable squad with a consistent style; he could only promise that the squad would perform to the best of their ability. Murph later admitted to the *Viet Nam News* that after the defeat against Malaysia, they were 'staring at death's door'. Vietnam would have to win their games against Indonesia and Laos to secure a second-round place, but he kept his faith in the grit and determination of his hastily assembled squad. In their second match against Indonesia, an 80,000-capacity crowd roared their support for the home nation. Yet Murph's boys refused to be intimidated. They survived a 52nd-minute sending off and treated the chain-smoking Indonesian coach to a dramatic finish; a final-minute equaliser and a gripping 2-2 draw.

Prime minister Phan Van Khai responded immediately with a personal letter of support to the team.

'I warmly congratulate coach Colin Murphy, the players and the rest of the coaching staff,' he wrote, 'for the effort and determination they displayed and for honouring the team, the flag and the nation.'

Former prime minister Vo Van Kiet praised the team with equal warmth but spoke less about the flag and more about the Singaporean referee.

'There were several reasons we failed to win the game, but the standard of refereeing was the main one.'

The dramatic scoreline fuelled the fervour of supporters back home in Vietnam. Thousands of cheering fans took to the streets of Hanoi. They wove their way through the '36 Streets' of the Old Quarter, flew red flags from the backs of scooters and motorbikes, and repeatedly honked their horns. Vietnam had to beat Laos and the Philippines in their remaining two fixtures, and hope that either group favourites Malaysia, or home nation Indonesia, would by some miracle lose. In the five anxious days before their next match against Laos, a country desperate for a footballing re-birth was daring to believe.

Vietnam marched on in their campaign with a confident 2-1 victory against their western neighbours. The local press reported they could have scored six or seven more. In their final qualifier against the Philippines, Vietnam had to win by at least two goals to have any chance of progressing to the next round. They did it in style and cruised to a 3-0 victory. And then the nation held its collective breath. The deciding Group B match between Laos and Malaysia played out later that day; the amateurs unevenly pitted against the professionals. Malaysia, the favourites with two wins and one defeat in their opening games, needed a win to progress.

'Now it's up to our Laotian brothers!' an excited Vietnamese TV commentator said.

By the 89th minute of the decisive game, Laos held Malaysia to an agonising 0-0 stalemate. The whole of Vietnam urged the underdogs to score. And somehow, against the run of play, Keolakhone Channiphone, Laos' number 13, ripped through the Malaysian defence and blasted a rocket of a long-range shot into the corner of the Malaysian net. The final whistle blew. Laos had beaten Malaysia by the slimmest of margins. And Vietnam had leapfrogged their way to the semi-finals of the SEA Games.

Two thousand miles away, the incredulous city of Hanoi erupted with spontaneous joy. Thousands of people took to the streets; young and old, men and women, die-hard supporters and football agnostics alike. Vietnam broke out into wild celebrations; an outpouring of emotion which the younger generation had not experienced before. Late in the night, they surged to Ho Chi Minh's Mausoleum in the heart of the capital city, curiously drawn to the solemn site, sacred to all of Vietnam. A site where over 50 years before, Ho Chi Minh, the father of modern Viet-nam, read the Declaration of Independence and broke the ties of almost 100 years of French colonial rule.

Ba Dinh Square, the home of Ho Chi Minh's Mausoleum, could accommodate 200,000 people on state occasions, but informal gatherings were discouraged. The *Viet Nam News* reported that the young people who flocked to Ba Dinh Square had grown up with their parents' definition of what it was to be Vietnamese. For the first time, they felt they could write their own rules.

The human crocodile of fans swept through the teeming streets. Motorbikes laden with three or four passengers jostled with jam-packed cars. Young people hung out of street windows and clambered on car roofs, waving their red and golden flags.

'Long live Vietnam! Long live Laos! Long live Uncle Ho!' they shouted.

As they snaked past the Hoan Kiem lake on their way to pay homage at the Laotian Embassy, they banged their drums and sounded their horns. And they acknowledged the two unlikely saviours who had made it possible.

'Long live great Colin Murphy! Long live Viet Laos!' they shouted.

Vietnam hosted street parties when they made it through to the SEA semi-finals in 1995, but nothing compared to the scale of these celebrations. The *Viet Nam News* reported how people showed a new sense of self-belief, not just in football, but in the country's future. Their previous success needed no longer be dismissed as beginners' luck. A country ravaged by war was united by sport. It could believe in its future. But first, the national team had a job to do. Group B runners-up Vietnam, would meet Group A winners Thailand, in the semi-final. Thailand had long been the front-runners in Southeast Asian football and Vietnam's nemesis at the SEA Games. From Hanoi to Ho Chi Minh City, an anxious nation awaited their sporting fate.

Murph's boys walked out on to the pitch at the Senayan Main Stadium, surprised at the warmth of the reception. A near capacity crowd of 100,000 roared their support for Vietnam, eager for the underdogs to face the home nation in the final. But like his Notts County team in the Wembley play-offs, Murph's boys struggled to settle into the game. Within three minutes they were a goal down. In a game of cat and mouse, the reigning champions overpowered their opponents and dominated possession. Until a Thai defender clambered on the back of Vietnam's Maradona in an aerial challenge and gave away a penalty.

Against the run of play, in the 35th minute, the boys in red and gold scored an equaliser. But Thailand returned in the second half at a breathtaking pace. A 56th-minute goal was disallowed and then re-instated. Murph's boys were 2-1 down and couldn't break the Thai defence.

The fans at home urged them to keep up the fight. In the 89th minute, Vu Minh Hieu, Vietnam's attacking midfielder, took a last-ditch free kick from the edge of the Thai box. His right-footed strike beat the keeper, only to curl narrowly wide of the post. Murph clasped his head in his hands. And millions of Vietnam fans the length of the country followed suit. The final whistle blew on a 2-1 defeat. Thailand had denied Murph and his fledgling national team their fairytale ending.

They had only 48 hours to recover from the disappointment, and prepare for the losers' reward, a third place play-off match against Singapore. They were two teams only 12 places apart in the FIFA world rankings. In the 89th minute of the play-off game, Vietnam secured the result with a 20-yard belter. As the final whistle blew, Murph's Gold Star Warriors rushed to the side of the pitch, mobbed their beaming coach, and catapulted him high into the air. They had sealed football bronze. And along with it, Murph's reputation as the man who gifted football-mad Vietnam one of its greatest sporting comebacks.

In less than three months, he had not only transformed the morale of the national team. His new squad played a distinctive attacking game, no longer in danger of capitulating if the opposition scored an early goal. Thailand's head coach, Witthaya Laohakul, the first Thai to play for a European club in the German Bundesliga, complimented his English opponent. He said Vietnam were the only team which troubled them in the competition.

Murph had done more than enough to satisfy the Vietnamese people. After the team touched down at Noi Bai airport the following evening, over 10,000 supporters surged on to the runway to mob their returning heroes. The fans waved hastily drawn posters of their national coach.

'Hoan ho Colin Murphy!' ('Hurrah to Colin Murphy!'), the messages read.

A nation shows its love for their national coach, as Colin Murphy returns to Hanoi airport with his bronze medal winning team. (Photograph from the Murphy family collection)

The screaming fans swept Murph off the plane and threw him high above their heads; a commotion which forced the airport authorities to temporarily suspend all flights out of Hanoi.

'Mr Colin! Mr Colin!' the crowd yelled.

Mr Colin rode aloft a wave of supporters, soaking up the rapturous welcome; a bunch of orchids in one hand, and a slouch hat and briefcase in the other. Bundled into the team coach,

Murph and his boys heard the fans scrambling on to the roof above them. As they drove the 25 miles from the airport to the city centre, thousands of cheering fans lined the streets. An impromptu cavalcade of 500 motorbikes blocked the way ahead. In Hanoi, the fans forced Murph and his players to seek shelter in the central police station. At three o'clock in the morning, wearing a police helmet as a disguise, Murph was driven at 90mph through the crowded streets, still laden with national flags and banners. The warmth of the homecoming astounded him. It took some time for the reaction of this football-loving nation to sink in.

Encouraged by their bronze medal success, Murph outlined his major goals for the year ahead; to win the eight-nation Tiger Cup in Jakarta and reach the semi-finals of ASIAD 98 (the Asian Games). To win the Tiger Cup, they would have to beat Thailand, now eight-time champions of the SEA Games. Despite their ill-matched FIFA world rankings (119 played 65) Murph believed the Vietnamese team could bridge the gap in the months ahead. He was right. Vietnam did beat Thailand in the Tiger Cup, although as events unfolded, it was no longer with Murph as coach of the national team.

To mount a serious challenge on the world stage, Peter Velappan, general secretary of the Asian Football Confederation, told the VFF they needed to introduce professional football and stamp out the 'evil of match fixing'. Murph agreed with the pioneer of the commercialisation of Asian football, admiring the Malaysian's quiet demeanour, which hid a steely determination. The football administrator was a relentless advocate for Asian football in FIFA's European- and South American-dominated corridors of power.

Vietnam's top league would not turn professional until the year 2000, and it would not cure the plague of corruption in the domestic game, but the country was already embracing significant change. The state-run broadcaster, Vietnam Television, showed several hours of English and European football each week, and state-controlled publishers produced weekly football magazines.

Murph had developed a local cult following; schoolchildren

would cycle for miles from their rural homes simply to catch sight
of him. It didn't matter that he wasn't a well-known Premier
League manager, they were proud to have their own English
coach. Ian Chadband from the *Sunday Times* picked up on
Murph's story and interviewed Steve Boyle from the *Viet Nam
News*. Boyle confirmed an unlikely truth; a handful of faces were
instantly recognisable and revered in Vietnam; the first was President Tran Duc Luong, the second, prime minister Phan Van Khai
and the third, national team coach Colin Murphy.

'He's a sort of demi-god now,' Boyle said.

Chadband asked Murph what the Vietnamese people made
of him.

'Difficult to say, because you need to try to behave with an
element of modesty,' Murph said. 'The adulation is really embar-
rassing. You can't walk down the street without them coming up
to you, putting their arms round you, offering you lifts on their
rickshaw things. It's unadulterated enthusiasm, which is sometimes almost frightening, but they are lovely, lovely people.'

After the negativity he experienced in England, it was difficult
to adjust to adulation in Vietnam. But he had immersed himself in
an alien culture. He shopped in the teeming outdoor food markets,
had his hair cut in a barber's chair on the side of the street. And he
ate snake and dog at banquets, which were held in his honour.
This unusual sensitivity to local customs brought its own rewards.

'As long as you're courteous and democratic, you can be in
charge of your own destiny,' he said to Chadband. 'I'm not a
Hoddle or a Maldini, but I'm controlling football in a country
where the potential is surely unsurpassed.'

It's unlikely that Glenn Hoddle or even Paolo Maldini,
captain of the Italian national team, experienced hero-worship on
such an extraordinary scale. Though flattered by the adulation
and not averse to the media attention, Murph didn't allow it to
turn his head.

'I don't go far,' he said to Jonathan Birchall from the *Finan-*

cial Times. 'I have a beer at the Verandah Pub, and I go to the Metropole Hotel. It's bloody expensive, but I only go there to read the football results in the *South China Morning Post.*'

The Metropole, a five-star hotel nestled among French colonial architecture in the Old Quarter of Hanoi, had welcomed writers, heads of state and foreign dignitaries for the greater part of a century. And now football managers came to relax in its opulent surroundings. It was a world far removed from the lower leagues of English football, but it might not hold Murph's attention for long.

Five months after his first visit to Vietnam, Dennis Coath returned to film Murph in Saigon. As the two men rode through the streets in adjacent rickshaws, Murph smiled to camera and talked about his new life.

'It's an adventure. It's all about really wanting to seek new horizons, learn about new things and, of course, the boys, the team, have been marvellous,' he said.

Murph grinned at his travelling companion.

'Yesterday afternoon, Dennis, I was summoned to the chairman, and he said to me he was so pleased with the progress the team had made, they were going to give me a club car. Would I come along and meet him tomorrow at two o'clock for the handing over ceremony?'

Murph looked at his watch, then at the bicycle taxi.

'It's now 2.30 and here you see me in my new club car. These chairmen don't change, do they?'

Murph laughed at his local-issue company car, but he had just signed a lucrative one-year contract; $7,000-a-month salary, free accommodation, travel expenses, 60 days' annual leave and two return plane fares to England a year. Success at the SEA Games catapulted him into the public eye. As he stepped down from his new club car, young men jostled to greet him. A middle-aged man plumped his chest out for Murph to sign his shirt. Police officers stopped in the street to shake his hand. Coath saw the adulation of Vietnam's national coach but asked Murph what he missed most about England.

'Well, I miss my cricket, Dennis. I miss it very much, Collingwood Cricket Club. But I think the way things are going here, I'm going to start my own cricket club. I'll call it Vietnam Wanderers and we're going to play all our games away from home. There's enough googlies out here, and there's a few Chinamen!'

The gaffer wasn't troubled by political correctness in the late 1990s.

Colin Murphy receives a ceremonial welcome on his return from the 19th SEA Games. (Photograph from the Murphy family collection)

Shortly after Coath completed his mini documentary, Murph requested a two-week holiday to return home to Lincoln. With preparations underway for the Tet Festival, the Vietnamese Lunar New Year, the VFF approved a one-month break for their national coach. Four weeks passed, then another two. There was no sign of Murph, and no explanation of his unauthorised leave of absence. The local press speculated about problems with his contract of employment, recalling the hasty and acrimonious departure of

Murph's European predecessors. VFF contacted the Strata sports agency to track down their man. In early March 1998, the federation received a letter of explanation from their absent employee.

'It is with extreme personal and professional regret that I am unable to return to Vietnam to continue my position as national coach to the VFF, due to solely personal circumstances,' he wrote with great solemnity to the governing body.

Murph listed a catalogue of circumstances; his children Ben and Lucy were at delicate stages of their university careers, his wife was experiencing difficulties with her job, and the family home was up for sale.

Murph didn't mention he'd received a job offer from Tottenham Hotspur.

The English Football League was never far from Murph's thoughts. And perhaps that's why at the start of a new and lucrative 12-month contract, he abandoned adulation in Southeast Asia for the lure of White Hart Lane. Murph accepted the post of director of Spurs' youth academy. He didn't work out his notice period in Vietnam.

The *Viet Nam News* interviewed fans about the unexpected departure of their national coach. With quiet resignation, one supporter said, 'Mr Murphy has somehow damaged the good sympathy Vietnamese football fans reserved for him.'

He had disappointed the fans, but their reaction was far less vitriolic than when he abandoned Stockport County for Lincoln City, a decade before.

Some 20 years later, on a family holiday in Vietnam, I rode tandem on a motorbike past the former national football stadium in Hanoi. Amid the constant blaring of horns in a city famous for its five million motorbikes, I shouted to the driver to ask if he had heard of Colin Murphy, the former national coach of Vietnam. His response surprised me.

'Oh, yes, Mr Colin, bronze medal!' he shouted back, excited to hear that I was writing the life story of such a famous man.

After stopping at the stadium entrance to look through the

gates, I wandered on to the side of the pitch through a gap in the wrought-iron railings. The peeling pastel blue and yellow paint-work on the stands recalled the national stadium's former glory. The stadium has since been re-housed in a National Sports Complex, north-west of the city. Its new home deemed more befitting of the hosts of the 2003 SEA Games.

The former Hanoi stadium, now the Hang Day Stadium, looms over local streets lined with vendors selling replica Premier League football shirts. Ho Chi Minh's painted image looks down solemnly on the pitch from high above the main stand. His stern gaze seems to make judgement on the match fixing and the corruption scandals which plagued the national league in the 1990s, and still mar the reputation of Vietnamese football to this day. My driver beckoned to me from the shadows of the main stand. He was talking to a man in his early 30s, who stepped forward to shake my hand and subtly bowed his head.

'Mr Colin, very good man!' he said with some deference to the lady he now knew had the good fortune of knowing Mr Colin.

The man, wearing an unbranded, tight-fitting football shirt, could only have been a young boy when Murph coached Vietnam for less than a year. Two decades after their change of fortune in the 19th SEA Games, the country had not forgotten its first and only English coach. The top role in Vietnamese football does not include longevity in its job description. The memory of Murph was undimmed by the 18 coaches who had followed in his wake.

It made me wonder why Murph had left behind a football-loving nation which revered him. He smiled when I later told him of my chance encounter in Hanoi. He couldn't recall why he had left Vietnam, the detail fogged by the aftermath of his stroke. But he was certain of one thing; by leaving Vietnam, he had made the second biggest mistake of his life.

WANDERLUST

TOTTENHAM HOTSPUR, MYANMAR NATIONAL TEAM, ENGLAND U21S, CORK CITY, LEICESTER CITY, AND STOCKPORT COUNTY

A wanderlust, a taste for adventure, a nomadic character; all descriptions of Murph from people who know him well. Expressions which go some way to explain why he left Vietnam at the height of his success and returned to England as director of the youth academy at Tottenham Hotspur.

'I thought it was the ideal role for him,' said David Pleat, who invited Murph to work with him again at White Hart Lane.

'It's a massive job. Overseeing all the players, having a budget for contracts, being an overlord. I saw someone who was a very good organiser, an administrative coach. He could see other people and say he's a good coach, he's got imagination, he's not so good. Colin was good with his brain and his pen. He was ideal for the role. The job didn't last long though, did it?'

The restlessness returned. Murph left the Tottenham job after only 15 months. He couldn't resist an offer to go back to South-east Asia, taking charge of the fledgling national side of Myanmar, also known as Burma. A country placed 127th out of 202 FIFA-ranked countries in 1999. The constant yo-yoing between clubs didn't seem to diminish Murph's reputation or affect his ability to get a job. His amiable attitude, dedicated hard work and persistent networking always brought new opportunities.

Murph had arrived in Vietnam three months before the 19th SEA Games. Two years later, he landed in Burma with only a month to prepare for the biennial tournament. At the 20th SEA Games hosted in Brunei, Myanmar's national team faced a group of opponents all familiar to Murph: Laos, Philippines, Thailand and Vietnam. Their respective FIFA world rankings gave a fair reflection of results. In the opening matches Myanmar scored a 4-1 victory over the Philippines, a 2-0 loss to Vietnam and a 0-0 draw against Laos. The results took Myanmar into their final group stage match against Murph's nemesis, Thailand. The Thai team coached by ex-England international Peter Withe were the kings of FIFA world rankings in Southeast Asia. They sat in 78th place.

Murph thought his time in communist Vietnam had prepared him for the Myanmar job, but he vastly underestimated the challenge. He stood on the touchline in the Berakas Sports Complex in Bandar Seri Begawan, shouting instructions to his Burmese team. In the 36th minute, 2-0 down against Thailand, one of his substitutes stepped out of the dugout. Murph asked his assistant what was going on. He hadn't told the player to warm up. The assistant explained. A general from the military junta sitting in the stands had rung down on his mobile phone to order the substitution. Thirty minutes later, the general did it again. Some minor consolation for Murph, he didn't have to take full responsibility for the result. And only 5,000 fans watched the match in Brunei's capital city. Myanmar lost 7-0.

I asked Pleat why he thought Murph took the job in Burma.

'He enjoyed being in those countries, it broadened his experience,' Pleat said. 'They wouldn't know if he had been a great player or a poor player, or if he had a great reputation in England or not. They looked up to him. He was the manager of the national team. Maybe he felt more important out there. I think he probably did.'

Murph accepted the role of national coach without dwelling on the pariah status of a country which for almost 40 years had been under the rule of an oppressive military junta. On a personal level, Burma was a safe haven. Living in a hotel, formerly the home of Lord Mountbatten, Murph was looked after by the military. Yet as soon as he started the job, he saw the cruel workings of the regime. A decade earlier, the ruling military government quashed a pro-democracy uprising by killing thousands of civilians and changed the country's name to Myanmar from Burma.

Murph discovered players could be removed from training camps on a general's say-so. If a youngster made selection for the national team, his mother or father would receive a job in a government ministry. The player's full-time status would save his family from poverty, but the authorities held him in their clutches. If the player misbehaved, he would take his family down with him. Murph admired the qualities his team displayed; commitment, desire and discipline, but he recognised they were also the by-products of fear.

He regretted the move to Burma, and only six months into his contract, he made his excuses and left.

Player recruitment and opposition observer for England U21s sounded a much better fit. Murph joined the England organisation where Howard Wilkinson, a good friend for almost 30 years, had taken charge. Murph kept in regular contact with the former technical director of the FA.

'He would ring out of the blue to talk to me about something,' Wilkinson told me. '"Have you got five minutes?" would turn into 55 minutes. "What do you think about this?" would be the usual opening to the conversation. It might be a centre-half or three centre-halves, or the best way to gain aerobic fitness. But it was always about something interesting, it wouldn't be gossip and chatter.'

Murph's appointment didn't surprise Peter Taylor, who managed the England U21s for the previous four years.

'People like Howard and Sir Alex had so much time for Colin. And they knew what a waste he was if he wasn't working. He was a good spot of a player who knew the opposition. He was perfect for the role.'

If Murph came up with an idea, he used Wilkinson as a sounding board. They held each other in mutual high regard.

'We had people out in the game who we trusted. Colin would be someone whose opinion I respected,' Wilkinson said.

Murph enjoyed the England U21s player recruitment role, but it was only a stopgap appointment to tide him over. Three months into the job, he heard that Dave Barry, manager of League of Ireland Cork City, was due to step down at the end of the season. Murph fancied returning to the city where he had briefly turned out for Cork Hibernians in the early days of his playing career. He threw his name into the managerial hat. A dozen candidates were said to have joined him, including former Everton defender Derek Mountfield, but Murph had the upper hand. He made a good impression on the League of Ireland in his brief appointment with Shelbourne, five years before. The club hadn't wanted to let him go.

Murph topped the Cork chairman's list of prospective replacements and after a lengthy interview process, Terry Dunne offered him the job. Murph accepted the position, but the Premier Division club delayed the announcement until he severed his ties with the England U21s. It gave Barry a chance to enjoy the run-in to his last game as manager after five years in charge. In the Munster Senior Cup final against Cobh Ramblers, City won 5-0.

Not for the first time, Murph had chosen a tough act to follow. Barry, a former Gaelic footballer with St. Finbarr's and midfielder with Cork was a local sporting legend. He had taken City to two consecutive second-placed league finishes and the club had qualified for the preliminary round of the UEFA Cup for the fourth year in a row. Murph didn't feel concerned by Barry's legacy. He threw himself into preparations for the start of the domestic season, and the challenge of landing Cork their first league title in seven years.

As soon as Murph arrived at Turners Cross, one player caught his eye: a powerful 18-year-old full-back, fresh from the youth team. Murph's first game in charge was the FAI Super Cup semi-final against Bohemians. The cup, introduced in the summer of 1998, gave the top four teams in the Republic of Ireland the chance to prepare for European competition. And it gave Murph the opportunity to assess his team. Damien Delaney scored the equaliser. The youngster's card was marked.

Twenty-one years later, three summers after he retired from Crystal Palace and the Premier League, Delaney still remembers Murph's impact on the League of Ireland club.

'He came in like a whirlwind to Cork City. His pre-season was notoriously difficult. I was always a fit guy and I think he took a shining to me. He put on these monster running sessions. He worked the players very hard, in an old-fashioned kind of way.'

Murph arrived at a League of Ireland club full of old-school players, big drinkers, smokers, hardmen. Many of them played part time. If there were ever a problem, they resolved it with a fight.

'Colin loved that,' Delaney recalls. 'That was his environment, where men were men. If you've got something to say, say it. And if you can't say it, have a roll about. When you have a squad full of players with those types of personalities, the manager needs to be the biggest personality. And Colin most certainly had the personal skill set to deal with men. If there wasn't a fight in training, Colin would worry the lads were a bit soft.'

Murph's views were the product of a tough, lower-league apprenticeship. At the same time as the gaffer was delighting in fisticuffs, Peter Taylor took a phone call about the vacant manager's job at Leicester City. Martin O'Neill, one of the club's most successful and popular managers, had left Filbert Street for Celtic. Like O'Neill before him, the Foxes' board saw Taylor as a bright emerging talent. He had gained promotion for Gillingham via the play-offs into the First Division, and with no contract at the Kent-based club he was a free agent.

Taylor remembers his interview for the Premier League job.

He lobbied hard for Murph to join as his assistant. He hadn't spoken to Murph about the possibility of teaming up again.

'But I knew if there was an opportunity to go to Leicester City, he'd be there,' Taylor told me.

The Leicester board weren't keen on Murph returning to the club as assistant manager. His supporting role to David Pleat had been unsuccessful a decade before, but Taylor put a strong case forward. He said Murph could do anything, including building up the scouting network. As soon as the board offered Taylor the manager's job, he picked up the phone to his old running mate. How did Murph fancy taking a football coordinator's role in the Premier League? The gaffer didn't have to ask twice.

'That title of football coordinator came from the board, but really he was my assistant,' Taylor said. 'He was the person I spoke to and turned to for everything. I really just went into Leicester with Colin. Steve Butler joined us a month later from Gillingham.'

After six weeks of training at Turners Cross, and only one competitive game in charge, Murph handed in his notice. Cork City was consigned to a growing list of jobs which don't appear on Murph's CV; brief interludes carefully masked by employment dates which have expanded in time.

Murph's resignation, six weeks before the start of the league campaign, threw Cork's UEFA Cup preparations into chaos. The fans might have forgiven him if he left quietly, but he didn't. Soon after Cork turned out against Lausanne in the UEFA Cup qualifying round, Murph made a phone call to Derek Mountfield, the club's second choice of manager. Murph didn't phone the player himself, but he wanted to take Delaney on trial at Leicester.

After a week's training at Filbert Street, Murph called the player into his office on Friday afternoon.

'Peter Taylor wants to see you at five o'clock,' he said.

Delaney was resigned to returning home to Ireland. He certainly didn't expect the gaffer to offer him a contract in the

Premier League. And when he received the unforeseen news, he didn't own a mobile phone to let his family know.

Murph stuck his head round the office door and said to the youngster, 'I don't know what you're gonna be, or how far you're gonna go, but you're six foot four, and you can run and that'll do for me. I'll see you on Monday morning.'

Delaney didn't know if he'd received a compliment or not, but he remembers Murph's parting words, 'I'll teach you the rest.'

The gaffer kept his promise. The move to Filbert Street launched Delaney's professional career, but it also became a long-standing source of irritation to Rebel Army fans. He wasn't the first evacuee from Cork. Brian Barry-Murphy left to win the Second Division championship with David Moyes' Preston North End, the year before. Much to the disappointment of Cork fans, they would export more players to England than any other League of Ireland club.

Sixteen years after Delaney's exit, the Cork faithful had still not forgiven Murph for poaching their up-and-coming star. When Leicester stormed to an unexpected Premier League title in 2016, Ruairí O'Hagan, sports editor of RedFM and a lifelong Cork fan, talked about the bitter taste it left for his fellow supporters. On Newstalk's SSE Airtricity League podcast, he joked that his blood still boiled at the mention of Colin Murphy's name. Under Murph's reign, a link-up was proposed between Cork and Leicester. The partnership was launched at Guinness House at the Union Quay, home to Cork's sponsors. To the average City fan, there seemed to be little upside in a partnership with the Premier League team. The supporters acknowledged that the likes of Delaney would be tempted cross channel at some point, but it should be for a fair price.

O'Hagan recalled how he and a group of young Cork fans, fresh from school on a free Wednesday afternoon, made their way to Guinness House and protested against the link-up. They waved homemade signs, 'F*** off Leicester' and 'No to the Leicester link-up'. The protest was deemed a success. It got their glum looking

16-year-old faces in the *Cork City Evening Echo*. But it didn't stop Delaney from moving to Leicester.

Angry Rebel Army fans posted their comments on Leicester's online message board. One supporter wrote to *The Fox* fanzine saying, 'I can tell you if this deal goes through there will be a fans' revolt at our club ... Who do you English clubs think you are, coming over here getting players for nothing and laughing all the way to the bank?!'

Twenty years later, Peter Taylor recalls the Delaney transfer.

'If you look at the reality of it, he'd only played some football in Ireland, and some Gaelic football. We paid £50,000 for a player who could have made it or not made it. In the end, Damien had a wonderful career. If I'd been the Cork chairman, I'd have been delighted to say that one of my players played in the Premier League against Roy Keane and had a right old battle with him.'

On St Patrick's Day 2001, Taylor threw the 19-year-old Delaney into his Leicester side for an Old Trafford encounter, putting him up against Republic of Ireland captain Keane. Manchester United won 2-0.

When Murph left Cork it wasn't the first or last time his employers would try to claim compensation for an early exit, but he had no regrets about his return across the Irish Sea. By the beginning of October 2000, after 24 years of football management and an eight-game unbeaten run, he reached the ultimate pinnacle; sitting at the top of the Premier League with Leicester. He accepted the job of football coordinator, but really, he was Taylor's right-hand man. Murph took the job because he had huge respect for his younger partner. He described the gaffer as 'a gentleman and a very good coach with strong beliefs'. And Taylor benefited from his older assistant's perspective and experience.

Delaney recalls the management partnership well.

'Every good manager needs someone he can run ideas by, an experienced voice who says, "I'd do things a certain way" or "I'd advise you not to do this". I always thought Colin was that voice. Such an experienced guy, he always saw situations clearly. If I ever went into management, it would be someone like Colin I'd want with me. He was a very thoughtful man.'

Arriving at Filbert Street, Murph took a moment to reflect on his career. He brought a photograph to put on his desk; a picture of him celebrating with his SEA Games bronze medal-winning team. In the photograph, his Vietnamese captain clasped his arm around the boss. Murph considered the young man and his tragic past. The Americans had killed the boy's father, his sister had lost an arm, his village had been destroyed. Yet Murph remembered the player as the most delightful lad.

'So, if I ever get down,' he told John Wragg from the *Daily Express*, 'I look at this picture. Because we've got no problems compared to that, and I think: Well, we all ain't doing too badly.'

Murph joined Leicester at the dawn of a new era of football. Foreign players and coaches were driving a sea change in the culture of the game. Murph's reference points and the way he dealt with situations risked becoming outdated, but the football press recognised the qualities of Taylor's traditional lieutenant.

'Murphy is a football warrior, a survivor, a commuter from the back roads of football,' Wragg wrote, 'and a man with a contact book that is dog-eared with use and as full of telephone numbers as a dictionary is with words.'

Following in the footsteps of Martin O'Neill, Taylor and Murph's first season with Leicester was a period of transition. They would need Murph's book of contacts. The early euphoria of sitting at the top of the Premier League didn't last. The management duo kept the Foxes in the top six until March, but the letter-writing fans of Filbert Street maintained a constant barrage of complaints. They made unfavourable comparisons between Taylor's hands-on coaching style and O'Neill's more motivational approach, believing that the best managers, the Fergusons and Wengers of the Premier League, kept a distance from their players.

Taylor recalls his training programme at Filbert Street, 'Colin coached at Leicester, and he should have coached more. He did a session one day, and I thought cor that was good, that was a bit like Dave Sexton working there. But I was a younger fella, Colin's ten years older than me. I was probably thinking I should do all the coaching. I should have let Colin do more.'

The Fox fanzine wrote about a 'rumbling undercurrent of doubt' about Taylor's ability to succeed, following on from the club's charismatic Irishman. O'Neill had secured a bridgehead in the Premier League. It was Taylor and Murph's job to advance on it. A 13th-placed finish to the season was not what the fans wanted.

After a dismal start to the 2001/02 campaign, on 1 October, a year to the day since they topped the Premier League, Leicester were clinging on at the bottom of the table. They had lost 14 of their last 18 Premier League fixtures. The chairman announced the club would move to their new stadium, under fresh management 'to safeguard our Premiership future'. Murph and Taylor were out of a job.

The Fox's View from the Kop suggested, 'The club has simply fallen under an old Irish spell and has succumbed to the dreaded Curse of Murph. This condition appears at a club with Colin of that name and ensures more bad luck than the smashing of umpteen mirrors. He has now done for us twice in ten years.'

Unforgiving fans are the leitmotif of football. It was the first time the club had sacked a manager since David Pleat left Filbert Street. With Murph on his way out of the door for a second time, *The Fox* contributor pleaded, 'Let our elders and betters resolve here and now that the once is unfortunate, twice is careless but three times will be unforgivable.'

He needn't have worried. Murph wouldn't be coming back.

When I spoke to Taylor, he reflected on the trajectory of Murph's career.

'Colin took on some really hard jobs. When I do a talk, I say to people you haven't half got to be careful who you follow. And you haven't half got to be careful how you do it. I'm following Tony Pulis at Gillingham; he was a god. I'm following Martin

O'Neill at Leicester; he was a god. If you go in that changing
room saying the last manager was hopeless, you've got no chance.
Colin had to follow some top managers, David Webb at
Southend, Dave Mackay at Derby. They are incredibly important
names to follow. Which then means there's more chance ... Like
us, we were unsuccessful at Leicester, and that's probably because
Martin O'Neill was over successful!'

Murph wasn't out of work for long. Some 14 years after he
left Stockport County, he accepted an offer to return to his old
stomping ground. The First Division club faced relegation for
the first time since Murph saved them from non-league oblivion
in 1987. At 57 years old, a little heavier and a little greyer, but
with the unbounded enthusiasm of a much younger man,
Murph stood on the centre spot of the Edgeley Park turf for the
now familiar photo call. Wearing a pinstriped suit and a blue
and white County scarf, he leant his arm on the shoulder of
newly appointed player-manager, Carlton Palmer. The elder
statesman stood next to the young pretender, 21 years his
junior.

The *Stockport Express* wanted to know if Murph ever expected
to return to the club. He laughed, 'You can never say never in this
industry.'

Murph accepted the job as County's first director of football
and likened it to David Pleat's role at Tottenham Hotspur.
Murph, one league below Spurs, saw the extra tier of football
management as necessary to cope with the stresses of the modern
game. The manager's job had never been more difficult than at the
start of the new millennium. Player groups wielded more power,
supporters were more militant and media coverage had reached
saturation point. With Palmer on the pitch, Murph and assistant
Kevin Richardson could advise their rookie manager from the
dugout.

Murph savoured his return to Edgeley Park.

'It's always nice to be wanted,' he said to the waiting press.

He hoped he could repay the chairman's faith in him, but

with only eight points from the opening 17 games, bottom side Stockport would need a minor miracle to avoid relegation.

Chairman Brendan Elwood believed he had found his dream team; an ex-England international as player-manager, a former Arsenal midfielder as his assistant, and County's erstwhile saviour as director of football.

Palmer wasn't afraid of giving it to the Hatters' fans straight. On his first day in charge, he suggested they should 'prepare for relegation'. Palmer insisted he wasn't scared of the drop; it was the long-term future of the club which mattered most. He set out his stall to manage expectations and took a significant wage cut to launch his management career. But even in their worst nightmares, the Edgeley Park faithful couldn't anticipate what would happen next. Under new management, one away draw and one home win were followed by 11 consecutive crushing defeats.

Murph had made a call to bring Damien Delaney on loan from Leicester City; a three-month move which the player describes as instrumental in his early career.

'That was my first introduction to playing men's football,' Delaney said. 'Colin liked players who were brave, who were up for a fight. He could live with technical deficiencies, and I almost certainly had a few, but Colin loved people with heart. That says a lot about what he was like as a manager.'

Murph spent time with Delaney, trying to educate him as a player.

'What I learnt from Colin most, was he didn't care how you won games of football. He only cared that you won. If you had to use the dark arts, and alternative ways and means, then Colin was happy with that. I learned an awful lot from him. It doesn't have to be pleasing on the eye, it doesn't have to be nice, it's all about winning. If a certain player is getting the better of you, see if you can drag him down into the gutter. Stuff like that would never be taught to kids in this day and age. The coaching manual doesn't allow that, but Colin definitely had his own coaching manual. And it was very effective.'

*New manager Carlton Palmer and director of football Colin Murphy watch
in dismay as Stockport County lose 5-0 to Sheffield Wednesday at
Hillsborough, on 24 November 2001. (PA Images / Alamy Stock Photo)*

Despite a poor run of results, three months into their stewardship, the board gave Murph, Palmer, and Richardson a one-year
extension to their contracts. The comfort of job security allowed
them to make longer-term plans. Palmer wanted to abandon the
Scandinavian scouting system which brought the 'Flying Finn'
Shefki Kuqi to Edgeley Park. Murph's remit was to scout for
young talent closer to home. He predicted several players would
come out of Ireland over the next five to ten years, hungry to play
a part in the club's future.

Even a loan spell for Murph's favourite Irishman didn't
improve County's fortunes. Ahead of their next away match at
Wimbledon, the Hatters knew if they didn't come away with a
point, they were certain of relegation. They had only three league
wins all season, all from evening kick-offs. Peter Lansley reported
in his club-by-club guide for *The Times* that Palmer had ordered
the dressing room windows to be blacked out and the floodlights

switched on even for daylight games. If they created a night-time atmosphere, perhaps they would improve their chances. Or, as one County joker suggested, maybe they could get the team to drive into Edgeley Park in their pyjamas.

The tactics didn't work. County lost 3-1, and on 16 March, the Hatters set another unwelcome record. The earliest post-war relegation. There were seven matches still to play.

Early in the new season, in the recurring game of managerial musical chairs, Hull City approached Peter Taylor for the vacant manager's job, and Howard Wilkinson moved to manage Sunderland from his post as technical director of the FA. Murph and Richardson were linked in the press with a move to both clubs at two extremes of English football: relegation-threatened Sunderland in the Premier League and Hull on the bottom rung of the Football League. For Murph, there was no competition. The East Riding of Yorkshire was the bigger draw.

Peter Taylor met Hull chairman Adam Pearson in London and left the interview with a job offer in hand. The former England caretaker manager said he would go home and think about it. He had to make a phone call first.

13

THE UNSUNG HERO
HULL CITY

'Colin, how far is Hull from my house?' Peter Taylor asked Murph.

The Second Division championship-winning manager at Brighton and Hove Albion lived about 20 minutes from the Dartford Tunnel.

'Gaffer, it's about an hour and a half, no more than two hours,' Murph said.

Taylor accepted the job at Hull City before he realised it was a three-and-a-half-hour drive from his home in Kent to Boothferry Park.

'Colin lived in Lincoln,' Taylor told me, 'and it was a good move for him. He was desperate to take the job!'

Murph recognised Hull's prospects, and Taylor remembers his friend's advice.

'It's the chimneys round the ground. You should always go to a club where there's millions of chimneys. If you get that, you're gonna have good support, and a real chance.'

Taylor knew Murph was right.

'The place was absolutely buzzing. You didn't see any Man United or Liverpool shirts. Everyone in that town is Hull City supporters. It was a wonderful opportunity.'

In the 2002/03 season, the average home gates at Boothferry
Park were almost 13,000. Over three times the support of fellow
Third Division challengers Lincoln City and higher than Millwall
in the First Division. Murph convinced Taylor the Tigers might
well be sitting on the bottom rung of the Football League, but
they were perched ready for a biblical transformation.

Taylor didn't waste any time putting together his backroom
team. He signed coach Steve Butler, his number two at Leicester
and promotion-winning striker at Gillingham, on a three-year
deal. An appointment which irritated the chairman of non-league
Maidstone United, who objected to losing his director of football
to the 'big boys' who were 'taking advantage of smaller clubs'.
And after 20 years of intermittent rumours, Murph finally joined
the Tigers' management team. He was excited to tap into the
club's new-found positivity as Taylor's assistant. Murph had
followed Hull's fortunes throughout his career. He admired its
strong fanbase and knew the soon-to-be-completed 25,000-seater
stadium would invigorate the club.

Not for the first time, Murph upset the chairman he left
behind. Brendan Elwood recognised Murph's unstinting work
and the valuable contribution his director of football made to the
smooth running of Stockport County. He viewed Murph as a
long-term addition to the management team and was disappointed in the way in which he left Edgeley Park. Murph didn't
tell Hull they needed to agree a compensation payment. Elwood
wanted six months of Murph's salary. Hull offered two weeks and
then four.

In late October, Elwood spoke to the *Stockport Express*, 'At the
moment I haven't accepted his resignation, but I'm assuming he's
working at Hull, because we aren't paying him.'

Murph confirmed the arrangement when he returned his
company car and swapped a two-litre Jaguar for a 5 series BMW.
Murph liked a nice car and according to his son Ben, took a
forensic interest in vehicle tax brackets.

Almost two decades after Murph joined the Tigers, Richard

Gardham, a lifelong Hull fan, published a fabulous 400-page tome of oral history. In *The Decade: Ten Years That Transformed Hull City A.F.C.*, the former sole owner of the club, Adam Pearson, told Gardham that when he bought it in 2001, 'It was quite a scary situation – like walking into the worst-funded village team – but they had a marked spirit and determination that was going to take them places.'

Twenty months before Murph joined the backroom staff, the club was put into administration. But Pearson, the former commercial director at Leeds United and an ambitious new owner, provided a formidable transfer budget for a lower-league club. Over £500,000 had already been spent on building a new squad.

Gardham recalls the 'Great Escape' of 1998/99 when Hull narrowly avoided dropping into non-league football. Taylor and Murph were charged with producing the re-make of 'Great Expectations' and realising Pearson's long-term vision.

Brian Little was sacked as manager in February 2002, when Hull were sixth in the Third Division, the fourth tier of English football. Eight months later, his successor, ex-Liverpool legend Jan Mølby, left the club at the bottom of the Football League. Taylor and Murph knew they had to deliver.

The management team brought fresh impetus. Murph focussed on improving fitness levels and introduced high-intensity training to the squad. Taylor and Murph wasted no time in making their first signing. Within days, they paid £50,000 to cash-strapped Leicester for Damien Delaney on a three-year deal. Delaney, who was turning out for Leicester's reserves and on loan at third-tier Mansfield Town, jumped at the chance of a permanent move. He hated playing reserve team football in front of empty stadiums on a Monday night. He'd rather play regular football in the Third Division than sit on the bench in the Premier League.

'I loved Colin. I would have walked up to Hull City for him,' Delaney told me. 'I had that much admiration for him. He always looked after me. He played such a pivotal part in my development as a footballer. And I knew if Colin and Peter Taylor were going to Hull City, it wouldn't be a Third Division club for long.'

Delaney remembers Murph's unorthodox approach to pre-season fitness. The players arrived at Hull's sprawling training ground; 20 football pitches and 20 rugby league pitches stretching out as far as the eye could see. They looked out of the changing room window and saw a silver BMW driving across the football pitches in the distance, stopping at regular intervals, dropping cones out of the window.

'When you did a running session with Colin, there was no metres or kilometres,' Delaney said. 'He did it in miles. He was using the odometer on his car to map out the course. That sums him up, really, what a character he was. He probably looked at the new-fangled GPS system and thought that's not for me. This is how we've always done it.'

Taylor says he took Murph with him to Leicester and Hull because his assistant had so many contacts at all levels of the game. Anyone worth knowing in football had an entry in Murph's threadbare little black book. Taylor told me of a conversation he had with John Barnwell, former wing-half for Arsenal and chief executive of the LMA.

'As soon as I signed for Hull City and took Colin with me, John Barnwell said to me, "You're clever because you've taken an older fella with you. A lot of people are frightened of that because they think they want their job. You've taken Colin who's got all the contacts".'

Murph didn't just have the contacts. As soon as he arrived at Hull, he put his heart and soul into transforming the club.

'He even painted the changing rooms in the summer,' Taylor said. 'It was the first training ground we had at Hull. We shared it with the rugby club. Colin didn't want the players coming back looking at the same coloured walls as when they left. Little things like that, people just wouldn't imagine.'

Within two months of Taylor and Murph arriving at Hull,

the team played their final game at a dilapidated Boothferry Park, home to the Tigers since the end of World War One. Fans recalled with nostalgia, how they would file past the Kwik Save concession at the back of the North Stand, and dodge bits falling off the stadium's roof. Not all of them welcomed the move to the £44m council-built and owned KC Stadium, but Taylor and Murph realised it was the start of something special. They just needed the results to match.

Three months into his new role, embarrassed to be 3-0 down against his former club Southend, Taylor was almost ready to quit. Only chairman Adam Pearson persuaded him to stick with it, convinced his manager would get it right. Taylor took advice from Sir Alex Ferguson, who told him he couldn't just sign good players, he had to sign players who could deal with the expectations; individuals who could handle a big crowd in an impressive new stadium. Taylor saw that Ian Ashbee, signed by Mølby on a free transfer from Cambridge United, was a ready-made captain. Ashbee was Murph's type of player; a battle-hardened pro, the perfect leader for a group of young men who were finding their way in the game.

Taylor and Murph hunted for players who could handle expectations. Defender Marc Joseph came from Peterborough United and target man Ben Burgess moved from Stockport. Within four weeks, the imposing centre-forward, unfavoured by Carlton Palmer, christened the KC Stadium with its first hat-trick and took home the first match ball of his professional career.

At the end of May, Hull sat in 13th place, and Taylor and Murph prepared for a busy close season, a player cull and a quintet of new signings. Australian striker Danny Allsopp, forward Jason Price and a trio of defenders, Andy Dawson, Richard Hinds and Alton Thelwell, all arrived at the KC Stadium. They joined Stuart Green, a goalscoring midfielder, back in Hull after an ill-conceived and short-lived move to Carlisle.

Murph later wrote in the Tigers' matchday programme notes that smart recruitment was essential to success.

'If you get eight out of ten players right that you bring into this club, you keep your job because the boy gets better, the team gets better, the team wins, and the supporters keep coming through the gate (stops the chairman from putting his hand in his pocket!).'

Any less than eight out of ten, and you risked the sack.

The players knew the signings were right that summer, both on and off the pitch. Taylor wanted a top-notch full-time physiotherapist to join the team. Murph followed up with his contacts in the FA and interviewed candidates for the job. The gaffer took Murph's advice and signed FA senior research physiotherapist Simon Maltby to head up the club's medical team. Maltby brought new ideas with him; sports science was an unfamiliar concept for many players in the Third Division. His appointment underpinned the club's ambitions and had a long-lasting impact on its future success.

'I always say to people, a top physio or a top assistant manager is worth two or three players,' Taylor told me. 'And Simon Maltby was an absolutely outstanding signing for Hull City. He was a brilliant physio. We didn't have many players who played on a Saturday who broke down, because the physio knew what he was doing.'

Taylor remembers the interview process.

'Simon turned up once to speak to me, and he didn't have a tie on. Colin slaughtered him. It didn't bother me at all, but it was Colin's standards. That was how he was.'

The backroom staff were excited by what lay ahead. The team was in good shape, but Murph realised there were still changes to make. Delaney had a lot of attributes, he could play anywhere, central midfield, left-back, but he hadn't nailed down one position. Murph sat down with the player at the start of the 2003/04 season, took out an A4 sheet of paper and told him, 'You're gonna play centre-back. This is what I want from you.'

Murph wrote down a list of ground rules. The 'non negotiables' as he called them.

'Believe it or not,' Delaney told me. 'I kept that A4 sheet of paper with me for about ten years. Every now and again I would open it up. You know when you've lost form, or you've lost confidence, or you weren't playing very well. It was always a good reference point for me to go back to. They were very basic things, but sometimes those basic things anchor you and get you to play. I remember that meeting with him at the KC Stadium. He said if you do these five things, you'll have an unbelievable career.'

Murph was right. And Delaney still remembers the five things. Don't pass off your opponent in the box. Don't get too tight to centre-forwards. Avoid basic mistakes. Don't dive in. Make solid clearances.

Delaney laughs at the memory of the solid clearances advice.

'Colin said to me "When you're clearing a ball at centre-back you need to be an opening batsman." Colin loved his cricket, and I'm thinking what's an opening batsman? "An opening batsman in a five-day test, he'll be in there for the opening day and give a good foundation to the team. He doesn't swing at anything; he just blocks and gains a foothold in the game." I knew nothing about cricket, but I knew what an opening batsman was after Colin explained the rules to me for an hour! "Don't do anything special, just block and get in the way, stop the opposition from getting any momentum or enjoying themselves, if they get an early wicket, they'll feel good about themselves."'

The simple advice and the analogy worked wonders. Murph transformed Delaney into a left-sided centre-half who earned nine international caps for the Republic of Ireland.

Aside from the odd cricket tutorial, Murph didn't stop his scouting mission. He had his eye on a player at Northern Premier League Alfreton Town, went to watch him a few times and reported back to the boss. Murph said he'd found a player who had everything to offer; right-back, right wing, good in the air. Taylor agreed with him, and Pearson sanctioned the deal. Within days, Ryan France was on his way to the KC Stadium. He scored a goal after arriving from the subs' bench on his debut, a 6-1 rout against Kidderminster Harriers, and kickstarted the most extraordinary eight years of his professional career.

Murph took huge pride in signing players from non-league, unearthing characters other coaches had overlooked. From his background in the Southern League, he realised there were players who deserved a chance. He loved giving an underdog a shot.

He was tracking a 21-year-old goalkeeper, on loan from Aston Villa, turning out at Macclesfield then Stockport. Taylor remembers the chain of events.

'It would have started off with Colin making the original contact with Paul Barron, goalkeeping coach at Aston Villa. That's how it all starts. That's the lovely thing about Col, someone who's got all the contacts. He'd give you a list and say these are your choices. It were great.'

Taylor watched Boaz Myhill play, agreed with Murph's intuition, and told Pearson they should pounce. The chairman sanctioned a deal to bring the keeper to the KC Stadium for £50,000. A scouting triumph for a player who moved to West Bromwich Albion for £1.6m within six years.

Murph was excited by the team they had put together. The players showed confidence and self-belief. He could see their quality exceeded the league they were in and predicted many of them would play in the Premier League. The players laughed at his optimism, but with hard graft and a little bit of patience Murph's prediction might just be proved right. The end of the season took them one step closer to the impossible. A second-placed finish brought automatic promotion into the newly renamed Football League One.

With the rebranding of the Football League for the 2004/05 season, the First, Second and Third Divisions became the Football League Championship, Football League One and Football League Two.

Murph eulogised to the press about Taylor's achievements in gaining promotion. He couldn't help the odd hyperbole in describing his boss's attributes. The *Hull Daily Mail* quoted

Murph on Taylor, 'He's required the wit of Sergeant Bilko, the sleuthing abilities of Holmes and Watson, the humour of Tommy Cooper, the no-turn strength of Margaret Thatcher, the wisdom of Churchill, the fighting instinct of Colonel "H" who led the boys over the hill in the Falklands, the bravery of the Red Baron and the secrecy of MI5.'

Hull had achieved their first promotion since 1985. Nineteen years of waiting for the Tigers' fans. Murph could be forgiven his purple prose.

April 2004, the Hull City management team celebrate promotion at the KC Stadium. From left to right: manager Peter Taylor, coach Steve Butler, assistant manager Colin Murphy, goalkeeping coach Ron Arnold, and physio Simon Maltby. (Image courtesy of Hull City (Dave Lofthouse and Dave Richardson))

In an improbable turn of events at the season's close, Pearson took a call from the agent of a 23-times capped England international. The former Spurs, Everton and Liverpool winger was keen to return to his native Hull. When Pearson appointed Taylor, he raised the profile of the club. And when Taylor signed Nick Barmby, he sealed its future.

At the other end of the football pyramid, Murph spotted a goalkeeper playing for mid-table Conference team Burton Albion. Murph thought he would slot in well beside Myhill, the club's number one keeper. Matt Duke joined the Tigers for £20,000. Another bargain buy of a non-league player, who would make 21 appearances in the Premier League.

In the close season, still fresh from the success of automatic promotion, the FA invited Taylor to combine his full-time job at Hull with part-time management of England U21s. It was an irresistible offer for the gaffer, removed from the role in 1999 when Howard Wilkinson the FA's technical director, took over as his replacement. After lengthy negotiations with Taylor and the FA, Pearson sanctioned his manager's job share; a decision hotly debated by the fans.

A disappointing 1-0 defeat at home to Bradford at the end of August preceded a trip to play-off victors Huddersfield Town. With Taylor ensconced in a hotel in Poland on U21s duty, Murph as acting manager needed to secure at least a draw from the ill-timed and rescheduled East vs West Yorkshire derby. One point could take Hull to second in the table and might convince the Tigers' fans the job share could work. The master plan failed. Hull went two goals down from defensive errors within 20 minutes. By full time, the Terriers had comprehensively mauled the Tigers, who left the pitch, dragging a four-goal deficit behind them. Murph played down Taylor's absence when he spoke to the press. He couldn't criticise the players' work rate or attitude, but the result hadn't done Taylor or his assistant any favours.

'It wasn't just Hull City losing 1-0,' Taylor recalls. 'It was Hull City not playing well, losing 4-0 to a local team. If that had carried on, I'm sure Adam Pearson would have said it's not right. As I said to people at the time, I could have been on that touchline and still got beat 4-0. It doesn't mean because I wasn't there, that was the reason we lost. The greatest thing about Colin as an assistant, if he thought it was a nightmare and I shouldn't have been doing the U21s, he would have told me.'

Murph saw there were more positives than negatives from Taylor's dual role as England coach. It extended the management team's connections. And it wouldn't stop them from turning a small miracle in the East Riding of Yorkshire.

The team settled back into the season. Hull played host to Huddersfield on New Year's Day. Honour was restored. They won 2-1. In an article written for the matchday programme, Murph charted the Tigers' progress in the first half of the campaign. He acknowledged there was pressure from fans to buy players to strengthen the squad, but Murph gave the gaffer a rock-solid vote of confidence.

'He will only buy to manage the club for tomorrow, and not for today.'

Murph suggested that Taylor's success came from creating a group of players which 'has transcended team spirt into contemporary spirit'.

Murph explained the distinction.

'The difference between contemporary spirit and team spirit is that it goes beyond the pitch. If one of them got a phone call at 1am in the morning to say that a teammate was lying in the gutter somewhere, he'd ring three or four of the other ones and they'd go and get him. You cannot buy success. It has to be created through the medium of teamwork and a collection of good technical ability, good tactical ability, good physical prowess, desire, commitment, discipline, integrity and respect. Every time you buy, you put that particular set of standards at risk.'

He suggested that any criticism of Taylor's buying philosophy came from either a buffoon or a baboon and concluded, 'Nothing and I repeat nothing, will knock this manager off course. Ladies and gentlemen, roll over Beethoven and make way for Elvis.'

In May 2005, League One made way for Taylor and Murph. A second-placed finish behind Luton Town brought Hull a back-to-back promotion. The Tigers were on their way into the second tier of English football.

Manager Peter Taylor (right) and assistant manager Colin Murphy (left)
celebrate back-to-back promotions for Hull City in April 2005. (Image
courtesy of Hull City (Dave Lofthouse and Dave Richardson))

'I don't mind saying, and Adam Pearson won't mind me saying, Colin and Simon Maltby were the best signings at Hull City,' Taylor said. 'What people don't realise, the number of players we signed and sold for a lot of money, and the two promotions we got, that was all to do with Colin's contacts. And knowing where we could get players. We all said Hull was a sleeping giant. That second promotion meant a lot to everyone. I don't think Colin cried in the dressing room, but he definitely cried in my office.'

The first year in the Championship brought further progress; a respectable 18th-placed finish, ten points clear of the drop, and with it another enticing offer for the manager with the Midas touch. This time, the invitation came from Crystal Palace, a Championship side where Taylor had been a Player of the Season in the 1970s. Murph questioned his old pal's thinking. Why would Taylor defect from Hull after all they had achieved?

'Gaffer, are you sure you know what you're doing? You run

the show here,' Murph said, 'and you won't run the show at Palace, you'll have that Simon Jordan interfering.'

Taylor gives a wry laugh when he recounts the story.

'He was spot on!'

The gaffer ignored Murph's warning about the Crystal Palace owner and accepted the job.

'I had to go into Palace basically on my own. I should have been stronger and said I'm not coming unless I can bring my staff. Colin was right. I made a mistake.'

It didn't take long for Taylor to wish he had listened to his running mate. He lasted only 16 months at Selhurst Park. And he consigned Murph to a backroom staff reshuffle at Hull.

In the close season, Pearson targeted Phil Parkinson at Colchester United to take over as manager. While Colchester took out an injunction to prevent Parkinson from jumping ship, Nottingham Forest coach Frank Barlow arrived at the KC Stadium as caretaker manager. Hull agreed a £400,000 compensation payment to buy Parkinson out of his contract. With the new manager in place and Barlow as his assistant, Murph accepted the role as director of club development. He was going back to his roots, in charge of scouting and youth development. It was a backward step but Murph had little time to settle into the job.

Thirteen games into the season, and only two wins and nine goals to show for it, Parkinson dispensed with Barlow's services and reinstated Murph as assistant manager. The boss then made the cardinal error of job protection. He recruited a first team coach; a highly ambitious, out-of-work manager. Enter Phil Brown, formerly of Derby County.

Roll forward two months. After 21 games and less than six months in charge, Parkinson's team sat one spot off the bottom of the Championship. He was on his way out of the KC Stadium and Brown was on his way back into management, albeit on a short-term contract. The move brought Adam Pearson one step closer to bringing a much-fancied local lad back to his Hull roots. Taylor had turned down the return of an ebullient dressing room character in favour of signing Nick Barmby, but Brown welcomed Dean Windass home. Within ten days of Brown's appointment as manager, he and Murph met the local hero at the Medici restaurant in North Ferriby. A deal was agreed. Windass, sold by Hull in 1995 after 176 appearances, was on his way back to the East Riding of Yorkshire. The striker kept his promise. Eight goals in the last 13 games saved the Tigers from relegation.

The end of the 2006/07 season brought a changing of the guard. Brown accepted the full-time job as manager, and Steve Parkin came in as first team coach. The 63-year-old Murph dropped down the pecking order, to resume the role of director of club development. In the curious ways of football management, the assistant manager's job went to Brian Horton, 19 years after the club had sacked him as manager.

Four months into the new season, on Thursday 22 November 2007, Murph took a rare day off work. He was admitted to the Bupa hospital in Hull for a pre-scheduled operation. He met his son, Ben, and they discussed the medical consent form. It was a standard procedure. Among the usual contraindications, the operation carried a one in 200 chance of causing a stroke. Murph signed the consent form, unaware of the cruel price he might pay for his signature.

During the operation, some debris broke free and carried on through to his brain. The odds had fallen against him. Murph suffered a devastating stroke.

Judith phoned Gordon Simmonite and told him what had happened. She asked if he could visit Murph in hospital.

'But you'll need to be prepared, Gordon. He's got a very limited vocabulary.'

Simmonite arrived at the hospital and found his good friend pacing the room. A nurse came in to check on her patient.

'Is everything all right, Colin?'

'No.'

'Do you want to use the toilet?'

'No.'

'Can I do anything for you?'

'F*** me!'

Murph's well rounded vocabulary, feted by the British press, had been reduced to his three most used phrases, '"Yes", "no", and "f*** me!"'

Gordon wasn't surprised. It was Murph's favourite response. If a player had a good shot on goal, 'F*** me, Gordon, look at that shot!'

Murph's close friends and colleagues all have their own memories of the aftermath of his stroke. They speak of silent bedside visits, of Murph discharging himself from hospital, of photographs taped to his sitting room wall. Attempts to unlock his speech, to stimulate conversation, to remind him of the sport he loved. Visitors talked to him of matches won and lost, the insignificance of the everyday. And Colin watched and listened. Staring blankly at his visitors, repeating patterns of numbers, unable to communicate. It took months of speech and physical therapy, and a great deal of courage and determination for Murph to rediscover his voice.

In a cruel twist of fate, Murph's debilitating illness denied him the chance of seeing the transformation of Hull City through to its ultimate conclusion. At the Wembley play-off final on 24 May 2008, a sublime volley from a 39-year-old Dean Windass took the Tigers into the top flight of English football for the first time in their 104-year history. Murph wasn't sitting in the dugout for the triumphant result. He watched from a corner stand with his son, Ben. They didn't know how the after-effects of Colin's stroke would pan out over the months ahead, but they both knew that he would never work again.

On the same night, at Croke Park in Dublin, four months after he transferred to Queens Park Rangers, Damien Delaney made his first international appearance for the Republic of Ireland. After the game, he sent his framed jersey to Murph's home in Lincoln.

'I felt he deserved it,' Delaney said. 'If it wasn't for the faith

Colin showed in me when I was younger, I wouldn't have got that. And I wouldn't have had the career that I had.'

Colin Murphy, back at Wembley, for another play-off final in May 2008, with his son, Ben. Enjoying the beautiful game from a different perspective. (Photograph from the Murphy family collection)

When Delaney retired from English football at the age of 37, the BBC Radio Humberside *Sports Talk* team invited him to reflect on his long career. The player acknowledged the fantastic support which Peter Taylor had given him, but he described Colin Murphy as 'the unsung hero of the Hull City renaissance'.

When we spoke during the lockdown of 2021, Delaney explained what he meant.

'Colin was really the lifeblood that flowed through that club. He was everywhere, he did everything. If you lost a game, he sat down and said the right thing at the right time. That was his experience, but he never got any publicity for it. Everybody knew who he was, but nobody knew the extent of the job that he did. I think he deserves the recognition, because I can say wholeheartedly, what happened at Hull City wouldn't have happened, if it wasn't for Colin.'

Playing in the Premier League for the 2008/09 season, Ian Ashbee, Andy Dawson, Boaz Myhill, and Ryan France joined an elite group of players who have appeared for the same team, in all four divisions of English football. Murph was instrumental in bringing Myhill and France to the KC Stadium. From the Third Division to the Premier League in only five seasons, he was an integral part of the Hull City journey.

The club and the League Managers' Association gave Murph tremendous support in the months after his stroke, but Murph realised with great sadness that his illness had ended his career in the sport that he loved. He had spent over 35 years in the professional game, most of them in the lower two leagues of English football. When he was a player, he wanted to be a coach. When he was a coach, he wanted to be a manager. And when he was a manager, he wanted to manage in the First Division, the equivalent of today's Premier League. He achieved the latter only briefly, early on in his career.

Why did the youngest manager in the First Division in 1976 not receive a second opportunity to manage in the top flight of the English game? Would he have struggled to manage with a bigger budget, as some suggested? Or have been unable to run a higher profile club in the same way he ran Lincoln City? Maybe he was the victim of his own career decisions. In the late 1980s, he took his chance in Saudi Arabia and the money that came with it. As he did in Southeast Asia, a decade later. It would be hard to come back and start all over again.

As David Pleat said, 'Who would have blown Colin's trumpet

back home? Who would have known he was doing these wonderful things? Very few people. Certainly not chairmen who only knew the English leagues back in those days.'

I asked several of Murph's friends and former colleagues how he survived for so long in the ruthless world of football management.

'He was very determined, very strong minded, a hard worker,' Roy Hodgson suggested. 'He had the ability to take the blows and come out the other side. It boils down to his enthusiasm and love for the game of football.'

Lennie Lawrence was equally unequivocal in his response.

'Murph was a unique one-off, but that shouldn't detract from his talents, he was a bloody good manager. If you wanted somebody in League One or League Two to put your club in order, develop your players, recruit people you could sell for money, and have half a chance of being successful on the field for a long period of time, he was your man.'

'He was an intelligent person, that's why he survived,' David Pleat said. 'He knew the importance of networking. It's good to keep associates and friends, you never know when you might need them. He was very good at keeping in touch with people, he would be in regular contact with Howard [Wilkinson] at the FA. Colin knew what was going on, he kept himself aware of things, and he was a knowledgeable chap. He was a bit different. Maybe I was too.'

Howard Wilkinson made his own assessment of Murph's career.

'He never won the First Division. He never won the FA Cup, but within football he was very well respected for the intelligent way in which he approached whatever job he was given. He had a gift for working with younger players. And he had a philosophy which he applied when dealing with younger players. He was a teacher.'

Damien Delaney, one of the players whom Murph taught, has

no doubt why the gaffer survived for so long in the professional game.

'He loved everything about football. I think he loved the challenges, the banter, the freedom. Football then, was probably the last bastion of where men could be men. It was cut-throat, it was ruthless, it was dog eat dog. Colin loved that. He loved environments that were tough.'

Now well into his late 70s, football still permeates the fabric of Colin's life. More than 30 years since he left Lincoln as manager, he enjoys an enduring relationship with the club. A regular supporter at home games, he was honoured to become the first inductee into the Lincoln City Hall of Fame in 2018.

In a matchday programme from early 1990, Murph wrote there was no secret formula to success, but you needed 'undisturbing resolve as to what you are about, and what you are endeavouring to pursue and develop'.

He recognised you could be knocked off course with injury problems, an incompetent performance or 'at times, sheer, hard luck' but there was something more important to consider.

'Unfortunately, some people do not see beyond the next performance, they do not see beyond the next result, they just evaluate the circumstance from game to game, seeing no further than their nose, and thereby being unable to decipher the whole objective of valuable, safe and successful football club management.'

Murph always looked beyond the next performance. He didn't always get it right, and he wasn't always successful, but football club management was his life.

As Peter Taylor told me in 2021, 'New owners these days would be crying out for a Colin Murphy.'

Murph couldn't ask for more than that.

14

MURPH'S MESSAGE – A TOP 20

Lincoln City matchday programmes from the late 1980s were the vessel of Murph's thoughts and philosophies on football, life, conkers and everything in between.

A Top 20 of extracts from Murph's Message are reproduced below, with kind permission of Lincoln City Football Club.

1. On what football is all about, and what it takes to succeed.

(28 December 1987 vs Kidderminster Harriers)

'Certain tactics are under the microscope these days but I have always felt that people should visit a home for deranged ferrets if they feel that playing balls into the heart of the opponents' defence quickly, regularly, early crossing on every possible opportunity, shooting on every possible opportunity, are the only pre-requisites. Have the pundits considered that to be successful you need to have your team organised correctly, you need some concentration, you need responsibility, and you need willingness, spirit and determination?'

2. On the need to view victories and defeats as a campaign, and not in isolation, after winning the Vauxhall Conference.

(24 September 1988 vs Hereford United)

'In my opinion the times for such judgements need to be after 46 matches when after the cannibals have mixed the ingredients in the boiling pot then, and quite correctly in my view, we shall be eaten alive, held on simmer, or as was the case last year, obtain some tremendous taste from having formulated the correct recipe.'

3. On commitment to success.

(22 October 1988 vs Darlington)

'In my opinion, laurels were never shrubs, they should be emblems of victory. No rest.'

4. On local derby opponents and the pursuit of excellence.

(26 December 1988 vs Grimsby Town)

'One thing is for sure they will either, to use the colloquial expression, play entertaining football, or to use the professional technical analogy, will endeavour to pass the ball around the field in their efforts to obtain crosses and shots, and this is to their credit ... I hope during the Grimsby, Doncaster and York games we are in a position to satisfy your holiday lusts.'

5. On giving that little bit extra.

(28 January 1989 vs Peterborough United)

'Maybe the difference between the ordinary and the extraordinary is just that little bit extra and this we must strive to obtain in the ensuing games. This is developed from good attitude on the training pitch, good desire to perform competently, success in the state of the player's mind, and to apply all the disciplines that are necessary in the arena. These three areas have always been the basic requirements to succeed, and they will never change in anybody's lifetimes in any form of employment.'

6. On the need for positivity.

(4 February 1989 vs Cambridge United)

'Fatigue, whether it be moral, physiological or psychological will always make defeatists of us all so the positiveness of our actions in the coming games will determine our direction. We must ensure that the welcome hand can become the reluctant fist.'

7. On destiny.

(1 March 1989 vs Tranmere Rovers)

'I have always considered destiny is not a matter of chance, it really is a matter of choice. It is not something to be waited for, but something to be achieved ... Empires of the future are empires of the mind and if we dream, they do not become built.'

8. On accepting one's position in the league.

(1 March 1989 vs Tranmere Rovers)

'To expunge or not to expunge. We cannot expunge the last 30 games, what we can say is as a result of the last 30 games, whatever the variables, excuses or praises one wishes to implicate our position is as it is [*Ed: eighth in the Fourth Division*].'

9. On coming back from four consecutive defeats.

(25 March 1989 vs York City)

'Correctly or incorrectly people may well wish to gorge themselves in the fervour of our blood so it will now be certainly a most interesting test to see how we can handle this apparent "wobble". It is however disappointing that at the first opportunity some people act with chancre [*Ed: a painless genital ulcer – Murph may mean rancour*]. I suppose while we accept the pats on the back, we have to accept the Hoots. However discombulating we have been made to appear we shall genuinely endeavour to discoidulate the cleavage [*Ed: meaning unknown*].'

10. On keeping quiet when you leave a club.

(1 April 1989 vs Stockport County)

'I consider it never pays to wash dirty linen publicly. Or clean linen for that matter. When it dries out it either smells or it is stained. It is not necessarily of claudication [*Ed: a pain in the buttocks when you walk*] to adopt the view that you say what you have to say whilst you have the opportunity to say it whilst you are there. When you've gone you've gone. Credibility, dignity should always be of the highest order with regard to others but as this is less pis aller [*Ed: a last resort*] then they are difficult attributes to possess under various pressures.'

11. On whether part-time teams should be allowed in the Football League.

(1 May 1989 vs Burnley)

'Food for thought, digestible to some, intestinally concluded to others. One thing is for sure in all of these circumstance, if one performs with crapulence [*Ed: the condition of being intoxicated*] they will require a corroborant [*Ed: a medicine which has an invigorating effect*] which will need to give you the strength to perform the corroboree [*Ed: an Australian Aboriginal dance ceremony*] in order to become corrible [*Ed: meaning unknown*].'

12. On the correct way of doing things.

(6 May 1989 vs Leyton Orient)

'In all cases there are four ways to do a thing, which are, the right way wrongly, the wrong way rightly, the wrong way wrongly, but as I think you will agree, in the last two years as we have attempted, the right way rightly, then I am sure you will come again in these numbers, again, if we are to give you the good commencement.'

13. On a good start to the season.

(30 August 1989 vs Wolverhampton Wanderers, League Cup first round, second leg)

'I have often considered that early games in football are like babies, they are like plants. In other words they need a good start to give spiritful foundations ... The conker at the moment is a 2-er and at times it needs to be prickly to keep the opposition away from us. But they must possess consanguinity [*Ed: descended from the same ancestor*] together with concubinary qualities and we shall then be successful.'

14. On sitting at the top of the Fourth Division and staying there.

(16 September 1989 vs York City)

'We must not have dillusions of grandure, we cannot suffer from tertiary disease of grand paralysis of the insane. Whilst I appreciate that many great decisions and many great victories were achieved with such tertiaries and such insanities in days of old, then accordingly we must continue doing what has put us on top then we shall remain top, in other words we will not be topped.'

15. On the need for players to realise that their own sanity is dependent on their own strengths.

(16 September 1989 vs York City)

'If not, they will, or as I am the one who bears responsibility for all the manouvres, we will, realise that life is not like a bowl of cherries but more like a bowl of Hungarian Goulash, hot sticky and at times intestinately negative.'

16. On the name of the game.

(1 November 1989 vs Stockport County)

'Be under no illusions my friends, it does not matter what you purport on the literary note, the name of the game as a Football Manager is winning. In the final analysis it will be the sole criteria for the retention of managerial employment ... One must not become fantoccinical [*Google: it looks like there aren't many great matches for your search*]. So, I have no doubt if we do not win here a great deal more times than we lose, then I will be trussed up by various parts of my anatomy from the Cathedral. Whilst I have been Christened but not Ordained, it will be less painful for my theological arrangements with the Church to be that of a passing friendship with the Dean.'

17. On breaking down opposition defences.
    (1 November 1989 vs Stockport County)
    'Of the keys on the ring at the moment we should be selecting more correctly to unlock opposing mechanisms. However, there is not a lock that cannot be unlocked so we shall continue to endeavour to unlock the lock, but in doing so we must not get locked out.'

18. On external criticism and those who put you to the test.
    (11 November 1989 vs Gillingham)
    'I also suppose it is important to assume that there has never been much difference between the educated monkey and the uneducated elephant on the basis that they both spend periods of encagement and on freedom quite often suffer from mental aberrations.'

19. On match-winning Saturdays and leaving a legacy.
    (17 February 1990 vs Colchester United)

'The Establishment will always be here a great deal longer than you, I, or the pieman. Make no mistake, in the majority of walks of life different forms of management are best evaluated when you have long gone.'

20. On asking his players to give their all.
    (14 April 1990 vs Scarborough)

'That tremendous feeling that one might have when they are forty or fifty years of age, when they are sitting back thinking that they broke a nose to save or score a goal, that gave them the promotion medal that is upon their fireplace. Not much to ask for really.'

(Image courtesy of the *Lincolnshire Echo*)

AFTERWORD

When Colin started his professional career at Nottingham Forest in 1972, I was poring over my first collection of football cards. With grainy images of First Division heroes, they were gloriously amateur in their production. A random selection of head and body shots, awkwardly posed, but neatly packaged with sweet cigarettes.

In the late 1970s, when Colin managed Derby County, there was little opportunity for football clubs to make a profit. The average First Division footballer earned a basic wage of less than £90 a week (£500 in today's money). In the following decade, when managers had greater autonomy and players had less economic power, Colin flourished. At Lincoln City, he established strong principles of play with a clear footballing philosophy, bought individuals who were suited to the system he adopted and played to the strengths of those players.

In 2002, when Colin joined his last club, Hull City, I completed my first Merlin sticker book with a little help from my five-year-old son. A 95-page Autograph Edition FA Premier League bonanza. The players' pictures were more poised, more professional, more shiny; a lot like football itself. A slither of bubble gum inside each packet, deemed more fitting than mock carcinogens for the under-tens.

Colin's story spans a period of immense change in English football. Much of his career played out before football became too commercial. But by the time of his retirement in 2007, escalating TV broadcasting rights had fuelled a greater monetisation of the English game. This transformation brought with it increased pressure on managers and the need for a more sophisticated approach. Some 15 years after the introduction of the Premier League, the average top-flight player was earning a basic average wage of over £18,000 a week. By 2021, this figure had more than trebled.

Colin's particular brand of leadership, his gutsy hard work, his loyalty to his players and his total lack of ego, belonged very much in the era in which he managed. He survived a turbulent 35-year career because he earned the respect of his contemporaries and learned to expect the unexpected. Colin's story is about the lure of the impossible challenge and a life consumed by football. But most of all, it's the story of Murph, the undisputed bard of the English game.

MANAGERIAL AND COACHING CAREER AND ACHIEVEMENTS

In the summary of Colin's career below, I have applied the league names which were in use at the time. Up until the 1991/92 season, the Football League was divided into:
First Division
Second Division
Third Division
Fourth Division

From the 1992/93 season, the league structure became:
FA Premier League
Football League First Division
Football League Second Division
Football League Third Division

From the 2004/05 season, the league structure was rebranded into:
FA Premier League
Football League Championship
Football League One
Football League Two

Clubs and positions:

October 1972 to October 1973
    Nottingham Forest – Second Division
    Youth team coach

October 1973 to September 1977
    Derby County – First Division
    Reserve team coach / caretaker manager / manager

September 1977 to October 1978
    Notts County – Second Division
    Reserve team coach

November 1978 to June 1985
    Lincoln City – Third Division / Fourth Division /
    Third Division
    Manager

August to October 1985
    Stockport County – Fourth Division
    Manager

November 1985 to November 1986
    Al-Ittihad – Saudi Premier League
    Coach

November 1986 to May 1987
    Stockport County – Fourth Division
    Manager

June 1987 to May 1990
    Lincoln City – Vauxhall Conference / Fourth Division
    Manager

June 1990 to June 1991
Leicester City – Second Division
Coach

June 1991 to May 1992
Luton Town – First Division
Assistant manager

May 1992 to December 1994
Southend United – Football League First Division
Manager / director of football

December 1994 to June 1995
Shelbourne – League of Ireland Premier Division
Manager

June 1995 to December 1996
Notts County – Football League Second Division
General manager

June 1997 to March 1998
Vietnam Football Federation
National coach

March 1998 to July 1999
Tottenham Hotspur – FA Premier League
Director of youth academy

July 1999 to January 2000
Myanmar Football Federation
National coach

January to May 2000
England U21s
Player recruitment / opposition observer

May to July 2000
   Cork City – League of Ireland Premier Division
   Manager

July 2000 to October 2001
   Leicester City – FA Premier League
   Football coordinator

November 2001 to October 2002
   Stockport County – Football League First Division
   Director of football

October 2002 to November 2007
   Hull City – Football League Third Division /
   Football League One / Football League Championship
   Assistant manager / director of club development

Achievements:

1980/81 – Lincoln City – promotion to Third Division
1985/86 – Al-Ittihad – Saudi Premier League runners-up
1985/86 – Al-Ittihad – King Cup runners-up
1987/88 – Lincoln City – promotion to Fourth Division
1994/95 – Shelbourne – Football Association of Ireland Cup final
1994/95 – Shelbourne – UEFA Cup qualification
1995/96 – Notts County – Football League Second Division play-off final
1997/98 – Vietnam national team – bronze medal at the 19th SEA games
2003/04 – Hull City – promotion to Football League One
2004/05 – Hull City – promotion to Football League Championship

BIBLIOGRAPHY

All the following were valuable research companions while writing Colin's story.

Books:

- Ball, Peter and Shaw, Phil, *The Umbro Book of Football Quotations* (Stanley Paul Limited, 1993)
- Barrett, Norman and Rollin, Jack (Editors), *The Daily Telegraph Football Year Book 1987–88* (Telegraph Books, 1987)
- Bracegirdle, Dave, *The Legends of Notts County* (Breedon Books Publishing, 2005)
- Brown, Tony, *The Official History, Notts County, 1862–1995* (Yore Publications, 1996)
- Carter, Neil, *The Football Manager: A History (Sport in the Global Society)* (Routledge, 2006)
- Cheetham, Barry, *When Friday Night was County Night: Stockport Footballing Memories* (Sigma Leisure, 2000)
- Collymore, Stan with Holt, Oliver, *Stan: Tackling my Demons* (Collins Willow, 2004)

- Cox, Richard and Russell, Dave and Vamplew, Wray (Editors), *Encyclopaedia of British Football* (Routledge, 2002)
- Elms, Philip, *Claret and Blue: The Story of Hastings United F.C.* (1066 Newspapers, 1988)
- Fieldhouse, John, *From Bust to Boom: Hull City A.F.C. From the Brink of Extinction to the Barclays Premier League* (Great Northern Books, 2009)
- Firth, Paul, *Four Minutes to Hell: The Story of the Bradford City Fire* (Paul Firth, 2007)
- Gardham, Richard, *The Decade: Ten Years That Transformed Hull City A.F.C.* (Independently published, 2019)
- Goodman, David, *Hull City: A History* (Amberley Publishing, 2014)
- Goody, Dave and Miles, Peter, *Potted Shrimps: Southend United Encyclopaedia and History Update 1992 to 1999* (Yore Publications, 1999)
- Halford, Brian, *Past Imperfect: The Story of Lincoln City F.C.* (The Parrs Wood Press, 2000)
- Hamilton, Duncan, *Provided You Don't Kiss Me: 20 Years With Brian Clough* (Fourth Estate, 2007)
- Harrison, Paul, *Gravesend & Northfleet Football Club Official Golden Jubilee Year Book* (Gravesend & Northfleet Football Club, 1996)
- Lawrence, Lennie, with Brennan, Kevin, *Lennie: The Autobiography of Lennie Lawrence* (Green Umbrella Publishing, 2009)
- Longford, Sam (Editors: Mulholland, Robert and Hill, Barry) *Sam's Story: An Autobiography* (Caron Publications, 2013)
- Mason, Peter, *Southend United: The Official History of the Blues* (Yore Publications, 1993)
- Mortimer, Gerald, *Derby County: A Complete Record 1884–1988* (Breedon Books Publishing, 1988)

- Nannestad, Ian, and Nannestad, Donald, *Lincoln City F.C. The Official History* (Yore Publications, 1997)
- Neale, Phil, *A Double Life* (Ringpress Books Ltd, 1990)
- Nelson, Guy, *Legends of Stockport County F.C.* (At Heart Ltd, 2008)
- Piper, Geoffrey, *Stand up if you love the boss: A collection of poems written in support of the Lincoln City Football Club* (TUCANNbooks, 2011)
- Powter, David (Editor: Robinson, Michael), *Derby County F.C.: The 25 Year Record Book* (Soccer Books Ltd, 1995)
- Rippon, Anton, *Soccer: The Road to Crisis* (Moorland Publishing, 1983)
- Rostron, Phil, *We are the Damned United: The Real Story of Brian Clough at Leeds United* (Mainstream Publishing, 2011)
- Shaw, Phil, *The Book of Football Quotations* (Ebury Publishing, 2008)
- Slater, Colin, *Tied Up With Notts* (Reid Publishing, 2012)
- Vickers, John, *City's Centenary* (Queensway Publishing Ltd, 2007)
- Wade, Allen, *The FA Guide to Training and Coaching* (Heinemann, 1967)
- Wain, Paul, additional material, Slater, Colin, *Notts County: A Pictorial History, the highs and lows of the oldest professional football club* (Yore Publications, 2004)
- Warsop, Keith and Brown, Tony, *The Definitive Notts County F.C. The Oldest League Club in the World* (Tony Brown, 2007)
- Webb, Stuart, *Clough, Maxwell and Me: Explosive, the Inside Track* (North Bridge Publishing, 2016)

Academic Papers:

- Perry, Bob and Davies, Gron, *Director of Football, cosmetic labelling or a sea-change? The football manager's formal job role* (University of Wolverhampton, Wolverhampton Business School, Management Research Centre, 1997)

Podcasts:

- talkSPORT *My Sporting Life*: John Fashanu, with Danny Kelly (broadcast 17 March 2012)
- talkSPORT *My Sporting Life*: Stan Collymore, with Danny Kelly (broadcast 17 September 2012)
- talkSPORT *My Sporting Life*: David Pleat, with Danny Kelly (broadcast 7 April 2013)
- talkSPORT *My Sporting Life*: Barry Fry, with Danny Kelly (broadcast 25 January 2015)
- Newstalk SSE Airtricity League podcast: Episode 9, with Oisin Langan and Richie McCormack, (broadcast 4 May 2016)

Fanzines:

You can't beat a good football fanzine. Here are some of the best, though not all of them complimentary about the gaffer.

- *Deranged Ferret* – Issue 1 (August 1989)
- *Deranged Ferret* – Issue 2 (November 1989)
- *Deranged Ferret* – Issue 5 (August 1990)
- *No More Pie in the Sky* – Issue 12a (August/September 1995)
- *The Banker* – Issue 4 (1989)
- *The Fanatic* – Southend United Supporters' Club Football Club (13 December 1992)

- *The Fanatic* – Southend United Supporters' Club Football Club (21 March 1993)
- *The Fanatic* – Southend United Supporters' Club Football Club (3 October 1993)
- *The Fox* – The Leicester City fanzine – Issue 102 (January 2001)
- *The Fox* – The Leicester City fanzine – Issue 104 (March 2001)
- *The Fox* – The Leicester City fanzine – Issue 108 (October 2001)
- *The Fox* – The Leicester City fanzine – Issue 109 (November 2001)
- *The Roots Hall Roar* – Issue 17 (December 1993/January 1994)
- *The Roots Hall Roar* – Issue 18 (August 1994)
- *The Roots Hall Roar* – Issue 19 (October/November 1994)

Courses:

If you like football and social history, you'll love this online course:

Future Learn
English Football: A Social History
University of Leicester

Government papers stored at the National Archives:

Departments of the Environment and Transport
Application of Research Results
Bradford City football fire – Video
File number: BRE/64/2/8
Bradford City Football Club fire – Disasters – May 1985
File number: Prem 19/1448

Department of Transport report:

Accidents Investigation Branch
Aircraft Accident Report 2/87
Report on the accident to Lockheed TriStar G-BBAI at Leeds
Bradford Airport on 27 May 1985

Television:

Central News East documentary (dates broadcast shown in
brackets)

Murph's Mission – One (19 August 1997)
Murph's Mission – Two (20 August 1997)
Murph's Mission – Three (21 August 1997)
Colin Murphy adapts to life in Vietnam (22 August 1997)
Murph's Mission 2 – One (26 January 1998)
Murph's Mission 2 – Two (27 January 1998)
Murph's Mission 2 – Three (28 January 1998)
Murph's Mission 2 – Four (29 January 1998)
Murph's Mission 2 – Five (30 January 1998)

ACKNOWLEDGEMENTS

It has been an absolute pleasure to research and write *Murphy's Mission*. I am very grateful to Colin Murphy, who trusted 'the lady' to tell his story, and Judith Murphy, for providing over 35 years of scrapbooks and family stories. My thanks also to Ben Murphy, for sharing an encyclopaedic knowledge of his dad's career.

I am indebted to Colette Leong-Son, my inspirational friend and the Minister for Fun, who always has the best ideas. This book was one of them.

Huge love and warmest thanks to my biggest supporters, Cory Mears (statto, football editor, chief Gooner), and Freya Mears (artist, sounding board, football agnostic). I couldn't have done this without you. What a team!

Sincere thanks to those who readily shared their footballing memories: Chris and Doreen Ashton (Lincoln City), Tony Cunningham (Lincoln City), Damien Delaney (Cork City, Leicester City, Stockport County, and Hull City), Roy Hodgson (non-league days), Lennie Lawrence (non-league days and Lincoln City), Phil Neale (Lincoln City), Trevor Peake (Lincoln City), David Pleat (non-league days, Leicester City, Luton Town, and Tottenham Hotspur), Gordon Simmonite (Lincoln City and

Stockport County), Peter Taylor (Southend United, Leicester City, England U21s, and Hull City), Steve Thompson (Lincoln City and Notts County), and Howard Wilkinson (non-league days, Notts County, and England U21s).

Special thanks to Gordon Simmonite for regular welfare checks as the project progressed. I couldn't have hoped for a more enthusiastic beta reader. And to Steve Thompson, who shared his address book and after-dinner stories with equal generosity.

Grateful thanks to David Pleat and John Inverdale, who so kindly offered to write the forewords to Colin's story.

Sincere thanks to my brilliant editor, Helen Cox, who topped and tailed, and asked all the right questions to nudge me gently over the line. And to my excellent proofreader, Gareth Davis, who saved me from an embarrassment of rogue hyphens, unwanted commas, and inconsistencies.

Grateful thanks to my brother, Anthony McGurk, who claims not to remember the football card collection, but made a fine beta reader. And to my late-night texting buddy, Esther Grigg, for warmhearted edits, a forensic pass of the final draft, and for recognising the adventures in Colin's story.

I am grateful for helpful advice and additional material from those associated with Colin's former clubs – Andy Ellis (Derby County Collection), Gareth Griffiths, Dave Lofthouse, and Dave Richardson (Hull City), Chris Ashton, Roger Bates, Phil Hough, Gary Hutchinson, Geoffrey Piper, and Charlie Russell (Lincoln City), Mark Whiley (*Lincolnshire Echo*), Peter Miles (Southend United History), and Marcus Heap and Des Hinks (Stockport County Historical Archive).

Thank you to City Lit, London for nourishing a supportive community of writers and tutors. Nicholas Murray taught a group of aspiring biographers to conduct the research, then lose 90 per cent of it. My spare room full of football books, newspapers, magazines and fanzines proves he was right.

I have spent many happy days researching in libraries across the country. Grateful thanks to the staff from The British Library

Newsroom Reading Room, the Lincolnshire Archives, the Derby Local Studies Library, and the Media Archive for Central England. No request was too obscure.

Football statistics are drawn from 11v11.com, soccerbase.com, transfermarkt.co.uk, and the Football Club History Database (fchd.info). *Lincoln City F.C. The Official History*, by Ian and Donald Nannestad, kept me straight on 1970s and 1980s chronology, and Gary Hutchinson's excellent award-nominated blog staceywest.net helped fill in the blanks. I highly recommend taking a look at footballsite.co.uk – a cornucopia of football facts and figures across the Football and Premier Leagues.

I am immensely grateful for a fabulous group of friends, who know how to enjoy themselves, and include a natural introvert in their plans. Love and huge thanks to the mad Kellys – Helen, Graeme, Billy, Joe and Leah – who have kept us sane. Thanks to Lorraine Kerr, for unparalleled wisdom and a refreshing dose of left-field thinking. My thanks also to Louisa Barnes, Julie Clare, Fiona MacGregor, Katie Murray, Liz O'Callaghan and Lyndsay Waring, who have given me walking, talking inspiration over more years than we care to remember. And to my fellow readers in The Bookclub and The Travelling Bookclub, for bearing with me when I hadn't read the book.

Heartfelt thanks to Dr Marina Parton, Miss Fiona MacNeill, Farzana Baksh and Dunia Ali, and the fabulous staff at the Royal Marsden Hospital in Chelsea – lifesavers one and all, without whom there might have been no *Murphy's Mission*.

And lastly, love and huge thanks to my wonderful mum, Shirley McGurk. At 93 years young, she brought her sharp eye and ready wit to the editing process, and never stopped believing she would see the book in print. We got there in the end, Shirl. Time for a small celebration.

ABOUT THE AUTHOR

Sally Mears started her first football card collection in 1972, in a desperate attempt to impress her older brother. More recently, she has spent 15 years freezing on youth league football pitches across the country, and a decade sitting in the relative warmth of the Emirates Stadium.

A linguist by background, Sally married an East End-born West Ham fan, has raised an Arsenal-supporting son, and written the biography of a Lincoln City legend.

Writing non-fiction combines Sally's love of storytelling with social history. A researcher at heart, she has an ever-growing library of football books and fanzines, and thinks the British

Library is her spiritual home. Sally loves the camaraderie, the honesty and the humour of the beautiful game, and recognises all these qualities in Colin Murphy's life story.

Sally has two grown-up children and lives in south-west London with her border terrier, Chipper.

If you have enjoyed Sally's first book, please consider leaving a review on your favourite online bookstore. Honest reviews are a great way for an independent author to spread the word. Just a sentence or two with a star rating would be greatly appreciated.

Please visit sallymearsmedia.com for author updates and news of future books.

Sally was a late adopter of social media and invites you to boost her following!

 instagram.com/sallymearsmedia